When
Children
Ask

When
Children
Ask

Margueritte Harmon Bro

HARPER & BROTHERS PUBLISHERS
New York

To My Parents

Andrew Davidson Harmon

Alice Gadd Harmon

who will question some of the answers
suggested in this book and answer some
of the questions they will read
between the lines

Foreword

Seldom has a book about children been written under more
ideal conditions than those under which this was produced.
Our own children were safely at home exercising their assorted initiatives, curiosities and ingenuities while their
mother was on the Atlantic in a cargo ship somewhere between New York and the Southern Cross. She had a good
deal of time between these two points and back again to
remember questions each of the children had asked on some
occasion or other and to think of far better answers than
she had been able to supply at the moment; and she had,
too, the comforting if rather humbling knowledge that the
children were under the guidance of a father who is something of a question-answerer himself, and of a more-than-
housekeeper the mere recollection of whom added to the
sense we all have when out in mid-ocean of not being in-
dividually so very important in a world so big within a universe so vast. Perspective seemed to increase as the distance
from the young questioners grew greater. And since the
ship was manned by Swedes fresh out from Gothenburg,
and the ship's library contained no books in English, and
the other passengers were male and unmarried, the subject
of children — if and when she could wangle any conversation on the subject — was one upon which this mother was
practically and at long last an Authority. Hence the book.
At home under the chastening influence of the youngsters
themselves, even the most understanding of parents would
be given pause before presuming to write any theorem
about the bringing up of the new generation, and certainly
her audacious hand would be stayed before she proceeded

to a demonstration of the theorem for others. But in the middle of the ocean, bounded on the north by memory, on the east by hope, on the south by wonder, and on the west by a faint afterglow of wisdom, daring — and perhaps imagination — may have wide scope.

The geographical coverage of a typewriter, by the time it reaches Bahia Blanca, seems to free it for treating almost any problem; space is only one of the verities which take on new meaning. Hereafter I shall connect the children's questions not only with their own eagerness to find answers to a particular dilemma in a given situation, but also with the panorama of circumstance against which their questions and answers were written down: the fan-flare of light above distant Pernambuco; the rugged outline of Cape Frio; the tropical sunsets melting like spun sugar; the storm during which the ship rolled at an angle almost (but not quite) prohibitive of typewriting; the delivery of Christmas provisions to a sister ship at sea; the merry-go-rounding at anchor off the harbor of Montevideo; the gala ships of all nations under surveillance of Sugar Loaf in the harbor of Rio; the grounding on a sandbar at Ilheus; the second cook's jumping overboard, being rescued, put under guard till quarantine. . . . But actually, of course, such experiences happening to a usually routine parent are less amazing than that children should venture so casually into the strange land of human relations, or that adolescents should chart their own excursions into the far reaches of immortality.

Any parent will understand automatically the hesitation and honest-to-goodness humility with which any other parent tries to report what goes on in the mind of a child!

MARGUERITTE HARMON BRO

Frances Shimer College
Mount Carroll, Illinois

Contents

When
Children
Ask

Parents Who Answer

And children's faces looking up
Holding wonder like a cup.

Success in rearing children seems to consist largely in accomplishing the impossible without effort. The wonder is that we live and grow at all in the face of the high demands of our offspring. But we do. We even have our little islands of serenity upon which we stand looking upstream and down, wondering at the reefs we have passed safely, measuring the current ahead. Sometimes, for our own sake or someone else's, we pause to draw a sort of outline map of our journeys — using a light pencil — knowing that the course probably looked different to the others who were with us, remembering that our own sense of direction went askew now and then. Just the same, if we cannot stamp our map " official " — if we cannot say, " This is *the* way to bring up children " — it is something to know a hazard when we've passed it, or when it looms in the offing.

Probably the most difficult hazard which parents have to negotiate is the fact that when a child asks a question, no matter how suddenly, the parent has to reply whether he knows the answer or not. If he wants to maintain an enduring relationship between himself and his child, one upon which the winds may beat and the rains may fall, then it is just plain necessary for him to come through with an answer. But only a paragon could be prepared beforehand with all the answers, and a paragon, he consoles himself, would no doubt give his child a dreadful inferiority complex. No ordinary parent can even guess in what direction a child's mind is going to move because his next question may not have any apparent relationship to the things he has previously been saying and doing.

It is at this point — answering when he does not know what to say — that a parent eventually makes a discovery. He stumbles onto the important fact that if he does not know the answer to his child's questions offhand, then he has to go find out the answer and come back to share it. Becoming a good answerer is as simple as that, and as relentless. The parent of a questioner becomes an answerer only by unceasing endeavor and unremitting honesty in finding out. Lazy minds beget lazy minds, and haziness and laziness have more in common than seven-eighths of their letters.

On the other hand, when parents are as eager as their children to find the answers to things, then the children are already half-answered. The spirit of joint inquiry is probably chief among the bridges of integrity which span the gap between generations.

Now any parent knows a large, important question when he hears it, but the odd thing is that little questions are just as important as big ones because it is the questioning which matters. Questions are the child's growing edge. He has no other way to grow. Questions are his hold upon his universe. He has no other way to take hold. Thwart a thousand little roots and the tree is never made fast in the earth. A child in the same fashion takes hold of life by the hairroots without which the main roots cannot be fed.

"Why does the radiator make that noise? " asks Tommy as he stands, shoes and stockings in his hands, raptly listening to the sputtering pipes.

"It's the steam," says his mother. "Tommy, I wish you'd get dressed."

"But what is the steam doing? " Tommy persists.

"How should I know?" says mother. "You'll be late for kindergarten if you don't get dressed."

This mother is no answerer.

Another sort of mother might take a minute to explain: "These radiators are heated by steam which comes up through pipes from the boiler down in the basement. Sometimes when the radiators cool off, part of that steam condenses into water and settles in the bottom of the radiator pipes — right here. And then when the janitor makes up another hot fire and the steam comes up again, it has to bubble through the collected water until the water gets hot enough to be steam, too. So it's the steam bubbling through the water that makes the noise you hear."

This second mother is a "natural" answerer. (Of course, the noise Tommy heard may have been a different noise with a different explanation.) To be sure, the second mother may precipitate six dozen further questions about steam and have to explain every word she uttered in her original explanation. The breakfast hour may become an elementary physics class. But few breakfasts are put to as good use as that, and talk about steam may be at least as interesting as talk about who burned the toast. This second mother is a first-class answerer because, in this instance, she is armed with facts pertinent to the question at the moment of its asking.

But perhaps Tommy's mother really has not the least idea what makes the noise in the radiator. She has often wondered herself but never asked because she was sure she would not understand if someone told her. For herself she can accept the responsibility of not finding out. Her interests lie in other directions. But she cannot make such a choice for her child. His question, no matter how remote it may seem to her, is his right to an answer. Even if she wants to make a poet of her son, she has no right to withhold the answer to the radiator's racket, because her young poet may find his rhythm in steam and boilers, in pistons, cylinders and driving power. Or her son's creativity may not be the poet's creativity at all. It may be the physicist's creativity stirring him to question.

A third mother who does not know the facts involved says frankly: " I don't know what makes that noise. It's got something to do with steam. But we can find out from the janitor." (This is allowing for the chance that the child's father may not be steam-minded, either.) And then she finds out. She may even postpone her shopping trip or otherwise rearrange her morning to get that answer. It will not take long. Tommy cannot absorb a great deal of information but he needs as much answer as he can use.

This mother also becomes a first-rate answerer. Moreover, she will probably keep right on finding out as long as her son keeps on asking. In a sense hers may be a hard life in the way that an explorer's life or a scientist's life or a philosopher's life is hard because there will always be one more thing to find out. She can never take an examination and graduate. She has to live all the time in the seek-and-answer mood. Her reward is that she does indeed live and grow, even though a parent. Her child grows too.

Of course, the second and third mothers may be the same mother, for the most determined mother cannot know all the answers. But in either case she speaks with authority because there is no less authority in the shared quest than in the immediate factual answer.

Naturally, there are degrees of importance in the questions of a child. Sometimes it would be foolish for a parent to spend a day or even an hour hunting one answer. At other times the search for an answer is a necessity. In all common sense, much depends upon the question and upon the mood of the question. When a lad, made suddenly aware of death, asks, "Is this the end or *is there more?*" his question is a poignant demand upon reality, important out of all proportion to his casual questions of yesterday. Or when the young girl, made suddenly apprehensive of the meaning of sex, cries out, "Does it have to happen to me?" someone must answer, someone in whom the dignity of the sexual basis of life has found sure moorings. That girl's questions of yesterday and of tomorrow are incidental in comparison with her need for a true answer to the doubt of today.

A parent cannot let a shell of preoccupation shut him off from the urgency which may underlie a seemingly offhand remark. The child's mood frequently turns a question into a confidence, and then the parent must answer whether he has the time or not. The very fact that he takes time for an answer may far outweigh the intellectual content of his response.

Nancy is exceedingly shy and sensitive under a would-be blasé thirteen-year-old sufficiency. In her course on medieval history she reads the life of St. Francis and is imbued with the idea of adopting a life of voluntary poverty. She resolves that hereafter she will wear no better clothes, spend no more lunch money, have no more of anything than others in her class at school can afford to have, no more than the poorest of the others. She vows in her heart to be " the least of these " and to let her friendliness toward all become her " radiant garment." This attitude is new to Nancy, who has from childhood evidenced a special flair for being well dressed and having things. After three or four abortive attempts to consult her mother about her new vow, she finally takes her courage in hand and speaks.

"Mother, how old must a person be to become a saint? Do you think that if a person gave up her worldly goods entirely that others would soon begin to see something different — something sort of glorious, you know — shining around her? " Nancy is trembling beneath her casualness. So much depends upon the answer.

But her mother misses the mood of the question entirely. She is dressing to go out and in her haste she merely laughs, not unkindly but with genuine amusement. " Nonsense, silly. We don't have saints these days. Whatever put such a notion in your head? "

" But the idea is the same as it was back in St. Francis' time," insists Nancy falteringly. " People still have need and — and — you can't understand need unless you share it. You can't understand hunger if you always have enough to eat. Sometimes you have to be poor on purpose. Don't you think so? " Nancy concludes lamely.

Now her mother laughs more merrily. " What on earth will you think of next? " She calls to Nancy's father who is reading the newspaper in the next room. " Daddy, listen to your daughter. She doesn't think she's poor enough now."

Among all Nancy's acquaintances, probably no one has a kinder mother than her own. Nor a more generous one. Her mother has been known to go without a new fall suit in order that Nancy may have the kind of coat with fur collar that the other girls of her group are wearing. And yet in this instance her mother has done an ungenerous and stupid thing in failing to sense the mood of Nancy's question. If exigencies of time absolutely prohibited an answer at the moment when Nancy asked the question, then her mother should have managed some way to carry over both the mood and the question until she could give adequate consideration.

" I know what you mean, Nancy," her mother might have said. " It's a question I've often thought of, too, and never quite made up my mind about. Let's talk about it as soon

as I come home from this tea. Meet you here in my room
where we won't be interrupted. Don't forget, will you, because I have an idea of my own that I'll tell you about if you
promise not to laugh."

"Oh, I won't laugh, mother. Some of my ideas are kind
of — funny — too."

Whereupon Nancy goes off to do something else until
her mother comes home. But she has not lost her eagerness,
and the shyness is eased a bit. When her mother returns
and really has time to talk, both are a little better prepared
by the interim of "thinking it over." The delayed conversation is successful, however, only because her mother
made an immediate and honest answer to the *mood* of
Nancy's question.

Sometimes, of course, a mood cannot wait. The question
may be a kind of confession, or a desperate need which
blurts itself out at an unexpected moment. Then the parent puts aside his present occupation, no matter what it is,
and answers the mood, thanking his lucky stars that there is
a question to take hold of.

To be sure, there are times when a child's questions should
not be answered at all. Sometimes he is just talking to hear
himself talk, putting off the moment to go to bed, distract-
ing his parents' attention from a misdemeanor, trying to live
up to his reputation as "a great old questioner," or merely
being lazy in wanting someone else to figure out an answer
he ought to find himself. It is not always a favor to open
a door for a child; sometimes he ought to open his own
doors.

Over a period of months, Benny asks a stream of questions about airplanes. His father answers his questions, fac-
tually and completely, with many demonstrations. Finally
Benny himself makes a paper airplane. But when he tries
to fly it across the room the little plane falls to the floor.

"Why doesn't it go? " asks Benny. " I followed the directions."

His father senses the difficulty, which is simple enough so that Benny should see it, too. "You find out," he says to Benny.

" Aw, nerts, I'll just use Tubby's plane. He won't care."

"You'll not use Tubby's plane," says father firmly. " Find out about your own."

So Benny finds out — in time. He answers his own questions. But only a parent who is himself an honest questioner can demand such integrity of his son. Respect for the great human gift of curiosity is in the list of those nobler qualities which are not taught but caught. A child has a pretty clear hunch when he is dealing with an adult who demands of himself the kind of integrity which feels a personal responsibility for finding answers.

Parents face another difficulty, less apparent but more far-reaching than the necessity for meeting every question with an answer. They discover that they cannot give answers larger than their own understanding, and yet that no answer is sufficient unless it points the way to larger experience than the parent has himself known. In an effort to appear more authoritative than he really is, the parent frequently overreaches himself and hence accomplishes nothing.

David, who knows that his father does not go to church, has been asking him what is meant by " the house of God." Does God live in the church? His father has told him that some people find God in church, but others find him in other places.

"Where do you find God, daddy? "

" In nature," says his father mechanically. " Out in the woods listening to the birds ' each in his separate language.' Looking at the flowers. Walking under the stars."

David makes no comment. He is lost somewhere between memory and reason. For David has lived nine years with his father and knows quite well that his father cannot tell the birds apart, except the sparrow and the robin. He has gone walking with his father in the evening, but he has never seen his father look up at the stars. David does not put his contemplation into words, not even into clear thoughts. He does not impugn his father's honesty. He just fails to register the fact that his father finds God in nature. His father had tried to give an answer larger than his own actual experience and his words were meaningless.

Emily, whose mind is as quick and nimble as her little brown fingers, brings home a red mark in language study. She acknowledges that she failed because she did not learn the fifty lines of poetry assigned to her grade.

"Emily Williamson," says her mother sternly, "it isn't just that you could have learned those lines in an hour if you had put your mind to it. It's that poetry is important. Poetry contains the best thoughts of the ages. I certainly don't want a daughter of mine to grow up without real love of poetry."

Emily listens unmoved. Perhaps she is vaguely proud of her mother's defense of poetry and she supposes that her mother subscribes to the theory she has just set forth; but Emily has never seen her mother pick up a book of poetry when she wanted to read something. Indeed, there is no poetry in the house except books left over from her parents' college days, and they are up on the highest shelf of the bookcase which no one can reach. Her mother's words are the belligerent defense of an ideal, and in that sense they are honest, but the mother has never experienced her ideal. Therefore her words, which might have been seeds to bring forth harvest, lack the germ spark. For all that will ever grow from them, they might as well be pebbles.

Naturally most parents are not deliberately trying to deceive their children. Indeed, the very vehemence of their answers is frequently proof that they are trying to give their children a larger measure of truth than they themselves have been able to take in. Thus they may steadfastly affirm that the universe is friendly, though they have never found it so. Or they protest that the homes of other families are broken, feeling the foundation slipping beneath their own. The intent of their answers is reassurance. They want to preserve for their children a few firm pillars which will not crumble in bad weather. And so they confuse reiteration with genuine reinforcement. Sweeping affirmations are an attempt to answer not only their children's doubts but their own. But the end result is, of course, the same as if they had dedicated themselves to deception. It is simply an impossibility for a parent to give an answer larger than his own understanding. Nevertheless, a parent must somehow make plain to his child that the final answer to any question is probably larger than the parent's own experience or understanding.

The father of Edward is a nationally known political figure who has devoted his life to the promulgation of a certain political philosophy. He has made an imprint upon the political thought of our country. One day Edward, aged eleven, says to his father: " You always lose, don't you, pop? A lot of people say you're right but you never get elected. Maybe your ideas aren't practical, just like people say."

" Maybe," says his father slowly. " There's always that possibility."

" Oh, no," cries Edward, who was really asking for reassurance both for his young ideas and for the prestige of his father.

" Maybe," insists his father. " On matters of government you can never be completely sure until your theories are tried. You can only figure things out the best you can and then go ahead and work for those things. Now it seems to me from what I know of history that — " And he expounds again in simple words his political philosophy. His conclusions are the result of long-time study of history and current affairs. It is his habit to listen more than he talks, although he does a good deal of talking in public. He believes in his platform and convinces others. But he does not claim that his theories and his performances could not be improved upon. He has enough humility to make room for doubt. When he talks with his son, the boy is getting a surer answer than if his father had been too sure.

A further hazard which a parent has to deal with is the double necessity of his child's having " to learn to live " and, at the same time, of his needing to live as he learns. Many of us spend twenty-one years, or at least sixteen, getting our children ready to live, without ever realizing that they are living in childhood just as fully, probably, as they ever will. Unless they enjoy life as they go — relish each new day, savor each new experience, have a lively sense of adventure for each new task — the chances are not great that a sense of adequacy and elation will suddenly bloom within them when they are " grown up."

" I don't want to practice, mummy," says Ethel, aged ten.

" Why, yes you do, dear," says mother cheerfully. " When you grow up, you'll love being able to play the piano."

Ethel shrugs her shoulders. That future day is too far off to matter. At the first opportunity she slips out to play.

That night her mother speaks to her father. " She'll be sorry when she's sixteen and the boys want to sing and she can't play for them. I know that when I got into high school, I was sorry I couldn't play the piano. I often told my mother that she should have made me practice whether I wanted to or not."

" Just tell her that if she can't practice, she can't play out-doors," says Ethel's father in his that-will-fix-her voice. " If I'm willing to pay for her lessons, the least she can do is to practice. I want her to have things I never had." He scowls as he opens his paper. When he was a boy he longed for a flute but his father could not afford the flute and his mother thought it made too much noise.

Both of Ethel's parents are right enough, as far as they go. The difficulty is that they forget that the child needs to en-joy her music *now*. She is living *now*. She is living a ten-year-old life just as fully as she will later live a twenty-year-old life. More fully, probably and alas, than she will live a forty-year-old life.

To be sure, even a little girl may understand what is meant by working for a future good. If it is necessary for Ethel to go on with the teacher she has, then her parents will have to help her understand some reason for working now for the sake of a future satisfaction. But if she is to understand, she has to have some element of experience through which to interpret the future. Perhaps Ethel has seen her aunt play-ing for the family to sing, or has seen one of " the big girls " cashing in on a bit of prestige because of ability at the piano. If so, then she has a measure of experience by means of which she may be able to visualize herself at the piano and to work toward that future. But more important to the quality of her whole life is Ethel's enjoyment of her music in the present. For emotional appreciation of living is a habit just as truly as chromatic technique is a habit. No matter how high-priced her music teacher may be, how skillful, how devoted to her art, she is probably the wrong teacher for Ethel, because teachers teach joy in the doing or they do not really teach. And if they teach joy in the doing, then the pupil *is* living now.   The years ahead may give Ethel greater understanding of her mother's interest, her father's support, her friends' appreciation, but joy in the doing will still be the primary quality which gives her music and her living its full zest.

Emil, half a dozen years older than Ethel, comes suddenly upon the realization that he lives as he learns.   One day he is bending over a rowboat from which he has been scraping old paint preparatory to applying a new coat.   Overhead stand tall pines with the sun splashing through their needles to make patterns on the waves which nibble at the shore. Suddenly Emil looks up from his work and speaks to his father who is mending the torn leather on an oar.

"A fellow doesn't mind this sort of work if he keeps his mind on next week when the boat will be finished and have the motor in it."

His father also looks up quickly but responds slowly. "What do you mean — 'next week'?   Lots of us miss half the fun of living because we keep our eyes on tomorrow."

"Maybe that's so," says Emil, looking intently at the paint scraper while the idea soaks in.

His father smiles broadly.   "My Cousin Becky now, she's that sort of procrastinator.   She never will know that life's best tense is its present tense.   Ever since I can remember, Becky's spent her spring in housecleaning in order to get ready for summer.   She's spent her summer canning fruit and knitting sweaters to get ready for fall.   She's devoted the fall to preparation for the winter and the winter to getting the family ready for spring.   She can no more fill her children with the joy of living *now* than a tin hen could gather chickens under her tin feathers."

"You're kind of down on Cousin Becky, aren't you? Maybe she's happy in her own way."

"No, she isn't.   She's always getting ready to be happy.

Tomorrow is going to be a big day but today is a terrible burden. She doesn't do a thing about collecting daily joy."

" Maybe you're right," says Emil, again gazing intently at his scraper but seeing something far, far within his own spirit. "Maybe you're right."

"Now take us," his father persists. " The hour is pretty swell just as it stands. Maybe there's an added quality in knowing that we'll have a big time when the boat is finished, but I doubt if we'll really have a better time than we're having right now."

Emil goes back to his work and — we have it from Emil — from that moment he has a greater zest for living, as if someone had pushed back a curtain and given his days new dimension. In a new way, he is learning to live by *living*.

One of life's major tragedies, both for parents and for children, lies in the fact that the joys of today are all about us, unrecognized. Obviously, a father would defeat his purpose (and be a bore) if he studded the family conversation with rhapsodic exclamations, " What a good time I'm having shining my shoes! The rhythm of the brush! The redolence of the shoe cream! The highlights that the sunshine makes upon the polished leather! " Likewise a mother would kill the thing she tries to foster if she went about exclaiming, " Ah me! the silver egg-beater in a yellow bowl whipping thick white cream! What color! What texture! What beauty! " And yet it is just such unexpected homely incidents which make the sensitive individual catch his breath with wonder for the manifold beauties of everyday life: sunshine edging the drawn window shade and falling slantwise across a dark rug; a child bouncing upstairs with her own joyous rhythm; dandelions rioting in a vacant lot; rusty grasses along the roadside — these and a thousand other wonders crowding the most commonplace day.

Awareness, or learning to live as one goes, is distinctly a

habit. A parent may have to cultivate the habit in himself
before he can cultivate it in his children. But once awareness becomes a habit, then the spirit rushes forth with ecstasy
to moments of aliveness it would otherwise have missed —
and never know how great was its poverty in the missing.

Parents face still another dilemma in the fact that a child's
growth springs from his " doings," from his active participation in the world about him, and yet just as surely springs
also from absence of doing, from apparent withdrawal from
the world of goings-on. We fail to sense the balance between the two necessities. At times most of us belong to the
type of parent who cannot bear to see an idle child. Perhaps
impatience with our child's apparent idleness springs from
the realization that our own tasks are never finished. Perhaps we unconsciously inherit the tradition that " Satan finds
mischief for idle hands to do." Perhaps we feel that " doing
is learning," or that the silent child will become " intro-
verted," or that his inactivity reflects upon our lack of ingenuity. Or we may feel that noise and laughter and action
are synonyms for happiness.

Young Herbert lying on the grass looking at nothing and
apparently thinking about the same thing is a target for
parental suggestions. " Herbert, did you finish piling the
wood? " Herbert did. " Herbert, did you do your practicing? " Yes, that too. " Herbert, why don't you read your
book? " He doesn't want to. " Herbert, what are you
thinking about? " Nothing, just as his mother thought.
But by and by from Herbert, who has continued raptly to
do nothing for an hour, comes this question: " Can ants if
they hurry and do their work well ever be anything but
ants? Will they be men some day? And what's the use of
being men if they still have to hurry and hurry and hurry? "

Probably the measure of a child's repose, of his silences, is

the best measure of the man he will some day be. But unfortunately there are no " silence quotients " nor any other
indexes by which the quality of silence may be measured.
No doubt it is true that some children dwell too much apart
and develop a strangeness toward their outer world. But
for every child who dwells too much in silence there are
probably a dozen whose growth is frustrated by too little
being left alone.

Fortunately some children can feel themselves alone when
surrounded by any amount of grownup chatter and irrelevant clatter. They can set aside the outer scene and prepare a scene more congenial to the need of the moment. If
their silence seems unsocial, it is merely because the onlooker
cannot mount the invisible stage where the real play goes on.

The Harrisons had " unexpected relatives " for lunch and
everyone talked at once in the pleasant way of families full
of news. Jeanette, a pensive blonde of seven, tried to follow
the many exciting avenues of conversation until she was
dizzy with turning her head from aunt to uncle to cousin to
parents and back again. Gradually she lagged behind and
then gave up entirely, wending her own way down paths of
her own choosing. Suddenly, as the meal was finished, she
looked up at her mother with radiant face, " Mother, how
long before — " and then she caught herself and laughed
aloud. " Do you know what I was going to say? I thought
we were all up at Bass Lake and I started to say, ' How long
before daddy is going to get his fishing license? ' "

Reality for Jeanette was in her fruitful silence. She only
happened to give her parents a clue to what went on within
her mind. Usually parents have to trust the silences of their
children, without token.

But here again the quality of the child's silence is partially
determined by the quality of his overt experiences. No
child dwells in fairyland who has never heard tales of the

fairies. He does not dwell among the stars unless he knows something about stars and their myths. He cannot " play like " Napoleon or Pasteur or Lindbergh unless he has heard of their feats. Likewise, he cannot amuse himself making rhymes unless he has heard some sort of poetry. He does not imagine the shapes he will carve with his jackknife unless he has used a knife and tried his skill. He does not hear melodies singing in his mind unless he has listened to many songs, or played in the out-of-doors where nature's melodies rise.

Balance between action and contemplation is just as necessary for a child as for an adult — perhaps more necessary because a child is learning to achieve this balance. The parent's part is to use care and common sense in directing the child's activities when he seems to need direction and then to leave the child alone to experiment with doing nothing.

Hazards — on every side as well as behind and before. But sometimes they need only to be pointed out to be avoided. And sometimes we sail serenely over a jagged rock without ever knowing it threatened our keel. Parenthood is always exciting and usually a rather satisfactory vocation.

Paradox For Parents

You parents all that children have,
And you too that have none,
If you would keep them safe abroad,
Pray keep them safe at home.
JANE AND ANN TAYLOR (*London, 1662*)

Most of us become parents before we have figured out exactly what the parent's part is in giving life and eventual maturity to new human beings. But of two things we are reasonably certain: We must make our children independent of our care and, in the process, we must give them sufficient security so that their growth will be sturdy and unhampered. Almost from the beginning of their lives we try to foster their independence. We teach them to crawl after their own toys, to stand on their own feet. We wean them not only from the mother's breast but from a thousand other dependencies upon us. We want them to wash their own hands, and eventually their necks and ears, to put away their own clothes and toys and books, to devise their own games, to do their own lessons, to make up their own minds. The weaning process is a long one extending from infancy through adolescence for the fortunate children whose parents are really determined to make them truly independent individuals. For the less fortunate, the weaning process may never be fully accomplished and they go through life tied by invisible strings to parents who have let the possessiveness of their love prove a fatal embarrassment to their children's maturity.

But all the time that we are fostering independence we are

also protecting our children. We want them to feel that we stand between them and the world. Whether it is a matter of untying hard knots in small shoe laces, or going to school with an umbrella in an unexpected shower, or providing warm houses and good food, we are always devising ways to keep them from feeling overwhelmed by circumstance.

To manage the weaning process within a framework of security is difficult for a variety of reasons. The older generation tends to set standards in terms of the customs of yesterday while the new generation is trying to invent the folkways of tomorrow; the rules which one highly successful parent uses for one highly successful child may not work at all for his next child or for the neighbors' children; the rope which appears to be a tether to one boy is sufficient to hang the next one; the alacrity with which one daughter copies her mother's manners and attitudes is matched by another daughter's flair for doing everything in exactly her own way. The entire parent-child relationship is such an individual affair that rule books seem to be more useful on the shelf than in the hand. And yet, of course, we all know that we have a heap of problems in common; that children are pretty much alike even when most appallingly different.

Certainly there are a few basic considerations which all parents have to meet — or to ignore, which is just another way of meeting them. The child may state the problem for us. "Listen, dad, why are you all the time telling me what I can do? I'm old enough to make up my own mind." (He may be seventeen when he speaks or he may be only seven.) Or a mother may say to the father, "Just what can a home provide after all?" Or the father may ask of society, "In a changing and precarious world, how shall we give our children security and still make them independent?"

What *is* the home for?

In a child the love of the home has always been very

strong, even in the exceptional cases when he appears to have small reason for clinging to it. Every day so much that is new crowds in upon him from the outside — new scenes, new people, new experiences. Automobiles, telephones, radios, the whole machine environment, complicate the life they serve. Sense impressions come in faster than they can be assimilated and the child must swallow his day whole and digest it later if he can. At the same time welling up from within are new emotions, new desires, new needs. From the strain of continual adjustment, without and within, he turns to his home and to the heart of his home, which is his parents, seeking security in familiarity and affection.

Different homes offer different sorts and degrees of security. Sometimes, but not often, there is a home which offers quiet as a part of its protection of the child — a home, for instance, which by common consent bars the continual operation of the radio; a home in which a mantle of silence is thrown about the individual who is reading a book even though that individual be a child; a home in which every effort is made to reduce the tempo of life — soft bells on the telephone, soft lights to eat by, conversation which lingers around the dinner table. Serenity at home becomes the child's defense against the noises and distractions which batter at him from all sides during his hours away from home.

Another of the things which help to create a feeling of security and independence within the home is order, just old-fashioned order. Sometimes, to be sure, there is a highly successful home which does not know the meaning of the word. Occasionally there is a finely tempered personality which has withstood the bangs and bumps of great confusion. One of America's best known brain surgeons whose skill depends, so he says, upon the even ordering of his ways and days, grew up in a household in which the beds were never made, the dishes never washed, and hilarious disorder reigned in every room. But in that home every stray cat and every wounded dog found instant care. The boy found unusual security in the hospitality of his home and he was taught to exercise unusual independence and ingenuity. Thus factors have a way of canceling one another in arriving at a quotient. Nevertheless, for every personality which achieves distinction in spite of confusion and disorder within the home, there are probably several who have been maimed by such circumstances.

In general, some part of the security which the child needs to find in his home must be made up of order, plain physical order. A place for things, and things in their place. This is a theory which any parent may prove — or disprove — for himself. If the child is accustomed to finding his undershirts in mother's dresser one week, among daddy's socks the next week, on the back stairs the third week, let him have a dresser drawer of his own and see with what relief he turns to it. He may not turn instantly because, of course, one spot of his own is not enough to build complete and immediate security. But if a big box is provided for his toys, a closet for his clothes, a shelf for his books, a low hook for his coat and hat — particular places for keeping all the things which are his own — his response will be worth watching. Naturally the habits of five long years in a family habituated to disorder may take some weeks to reset themselves. Neither Rome nor the Romans were built in a day. But habits will reset. And in the process the child will gather together his "self." He will learn something of independence within the framework of security.

Naturally families differ in their patterns of order. One individual, looking back, says: "In my father's house, the furniture stood in the same place for fifty years. I could get up in the night and no matter how dark it was, I knew where each chair stood in the living room. In the kitchen I could reach for the salt or the vinegar and mix a gargle in the dark as well as if the light were on." But another may recall: "When we went off to school in the morning, we never knew how we would find the furniture when we came home at noon. Mother loved to change things around and could make that old parlor look like forty different rooms."

At first glance it may appear that the household which never moved the furniture was the one which made the greatest contribution toward security. But in the second household, although the order kept changing, there was still order. In both cases the children of the household felt that things belonged in place. And in both cases, order was not an end in itself. It cannot be an end in itself if it is to produce a liberated and competent personality; it must be balanced against other family needs.   Some of the most blessed homemakers of every generation have had to be on the move continually, carrying their order and their " security " with them if they wanted their children to have any at all. It is said of Miranda Stateler that she could move into the coldest, drabbest parsonage, hang up a curtain and have a home going full blast in half a day. Many another pioneer's wife had the same gift. And the wives and mothers of actors are frequently past masters in the art of carrying the home in a trunk or two, of transplanting the family spirit without disturbing the tenderest blossom. Such gifts of homemaking cannot be counterfeited. There is a world of comfort for the must-be wanderer in the knowledge that the finest security is not necessarily made up of walls, windows and furniture. Resourcefulness becomes security just as it fosters independence.

Another factor which helps to establish the child in both security and independence is the extent to which he can depend upon his parents' responses to his conduct. How can a child find his way in a universe which depends so largely upon immutable law if the parents with whom he deals most intimately have one reaction on Tuesdays, when they are rested and serene, and another reaction on Fridays, when they have been up all night?

A kitchen stove, if it has a fire within, will burn the child each time he makes the mistake of touching it. But the child's mother has no such constancy of response. She probably scolds him for losing the dime with which he was to buy a loaf of bread only if she really needs that loaf of bread in a hurry. Otherwise she may give him another dime and an absent-minded word of caution. She has no law for lost dimes nor for scoldings. Or perhaps father is the variable. One night he brings home a guest who thinks it is "awfully cute" in little Junior to take the evening paper apart and spread it like a sidewalk down the full length of the living room. But another night father comes home without a guest and wants to read the paper immediately. On that night he thinks it disgraceful that a three-year-old should not know enough to leave the newspaper alone.

However, the point need not be labored to parents who so often meet and mourn their own inconsistencies. Most of us have a deep and poignant desire to deal fairly with our children. Our inconsistencies burn secret scars upon our souls.

After the parent has fostered that deep confidence of the spirit which eventuates in independence and security, then the home has at least one more large gift to offer, a gift more lasting and more significant than all others. That is freedom from fear. It is fear which honeycombs the bulwark of security which a home might otherwise offer and makes it useless as protection for the sensitive young mind. It is fear which blocks initiative and independence. Unfortunately fear is not an adult emotion alone. All across the land, discussions in high school history and civics classes bear testimony to the adolescent's fear of political, economic and social change, with their attendant personal insecurity and misadjustment. Younger children also reflect the assorted fears of their parents — "afraid we may lose the house," "afraid Tom can't go to college after all," "afraid we'll never get the doctor paid," "afraid we'll have to move." The variations are endless.

Of course it is not strange, when political and economic changes snap insistently at our heels forcing us to a faster pace than we want to travel, that we become jittery. The current scene changes too rapidly; we lose our landmarks. And apprehension accompanies change as the tail the kite. Probably we think we are keeping our fears from our children. We say in confidence to another adult, "I'm almost worried to death for fear John will lose his job, but I don't let the children know it." Perhaps we do refrain from directly discussing our fears with our children, except in the provoking and altogether impolite way in which parents talk to each other over the heads of their offspring. But we convey our anxieties in the tones of our voice, in our quick, nervous movement, in our trigger responses to small annoyances. It is impossible for the most strong-minded to keep his fears to himself, and parents are seldom strongminded at home.

Probably the only sure way to keep fear from a child, financial fear or any other kind, is not to have fear. But such a resolve is easier to write about than to carry out, for in daily life we do not deal with fear in the abstract but with concrete, immediate fears. A large number of our fears are naturally enough concentrated in the region of our pocketbooks, and when we see the economic order threatening to change the shape of our pocketbooks, we are afraid that our children will be deprived of their just due. But what is it,

exactly, that we fear they may lack?   Tomorrow's food?
Tomorrow's clothing?   Our science of production is such
that we can scarcely imagine a shortage of these things, if
we proceed confidently to experiment in ways of dividing
the work of our hands and minds more fairly.   Fear makes
us want to bind all our tomorrows within today's limitations, leaving nothing to the inventiveness and courage of
the days to come.   In our more sensible moments we know
that we are much more equal to coping with our problems
when we are not afraid of them, and that we are free to roll
up our sleeves and have a hand in directing the change that
seems inevitable when we do not let ourselves be frightened
into paralysis lest it run wild.

After all, it isn't as if fear could do anything about the ills
it dreads.   Fear never held back a war nor the ultimate defeat which rides in on wings of victory.   It did not avert
the last depression nor save those hearts it fattened on.   It is
a primitive hangover from the days when men had not lived
together long enough to understand the power of cooperation.   Although the human race learns slowly, it would
seem by this time that we could get along without goblins,
witches, asafetida bags and fear of changing circumstance.

Perspective is the great old antidote for parents' fears.
To look back upon the fears of our fathers as reflected in
their daily arguments is to laugh at our own anxieties.   The
apprehension of our parents was voluble on such matters as
man's descent from the monkey, the infallibility of the Holy
Scriptures, the disappearing frontier, not to mention free
silver, the Spaniards in Cuba, parcel post, the subsidy of
railroads, and local option.   Against the sounding-board of
current affairs, the echoes of most of the fears of yesterday
have a hollow rattle.

But if we have already become myopic with fear and cannot register the values of perspective, then we may relax

the hold of our fears by asking ourselves whose children it is that we fear may not have their chance. Our own? Our neighbors'? The children of our community? Of our country? The wider the circle, the less one fears. To be sure, imagination is demanded of the parent who risks his own children's going hungry in order that multiplied numbers of other men's families may eat. An extension of patriotism is demanded of parents who let American children eat only two meals a day in order that children in other lands may be sure of one meal a day. But imagination has its practical uses. It frequently begets courage which, welling up, drives out fear. And ultimately, of course, the other children must have their food. To look at the world from the perspective of future history is to shift the basis of our fear from anxiety for personal security to concern for personal integrity. There is parenthood so proud that it will not ask nor take for its sons and daughters that which it does not strive to share with the sons and daughters of all.

In a precarious social order, preparation for threatened danger is obviously a very different thing from fear of it. To live in a cyclone country and not provide a cyclone cellar or its equivalent is foolhardy. But once one has provided a cellar large enough to hold the family in time of need, it is ridiculous to spend one's time constantly enlarging the cellar or covering it with flags. Even to dwell on the thought of it is tremendous waste of energy. It is needed; it is built; it is ready. And life goes on without fear. So in the realm of physical sustenance. It is true that our children must eat. Therefore, one plants and plows, harrows, harvests and stores. One allows a margin for the years when rain is scarce or when blight may shrivel the grain. These things done, nothing is gained through fear.

Let it be admitted that getting rid of fear is not easy. The dangers which threaten are real enough, as every parent knows. But to remind ourselves that most of the things we have feared to date have never really come to pass is not merely to apply a soporific. Half the time we are in a stew of anxiety all to no purpose. We are merely being driven by our habit of fear. An understanding God may forgive us our fears but there are still the paths in our brains to contend with. We *are* habits, and to extract the habit of fear may be to untangle the threads of our being. It can be done only by realizing that the rapid hold of a new habit is even more amazing than the tenacious hold of an old one. And confidence — outgoing, joyous trust — may become a habit as readily as fear. " Be not anxious " is more than a maxim. It is the warmest cloak a parent can throw across the straight young shoulders of his child. Freedom from fear *is* security in a high degree, and is also the fomenter of independent growth.

If our path as parents seems beset with hazards which trip us up so that we lose our balance if not indeed our sense of direction, there is some comfort in remembering that many generations have traveled the same difficult and exciting journey. They made their mistakes — some of them utterly stupid mistakes — and so shall we. But in every generation there are some parents who pause to scrutinize their convictions and prejudices, their attitudes and actions, their failures and achievements, and it is from such scrutiny that wisdom stems.

Amateur Theologians

Children of yesterday, heirs of tomorrow,
What are you weaving? Labor and sorrow?
Look to your looms again; faster and faster
Fly the great shuttles prepared by the Master.
Life's in the loom. Room for it! Room!

AUTHOR UNKNOWN

An editor of one of the national magazines for parents remarks that she receives more letters about the child and religion than about any other concern of parents for their children. Also that she finds these questions the most difficult to answer, either by personal reply or by article. In other sorts of problems — education, sex, food, play — parents across the land have enough common experience and enough common vocabulary so that a writer can speak to a great many persons at the same time. But in matters of religion, says the editor, neighbors who live next door to each other and apparently carry on a common social and business life, may be decades, if not centuries, apart.

At first glance it seems strange that religion, which deals with the meaning of life, should signify such different things to different people. The materials of living are more or less the same for all of us. Why then should we interpret them so differently? But after all, no matter how much individual experience appears to conform to the general cycle, it *is* different for each person. From the beginning, for instance, life has been one thing to the well fed, another to the hungry. The emotions of the successful hunter are not the emotions of one who was maimed from childhood and has to watch the chase from afar. Back when the world began or now, what could the hunter say about life to the one who sits apart? Or what could the man of contemplation say to the hunter? Each has to find for himself the meaning of his life, and having found at least a measure of meaning, he is likely to decree, " *This* is the meaning for all. And because the meaning is thus and so, you must do this and that."

Man tends to explain his actions after he has acted, and then to order his further actions — and everybody else's — in the light of his explanations. The process is a continuous one, neither the acting nor the explaining ever being finished. We have come to use the word " religion " for this acting-explaining process of working out the values of life. We are likely to share what we have found, sometimes spontaneously, generously, sometimes with coercion. We may *want* other people to see things the way we see them, to act the way we act; or we may try to *make* them conform. And in this respect parents are no different when dealing with their children than when dealing with other people.

The child's " religious " questions are his questions about the nature of the universe and his place in it, including his relation to his fellow humans. Obviously, such questions may cover pretty much the whole range of experience, and so the answers, although religious, are not exclusively religious. Sometimes the questions are about birth or death and then the answers are physiological as well as religious. Sometimes the questions deal with the duties and privileges of other children, other members of the family, and then the answers are sociological or psychological as well as religious. But whatever else they may be, if the questions have to do with the meaning the child is trying to find in life and with the ordering of his conduct in the light of that meaning, then his questions are religious.

Sometimes it is not the intellectual content of the child's question which makes it religious, but the mood in which he asks it. There is a difference, as the parent usually knows, between the child's exerting a little offhand curiosity about his physical well-being, and his reaching out to steady himself in a universe which already seems precarious. Sometimes this need to lay hold on ultimate assurance is very apparent, as when the seven-year-old between the short gasps of pneumonia looks directly into his mother's eyes and asks, " Am I sick enough to die? And if I die, mother, what then? " That child's question is religious. At other times his need to relate himself to time and space and persons appears more casual. " If time doesn't have any end, then how did it start? " " Why shouldn't I throw paper on the street for someone else to pick up? " " What if the sun bumped into the earth and killed everybody? " Probably these questions are not religious. But if the child is genuinely seeking his place in his world, the answers may be religious while at the same time they fall into other categories also.

It is the failure to realize that religious questions do not deal with a given and limited body of material which causes confusion in the minds of many parents. Questions about God we can classify at once as religious, as well as questions about prayer and the church and immortality. But where does "God" leave off and "nature" begin? When the child talks about the thing he wants most and wishes for every time he sees the evening star, is he unconsciously talking about prayer without naming it? When he asks about church services on Sunday his question seems plainly religious, but when he asks about a soup kitchen or the coming election, may his question be religious also?

The old division between things of the flesh and things of the spirit still rises to confuse us and we try, often unconsciously, to draw a line between "spiritual" concerns and "worldly" concerns. We try to answer certain questions with a patently religious vocabulary regardless of the fact that the vocabulary doesn't fit the child's experience. Many of us inherited a set of religious words for dealing with matters we feel to be religious. Sometimes the words still function in our daily lives and are consequently coin of the realm to which the child is accustomed. But at other times we have to get our religious words down off a high shelf of memory and dust them off before we can display them to our children. Yet we are amazed that the children view them as curios rather than as household necessities. Probably the test of the religious vocabulary is the pragmatic one that if words can express today's experience, as well as yesterday's, without strain, then they are still our words to pass on to our children.

This whole matter of religious vocabulary is important because we are likely to use theological words which tend to block off more understanding than they reveal. Once, and not so long ago, these theological words had meaning in everyday conversation. Children grew up knowing what they meant. They not only accepted the terms but frequently accepted their implications also. Today most of us simply do not realize how completely we have lost both terms and content until some incident brings the fact sharply into focus.

Horace, aged twelve, has grown up in a minister's family in which the concerns of religion are discussed casually and naturally. One Sunday he goes with a friend to Sunday school in a Jewish Reformed temple, where the boys of his grade are studying the great Jewish reformers, including Jesus. In the course of the lesson, the Jewish teacher explains a bit of the Christian theology which has developed from the teachings of Jesus. In great amazement, Horace comes home and calls to his mother: "Mother, where are you? Listen, mother, did you ever hear about the Three in One? "

"Did I ever hear of what? Come up here," says mother.

Horace bounds upstairs. "Did you ever hear about the Three in One — Father, Son and Holy Ghost, blessed Trinity in one Godhead? "

"Why, Horace," remonstrates mother, " you've heard of the Trinity all of your life."

"Not until this morning. Mr. Levy told the boys — " And then Horace repeats the traditional Christian tenets which, until that morning, he had been completely unaware of.

Horace is no exception to the general run of children in present-day churchgoing families. About man's responsibility to society he probably knows more than his father or his grandfather knew at his age. He will probably have to do less scrapping of childish concepts than his parents did in the process of growing up. But his theological vocabulary is a minus quantity.

If Horace's parents happen to belong to the group who hold that questions about the nature of God are in some peculiar way " religious " in contrast to the immediate, natural concerns of the child, then they will be bewildered in trying to state their religious beliefs without the help of the old theological terms in which those beliefs came to them. Their common-sense answers will not seem religious enough. If, on the other hand, they do turn to traditional religious terms which the child has never heard before, then the child is the bewildered one. At once religion seems to him something apart from life.

Horace's mother has to choose at the moment the question is asked whether to go into the unique divinity of Jesus as the son of God and to explain what she feels to be the meaning of the Trinity, or to outline the historical development of the terms (in a few simple sentences, please), or to say frankly that the concept of the Trinity seems impractical and beside the point to her, but instead she feels that. . . . This is the important part for her child: what she thinks herself. Whatever her answer, whatever the theological terms she expects to lead up to, she will save time and misunderstanding if she makes her explanations in the family-conversation vocabulary with which she passes on her attitudes toward other current concerns — traffic regulations, artificial flowers or the Supreme Court. The art for the parent to learn is to treat religious questions as though they were questions about *life* — as indeed they are — and to see that the child's curiosity is both satisfied and quickened.

Sometimes we forget that we have a " theology " to pass on to our children until their questions are hurled at us. We may call our theology a "philosophy of life." But whatever the name, we have in some way worked out a scheme of belief about the universe and man's place in it. If we can put this scheme of belief into simple words which sound respectable and satisfying to ourselves, then we have something to say to our children. But the fact that we are reasonably satisfied does not mean we can settle these religious concerns for our children, because a parent dare not speak with too much finality. As soon as we begin to talk *about* God, we frequently feel that we are talking *for* God. We say the final word. We become not merely theologians but *the* theologians. Nor is such dogmatism confined to exposition in behalf of the Christian theology. The no-god idea also may become an absolute about which we speak with the authority of high priests. All too-sure people are dangerous, especially parents.

But if we do not speak with finality about our religious beliefs, how shall we expect our children to abide by them?

In the long run of history, our religious beliefs set our ethical standards, our moral codes. We live by them. Frequently they seem so important that we sacrifice what appears to be immediate happiness for them. Then, because we pay a price to give our religious convictions reality in daily life, we want our children to live by them also. And yet — and yet — as parents we can never be too sure that we have found the final meaning or worked out the rules of conduct which are ultimately good.

It is difficult indeed to hold fast to verities of which one is not completely sure. But there seems no escaping the fact that we must live by our ideals although they are tentative. In all integrity we have to set up our values and then so order our days that we help to bring those values to pass. And while our mood and thought may be those of complete conviction, we have to leave room for other people, including our children, to differ in their interpretations and in their actions. Tough doctrine for parents!

Perhaps, in the end, our best answer to our children's religious questions is not what we say — although we must say the best that we can think — but in the fact that we are trying to help them find answers.

What Is God?

A fire-mist and a planet,
    A crystal and a cell,
A jellyfish and a saurian,
    And caves where the cave men dwell;
Then a sense of law and beauty,
    And a face turned from the clod —
Some call it Evolution,
    And others call it God.

      WILLIAM CARRUTH (*Each in His Own Tongue*)

" Mother, do you believe in God? " " Daddy, is there really a God some place? " In some form, every child asks these questions of his parents. And to these questions there are only three answers. The first answer is, " Yes, of course." The second is, " No." The third is, " It depends upon what you mean by God."

There are a variety of homes in which the first answer is the rule. To some, God is the just giver of the law, the dispenser of reward or punishment to those who live or fail to live according to his precepts. He is all-powerful, present everywhere all the time, his justice is tempered with mercy toward those who are saved, and salvation consists in accepting the fact of his being, both in himself and in his Son and Spirit, and trying to live the way he would approve. His law is made known in his Book interpreted in the "right " way.

Parents whose views can be summed up in this general fashion have a comparatively easy time answering their children's question. For one thing, they can turn to their book for the final authority on matters large and small as if God proved his own being by having a last word on every subject.

"Mother, do I have to wear my hat to church? The elastic hurts my head." Sally swings her hat in her hand hopefully.

"Of course you wear your hat to church." Rapid turning of pages, at least metaphorically, and Paul's admonition is delivered.

Or perhaps it is Ned who has been caught in an untruth. "Yes, I lied," he admits sullenly.

"Do you know what the Bible says about liars?" Out with the story of Ananias and Sapphira.

Susie squints into the cloudless blue sky. "Is heaven a real place we go to when we die?" Her mother, peeling apples on the back porch, answers almost without thinking and all the more emphatically because she needn't think. "'In my Father's house are many mansions. If it were not so, I would have told you. I go to prepare a place for you.' Of course heaven's a real place — somewhere. God says so."

At first glance, it might seem that the continual turning to the Bible as final authority is only an effort to establish its authority. However, the Bible derives its authority — in these cases — from being the word of God and it is used to prove his existence through his long-time ordering of history.

But some children, growing older and still struggling with the idea of God, are not satisfied with their parents' proofs from the Scriptures. "It seems to me that some people just wrote down what they thought about God in a book we call the Bible, but that doesn't prove there is a God. They might be completely mistaken. And even if there is some kind of God, he may not be at all as the Bible pictures him. Who is going to say what God is like?"

"The church." This answer is sufficient for many parents and they pass it on as sufficient for their children. In each generation the church has had ecclesiastical authorities whose business it is to make the final ruling as to what the Scriptures mean and what the term " God " shall signify. These specialists are set apart for their task just as specialists in medicine or law or architecture become authorities by dint of their studies and experience. Among the most successful parents of our generation, as of other generations, are some who are proud and glad to accord the final authority to these specialists. They expect common-sense individual application of the church's pronouncements about God as about other matters, but they think that the individual need not carry all the responsibility for figuring out his own idea of God and his relationship to God. He has access to the wisdom of the priest. All Roman Catholicism and much of Protestantism allow the church to make the final answer to questions about God's nature and being.

But to the question, " Is there a God? " some parents who answer quickly and unequivocally, " Of course there is a God," do not cite the authority of the Scriptures or of the church to prove their point. They rely upon what they feel to be their own experience.

" How do you know there is a God, daddy? "

" I have found him," says the father. " I am always aware of his presence. I turn to him and listen, and in one way and another he answers my need."

As the father goes on to explain his feeling of oneness with the rhythm of the universe as he finds it in nature, in some people, in his own creative work, the child may not know exactly what the words mean but nevertheless he picks up from his father a sense of the meaning for which the words are symbols. He has no doubt but that his father has found something very real and sustaining which he calls

"God." As the days go on, however, the father will have to keep answering that child's question by sharing his· experience if he wants to make the answer vital to the child.

The sort of parent who attests his faith in God by his experience of God may or may not identify himself with the church and the teaching of the Bible. He may be a Christian or he may be a Taoist; he may bear the name of any one of a number of "religions" or of no system· at all. He may feel no need of assembling himself with other people for common worship, no need of mediating priests or instructing parsons. There is no gainsaying the fact that the human spirit finds its sufficiency in a variety of experiences, perhaps all of them tapping at the same source. The most that a parent can do for a child, even when he answers the question of God with an unequivocal " yes," is to affirm that he himself is fed by certain deep springs and to disclose his way of reaching them.

The second kind of answer to the question " Is there a God? " may be a definite negative.

" Of course there is no God. ' God ' is an outgrown idea which man invented before he had figured out the laws of nature. The savage, for instance, could not understand the laws of rain and its capricious habits, so he laid the fact that it did not always come when needed to the whim or anger of some superior being who had moods like his own. He called this being ' God.' He did not understand the laws of health so he thought that someone outside his ken sent disease by way of punishment. He called this someone ' God.' He did not understand the nature of fire, the power of the sea, the habits of the sun and moon and stars. So he predicated some personality behind the universe making it work as it did work. He called this personality ' God.'"

Perhaps the child thinks over the answer for a while and then ventures, "But there are still a lot of things we do not understand." To which the parent replies, "Plenty of things. In fact we probably understand very little about the universe yet. But we have discovered that all physical movements are governed by law and that all life develops according to law. Our concern is to find out these laws and to understand their ultimate mechanics. The burden falls on us to live in harmony with the laws of the universe rather than to predicate some God to account for them and expect him to adjust the laws to our liking."

The conclusive "no" answer which maintains that reality is a machine expressing an unself-conscious amoral law, and the explicit "yes" answer which can attest the very nature of God and delineate his attributes, may have the same difficulty of failing to persuade by too great assurance.

There is a third group of parents who answer the question about God with the phrase, "It depends upon what you mean by God." Perhaps they know less than the first two groups. Perhaps they know more. Perhaps they are less diligent in pursuit of knowledge and experience than the others. Or perhaps they are merely fearful of any final word. They leave open a few windows for free winds of doubt.

Roscoe is a sturdy eleven-year-old, seldom preoccupied by speculative interest, usually absorbed in his many activities. His father is a physician who does research on cancer. He is not a churchman and has never discussed religion in any way with his children. Roscoe has been to church two or three times in his life when he trailed along with playmates who went habitually.

One day Roscoe comes into the house swinging a dead mouse which he has just taken from a trap. "Betty Lee says I'm a murderer. In her family they don't kill anything on account of it's God's business to give life and take it away. Pop, do you believe in God?"

His father puts down the book he is reading. "It depends," he answers, "on what you mean by God."

"I just mean — God," says Roscoe with an indefinite gesture. "You know, the God that made the world and made people and sits up in heaven and watches if you do right or not. Do you believe that? Do you believe he's always checking up on us?"

"Personally I don't use the word 'God,' son. I think there are better words for what we mean. I don't think that anyone 'made' the world. It came into being out of some vast chaos whose original form we do not yet understand. Somehow this whirling ball we call the earth shot off into space and found an orbit of its own. As its crust cooled, there finally emerged water and land, the oceans and the continents. Cells of living matter took on form. No one can positively say how living matter began — yet. We are just now at the border line of understanding something about radiant energy and possible sources of life. And we do not really know a great deal about the development of plant and animal life. Forms of life are still changing, evolving, adapting. Toward what end we are not sure. To say that 'God' does these things seems to me just a vague generalization. The important thing is to find out what is happening. Then perhaps we may be able to use our knowledge for our own good."

Roscoe does not understand all of his father's explanation but he gathers up the general meaning and thinks it over. Then he says, "If you did believe it was God that did all these things, then you'd have to go to church to worship him, wouldn't you?"

"Some people feel they have to go to church to worship. But it seems to me that one's respect for the processes of nature is intrinsic."

Father sees Roscoe's perplexity and tries again. "I mean

that as one works on the human body, let us say, or as one works in the field of chemistry, he develops such tremendous respect for the laws of nature that there is always some awe and wonder in his mind. He doesn't need a special time and place to express the profound humility with which he approaches his task of finding out more about life. When he accomplishes something, he does not need to gather his friends together to sing hymns of praise. His relationship to his work is a sort of steady compact with life. If he gets too proud over what he has done and rests back on his laurels, then nature just doesn't open any more secrets to him. But if he keeps on working, then life gives him more understanding to work with. I think the attitude of continual respect for life is more important than what you call 'worship.'"

Roscoe, hunched in a big chair, is obviously thinking over what his father has said. Suddenly he sums up his father's answers. "Well, I guess some people say ' God ' instead of ' nature.' They say ' God wants me to do something ' instead of ' Nature is waiting for me to find out things.' "

"It seems to me that ' nature ' is a simpler and more accurate word," insists father.

"It doesn't sound very simple to me;" says Roscoe. "It seems to me it's harder to find out about nature than about God because you don't have any Bible to help you with nature and you do about God."

His father does not follow the opening made by this comment. Time enough later, he feels, for Roscoe to consider what seems to him to be man's predilection for predicating his gods and then letting the gods speak with authority through holy books. He merely says, "We aren't after the easier thing. We're after the truth if we can find it."

Roscoe is impressed by that remark because his father's whole life backs it up. He slides out of his chair, still think-

ing, and starts back to play. Then he stops in the doorway.
"When I grow up I'm going to be a doctor, too. I'll operate on everybody and find out everything." A minute
later the kitchen door bangs. Roscoe is through with his
theological considerations for this day.

But he will come back some time. It may be years later
but he will come back inevitably to ask: " In an impersonal
world, how much do I matter? If I do ' right' or ' wrong '
how much ultimate difference does it make? Without a
God to hold me to accounting, it's pretty much my own
choice whether I'm a waster or a builder."

And then his father will have to.answer: " Yes, it is up to
you and to your fellows. You have high expectations for
yourself and if you choose to suffer the defeat of not living
up to them, then that's your own hell. And it's enough. If
you run amuck of the customs society has declared to be
good and useful, then society will make you pay one way
or another. But that's small punishment beside the gnawing
defeat of having let yourself down."

"And where do I get the power to hold myself up? "
cries this older Roscoe to his father.

" The power comes with the high expectations. You
generate it as you go. You build a reserve of power through
your habits of accomplishment. Nature never cheats.
She'll play your game and sustain your efforts as long as
you demand it of her."

Some other parent, likewise feeling no response to the
idea of God, might nevertheless profess his interest in gathering himself with others of his kind in some sort of religious service which celebrates the aesthetic and ethical
values that the group holds to be of greatest importance in
life. This religious service might lend itself to the use of
music and many forms of art in creating the mood of ex-
altation. Liturgy, created for the purpose of the service,

might have a place in setting and maintaining the religious mood. Nothing authentic in human experience would be sacrificed, this parent might feel, but the idea of God would be unnecessary as authority or explanation.

There is still another way of saying, "It depends upon what you mean by God." Jane's father is a physicist and Jane, now fifteen, firmly expects to follow in his footsteps. From much listening, and maybe some thinking, she has picked up some of the physicist's vocabulary and she dearly likes to ride cross-country with her father asking "large" questions. Something she has heard at school has brought up the discussion of matter.

"Well, father, when you get right down to it, matter isn't anything really. Maybe it's spirit and maybe spirit taken altogether is God."

"As far as we know," says her father, "matter is an immaterial element called force which does not behave with strict causality. But I don't see that you are anything ahead to call it 'God' instead of 'matter.'"

"But maybe there's something back of matter and *that's* God," Jane insists.

"If you're meaning to say that maybe there's more to reality than meets the eye, so to speak, then I think that's a fair assumption," her father agrees. "Our senses may shut out as much of 'realness' as they let in. Take a tiny electric explosion, for instance. We see it with the eye and we hear it with the ear. We even taste the tang of it, and we feel the prick of it. From our impressions we build up a mental picture of electricity. But probably we don't get all of the essence of electricity; if we had more senses we might perceive other factors now entirely unknown to us. But that doesn't signify that this larger reality which may now escape us, has the personal qualities which we think of when we use the word 'God.'"

"I suppose we do have to think of God as something of a person," Jane admits, "or there isn't any point to saying 'him' instead of 'it.'"

"There's where I think you're wrong," her father answers, "and you miss your own best argument for the idea of God. I don't know any good reason to conclude that there can be no consciousness except the individualized aspects of consciousness we know in ourselves and call 'personal.' There may be personality that transcends anything we ordinarily mean by the word. I tell you, when you see a thermionic valve in action you find yourself slow to say 'no' to a good many possibilities."

"You mean something to measure electrons and ions?"

"I mean an instrument for electrical detection of *thought*. Actually the brain has a field about it which perturbates with thought, and the fact that the brain is 'thinking' can be registered. 'Matter' and 'mind' aren't the antithetic terms they once were. If you want to call the ultimate mind-matter energy 'God,' and to feel that it is behind the laws we now know, perhaps even transcending them, I guess you have a right to do so."

"But, father, if I have a God, I want a God who is aware of *me*." Jane looks very young as she turns to her father, but her words are old as time and he answers them carefully.

"Maybe you can have that, too," he says. "Maybe we've been too long content with too easy assumptions. It's easy to say there can't be personality behind impersonal laws. But I think it has been a fundamental fact in human experience that the energy-radiation we frequently call 'spirit' will sustain and substantiate any consideration that creative desire calls upon it to support and fulfill. You might say that such a fact constitutes a personal relationship, if you take care not to measure the other end of the relationship in the limited terms of yourself."

Jane doesn't say anything for a while and then she turns a happy face to her father. "It's lovely, isn't it, to feel ourselves getting bigger ideas all the time." Whereupon she looks apologetic, almost embarrassed. "I mean there are so many kinds of curiosity and it's kind of nice when your curiosity sort of seems to get some place. That's why I want to be a physicist."

"You never need to apologize for curiosity whether it appears to get some place or not. It's the purest of the passions, Jane. Understanding just for the love of it is about as swell an experience as comes man's way."

They ride in silence for a while. Jane is in a state of alert passivity from which insight rises. Her father knows when not to intrude with words. Of course he knows that in their talk they haven't proved anything about God, one way or the other, but he feels that Jane won't use the word too specifically — which is quite as harmful as to make too vague use of it — for a while yet.

There are still other ways of answering, "It depends on what you mean by God." Karl, at sixteen, is more sensitive than most boys to the misery of the world. Pain has given him acute awareness of the place of suffering in human life. One day, driving along the river which skirts the miserable, crowded huts of the "Flats," he remarks to his mother bitterly: "I have no use for a God who allows such things to exist. If he is God at all, he could do something about it. He could allow a fair chance for everybody instead of sending poverty and misery to some."

"It isn't God who sends the misery," his mother answers. "Misery and pain are here as part of this growing, imperfect universe. God struggles against them as really as you and I do. He is the power of light and truth and understanding which works in the world for its ultimate perfection. But he can't do it all at once."

"Then he isn't an all-powerful, infinite being," says Karl promptly. "He is limited."

"Yes, he is limited," his mother agrees, bringing the car to a stop on a shaded boulevard where she can talk without dividing her attention. "I suppose one must acknowledge that God is finite. That he is a limited, growing God."

"There are evidently things he cannot do." Karl motions back along the road they have come. "He can't clean up those Flats."

"Not all at once. Not by divine fiat. He works through the laws of the universe. Unless he would entirely discard the growth of human personality, he has to wait for men to see and understand their responsibility to one another. He has to wait for them to invent methods of meeting their own needs. He has to wait for the slow process of trial and error, for the slow evolution of ideals and their even slower application to real life situations."

"But something in the universe works to tear it down, too. Something perpetuates pain." Karl's words frequently hold more of comprehension than sixteen years of living would seem to justify. "Something drives men to choose evil, to inflict poverty and stunt growth. There's an ultimate cause behind all that, too. You're just selecting the good in the universe and calling it 'God,' and ignoring the evil."

"I'm not ignoring the evil. Perhaps I might call it 'maladjustment' or 'error.' I think that what you call 'evil' is inevitably a part of any great scheme of growth because wisdom itself comes by degrees and the best intentions in the world do not save men from making tremendous mistakes. But you're right when you say I'm selecting the qualities I call 'God.'"

"Do you think that's fair? Isn't it kind of fooling yourself?"

His mother hesitates. " I don't think so.   When we talk
about the spirit of America or when we set up the intangible
figure of Uncle Sam, we are also selecting qualities which
we believe to be real and ultimately triumphant.   The experience of the race to date seems to prove certain qualities desirable, certain attitudes 'good.'   So we set them
apart as ideals, as goals, and then we throw our lives into
the task of bringing them to pass.   That's fair enough.   You
may call it setting up your God and then giving him life,
but I think it is just as fair to call it finding out God and
going along with him."

Karl debates the matter.   The fact that he has read more
than most boys of his age and spent much time alone, lends
insight to his quiet words.   " I believe I'd rather think of
God as the whole of the causal force behind the universe
making, or at least allowing, all that we call 'bad' as well
as 'good.'   I don't see any reason to worship him or to try
to placate him.   He just goes on his long relentless way,
handing out a lifetime of pain to some of us and a lifetime
of joy to others.   Maybe out of the pain comes wisdom
and out of the joy comes nothing.   But I don't think he
cares or is even aware which it is.   I don't think he has personal qualities at all."

The argument between Karl and his mother goes on for
months, each bringing to the other now and again some
new perception or observation.   After the death of a friend
in a tragic accident, Karl is impressed anew by the apparent indifference of God.

" Look, mother.   While Dave rode along in the ambu-
lance suffering horribly, the sky was a cloudless blue.   The
sun shone and the birds sang and trees cast their shade on
the boulevard.   Nothing in all nature cared."

" You mean that nothing in nature seemed to care.   But
perhaps the crudity is on the part of our dull ears.   You

know, Karl, if it's true that a falling apple exerts a pull of gravitation for the earth just as really as the earth pulls the apple and that the pull of each can be measured, then it isn't hard for me to believe that our tragedies pull at the whole of nature."

"Even so, we're still too small to mean anything," says Karl stoically.

"No, we aren't. We're small but we *do* mean something. We're part of the scheme of things."

"A big help that," says Karl, "when we don't understand the scheme."

A few weeks later the two have occasion to go through a federal housing project. Karl is enthusiastic. "It's a long way from the time when men lived in caves," he says. "If the neolithic man stepped in here, he might allow that the world had wagged along to some point."

"It's wagged along in more ways than one," says his mother, pointing to the crowded public playground across the street. "Just a handful of years ago, no one paid any attention to the children of the poor. Back when Rome was at its height, orphans without relatives frequently became child slaves. The insane were public nuisances but not public charges. Lepers were beggars, and goodness knows what happened to the blind and the deaf."

"And so, you're going to add, ' God is working his purpose out.' " Karl smiles at his mother.

"I think he is. The process is so slow that all our human minds can comprehend is less than a second's progress in the flow of time, but I do believe that consideration for human values is emerging. Slowly, unevenly, but surely. And at the same time man is mastering nature, or learning to cooperate with her, so that the very forces which now threaten his existence will some day be his friends."

As Karl sometimes comments, there is no end to the sort

of argument he and his mother carry on, partly because their experience is interpreted in terms of their emotions. Occasionally when Karl himself is suffering, his mother feels swallowed up by the vast impersonality of the universe. Most of the time she is sustained by her faith in the long-time process of the world's growth. Sometimes Karl partakes of that faith and is philosophical about his own life. "Maybe I'm merely an error in the process of the world's education," he says. "I'm just a misspelled word or a rummy bit of addition. But the educational system's pretty sound."

No final summing up is possible on children's questions or their parents' answers about the nature of God and man's place in the universe. Children will keep on asking; their parents will keep on answering; both will keep on learning from life itself. Perhaps the simple truth is that each man chooses whether or not he will have a God and how much God he can use. The man who negates a personalized power behind the universe does not easily dissuade the man who feels that his whole life has become buoyant and meaningful through contact with some sustaining, free-flowing power. On the other hand the burden of proof rests on the one who feels that he has access to that power. Eventually his life must sustain his claims or he must cease to answer "yes" when new generations of children cry, "Is there a God?"

Experiencing Values

As brother Lawrence had found such an advantage in walking in the presence of God, it was natural for him to recommend it earnestly to others; but his example was a stronger inducement than any arguments he could propose. THE PRACTICE OF THE PRESENCE OF GOD

Among those who accept the idea of God, it is one thing merely to accept an intellectual concept and it is quite another to go to work ordering one's days on the basis of that idea. In a practical sense, adults probably accept only as much of an idea of God as they can put to work in their daily lives. Certainly a child either "uses" his God or ignores him. The child's ideas and his actions are all of one piece. Sometimes an idea may push ahead of action; sometimes action appears to outreach the original concept, which merely means that the concept is enlarged as it is experienced. A child's experience of God, as of anything else, is as much in his play as in any of his real-life relationships.

Stuart was five the summer he went to the north Wisconsin woods to live on a lake. Day after day he accompanied his mother to an old farm at the head of the lake where milk and vegetables were sold. For the children, the farm was important because of the large crop of kittens, all "wild," living on the edge of the woods and refusing to come at any human's call. Through many years on that farm, mother cats had raised kittens who grew up and raised more kittens, most of them the color of burnished gold. In and out of the farm buildings, the plump cats and kittens played hide-and-seek. But only occasionally could one be coaxed to within a few yards of the onlooker. On various occasions Stuart had tried to play with the family of kittens who lived under the ice house. The roundest, coyest one of all he named "Fireball." Fireball got so she would go into an ecstasy of excitement over a moving string of grape vine and follow the boy all around the yard. But Fireball would not be caught. If she could be caught, the farm lady said, Stuart might certainly have her to take home "after she is weaned."

On one particular afternoon Stuart had a long time to wait at the farm. So he played with the kittens, particularly with Fireball who sometimes came tantalizingly near to him. Finally, tired out with play — or as nearly tired out as a kitten will admit — Fireball crept right up to the spot where Stuart lay on the grass — as nearly tired out as a boy will admit — and curled herself into a ball against his chest. There she purred most heartily. Mother from the porch saw the kitten and called the farm lady who called the cook who called the hands. Everyone surveyed the spectacle of the wild kitten curled in the arms of a small human.

At last it was time for Stuart to leave. He started down to the boat landing with the kitten jumping at his heels like a puppy. Onto the dock walked Stuart and onto the dock walked Fireball. The boy leaned over to give the kitten a last pat. She snuggled against his bare legs and scratched clawlessly at his ankles. Reluctantly Stuart picked her up and set her back on land, ran down the dock and hopped into the boat. The kitten leaped to the end of the dock where she stood mewing lustily, watched by the entire farm family on the porch and by the other cats peering out from beneath the ice house. The boat pulled away. And then, when the boat was some six or eight feet from the dock, the kitten jumped into the lake and swam for the boat. Back-paddling quickly, mother met the kitten half-way and Stuart leaned over the side of the boat to lift in a very wet bit of kitten.

Rolling the kitten into his sweater, Stuart turned to his mother with wide eyes. "Fireball thinks I'm God." And then to the kitten, "There, there, you don't need to shiver. God's got you all safe and warm."

The child continued in the role of God without comment from any member of the family. Each morning as soon as the fire was started in the kitchen stove, he heated the kitten's milk, poured it into her saucer and took it to her corner. "God's feeding you," he would say quietly. Or if the family were going away for an afternoon, he would pick up the kitten and carry her from her basket to her sandbox to her saucer of milk, and back to her basket, making sure she knew where everything was and then, giving her a final pat, he would add, "You think God's gone away but God will remember about you all the time and you'll be all right."

Evidently he had spun the theory that for all practical kitten purposes safety consisted in existing "in the mind of God," as the earlier theologians might have said.

One day a great-aunt came to visit and overheard Stuart's remark to the kitten, "God won't let Ben's dog come near you."

"Goodness me," she said in genuine concern, "it's pure sacrilege to let a child talk as if he were God Almighty."

"He'll probably never come nearer to God than when he's trying to act like him," said father calmly.

The idea of being God to the small cat wore off, as children's ideas do wear off. Stuart went away for two weeks. When he returned home he was still just as fond of the cat but he never again referred to himself as God — until one day when he was twelve years old. Walking along a country road one evening with his father, he said, "Once when I was quite young I had a kitten named Fireball. Do you remember?"

"I remember. She was about the cutest kitten we ever had."

"Wasn't she! Well, sir, I thought that the cat thought I was God so I used to try to act like God when I was alone. Evenings like this, I pretended I walked on the clouds and whenever I came to poor children's houses I dropped blessings on them. It seemed awfully lonesome for children to live the year round way out here in tar-paper houses and hardly ever have any company. I pretended I was God riding along the old roads with a wagonload of surprise packages and leaving one in every mailbox. I still think of that every time I go by country mailboxes and some day I'm going to do it."

"While you're at it, you might leave a little more livestock for the barns and a few washing machines for the women."

Stuart walked on without comment for a bit and then remarked: "I guess there are some things even God can't do without help. He can't make washing machines rain from heaven. And he can't make dairy cows walk down out of clouds. People have to help themselves."

"It's uphill work sometimes."

"I remember when Fireball thought I was God. I mean when I thought Fireball thought I was God. I remember telling her over and over, 'Even God can't teach you to use a sandbox unless you put your mind to it.'"

Father chuckled to himself, realizing how easily in a child's mind divinity concerns itself with practical affairs, realizing also how lightly and naturally a child may skirt the truths to which wise ones give a lifetime of searching. He spoke to that point. He spoke man to man.

"When you said there are some things even God can't do alone, you were saying one of the most important things about God, at least so it seems to me. He never transgresses human personality. He doesn't 'make' us do a thing. He doesn't even compel us to be good. If he did, he would be only a driving, arbitrary force in a world of automatons. There would be no choices for human beings to make, no struggle to know which things are good to do and which work harm. There would be no passionate devotion to finding out the secrets of nature, no sharpening of man's wits against the universe, no growth. It takes a really great God to leave man free to make his own mistakes."

The boy again walked along for a few moments without speaking. Just as he lengthened his stride to keep step with his father when they walked together, so he seemed to be lengthening his thoughts. "Well, sir, I'll tell you what I think. I think that maybe he doesn't make us do things, just like you say, but I think he wants us to do the right thing so much that you feel his ideas tugging at you. Maybe it isn't exactly his ideas you feel because ideas have to be about something. Maybe it's his spirit."

"His love," suggested father.

"Yes, that's it, I guess. You feel he cares so much about you that you can't let him down and so you sort of stop and wait awhile like you were listening and pretty soon you don't feel like doing the shady thing that maybe you were going to do. It just doesn't fit and you don't want to do it any more. And you feel like you'd had a sort of little visit although you didn't say anything. I mean you didn't pray or anything, and of course he didn't really say anything either." Stuart paused. "At least that's how we do it."

"We!" Father found his throat tightening. How naturally the boy said it. And here he had been wondering lately if his noisy young son, banging off to play with three whoops and a holler the minute he came in from school, ever had a serious thought.

One thing Stuart's father did not consciously realize, although any thoughtful neighbor could have told him. His son had been feeling the compelling love of God partly because he felt also the compelling love of his father whose quick understanding and high integrity were always behind the boy like a bulwark. Any child's experience of God is rather likely to be set in the mold of his experience with earthly parenthood.

But the child's idea of God is not always expressed overtly so that his parent can say, "Look, he is playing God." Sometimes, to be sure, a child may stand on a chair throwing imaginary balls into the air as he creates a universe and tosses the stars into space. He is plainly playing God. Or the fancy of another child may be caught by the story of the ark and, not content to be Noah, he is Jehovah the Lord God warning the wicked cities, calling on Noah to prepare the ark, finally rounding up the animals two by two so that Noah will have no trouble coaxing them to safety.

God the Creator seems to appeal to the small child, especially to the child who asks insistent questions about the beginnings of things: Who made me? How? How was the very, very first man made? How was the world made? Out of what? Who did it? How did he make the stars? Then who made God? How did it all start anyhow?

This sort of child, asking how-questions, is likely to relive the beginnings of all sorts of things in his play, although he may not go through the physical motions of making things. He may sit ever so still, a concentrated bundle of imagination, playing all the stories in his mind. Unlike the child who acts out his creations, he may not be aware that he is playing God. He is merely off on the edge of somewhere, stretching his mind to take in the ideas of time and space and an ultimate beginning. If he lives in a household which uses the term " God," he is unconsciously giving the word content for himself. He is letting his own emotions inflate the ideas which have come from his parents until, like a handful of tugging balloons, they almost pull him off his feet.

One way or another, the dominant characteristics of a child's God will almost always reveal themselves in his play. Even when he does not think of himself as pretending he is God, still he orders events on a large scale, giving himself tremendous power of the sort he would credit to God if his ideas were forced into words. Jack with his toy soldiers goes forth to fight the enemy, right and might on his side, daring storm and flood as well as bullets. Ellen, scarcely six, plays orphans' asylum with number-cards, letting the numbers stand for the ages of the children and gathering each child with its own particular story of hardship into the affection and responsibilities of the orphans' home. Day after day she plays the game, never seeming to tire of inventing new children.

Jack and Ellen are in the same Sunday school class. When a chance question about God sets all the children to answering at once, Jack says: " God punishes those that don't do right. He lets the good armies blow them to pieces. He makes earthquakes and shakes them up. He can do anything he wants to. No matter where they run to, he can always catch them in the end." Ellen says: " God finds out about everybody that's having a hard time, like children who don't have parents and people in hospitals and the poor and newsboys. Pretty soon he thinks up a way to help them get more to eat and have a birthday party and things."

Jack and Ellen listen to each other's answers, each ready
to fly to the protection of his own God but also uneasily
aware that perhaps there is something in the other's idea.
A week later, chance and a May morning make neighbors
of the two children. They begin to play together. They
play soldier and they play orphans. One play modifies the
other until, quite unconsciously, of course, both children
are also " playing God " from much the same point of view.

Playing God is so close to experiencing God that it is
difficult to say where imagination leaves off and participation begins. " Workers together with him " is a description of the human urge to bring high values to pass. The
child has his share of this urge. The parent may direct it
somewhat. Probably, in this matter as in most other matters, the unconscious influence is the only direct influence.
Our theory of reality makes its mark on us and all our ways,
and we " make " our child in the image of our God.

Does Prayer Make Sense?

*He had them then into another room, where was a hen
and chickens, and bid them observe a while. So one of
the chickens went to the trough to drink, and every
time she drank she lifted up her head and her eyes towards heaven. "See," said he, "what this little chick
doth, and learn of her to acknowledge whence your
mercies come, by receiving them with looking up."*

JOHN BUNYAN (*Pilgrim's Progress*)

Naturally, the family idea of God will determine the child's
attitude toward prayer. If God is an abstraction, an impersonal force pulsing in the universe as an engine pulses —
no more sentient, no more responsive to human need —
then prayer is a rather fantastic pastime. If, on the other
hand, the idea of God includes such qualities of personality
as awareness and sympathy and love, then it seems natural
enough to try to reach toward that personality, to try to
augment one's insufficiency by access to a limitless supply.
Prayer is also possible to those who view it not as an asking-
and-receiving process operating between person and Person, but as a "tuning in" on the creative energy of the
universe.

There are two sorts of homes in which children are not
likely to ask questions about prayer: homes in which a particular idea of God makes prayer a patent absurdity, and
homes in which prayer, and talk about it, are as natural as
any other family conversation. But a great many children
grow up in homes which fall some place between these two

categories, and these children are likely at some time to ask a good many questions about prayer.

Their questioning may come suddenly when some untoward incident makes them suddenly aware of their own prayers.

"But I prayed, mother. I prayed every day, a lot of times every day." Barry's voice betrayed incredulous disappointment. This was his birthday, his seventh birthday, the day to which he had looked forward so eagerly and from which he had expected so much. In spite of planning to be up with the sun, he had overslept and had almost been late for breakfast. When he bounded into the sunny dining room, there by his place at the table were packages of all sizes and shapes. True to the family tradition, he opened only the smallest one before he ate. It was a key ring just like father's. He smiled triumphantly. Of course, a key ring. He would have to have keys because the Thing he was waiting for — the biggest present of his life so far — would need to be chained to the fence and locked just like a bicycle when he went to play with Jack or Raymond. He laughed aloud. His mother laughed and his father laughed. Millie, the cook, stuck her head in the doorway; laughed, too, long and heartily. No doubt Millie was in on the secret. He hoped she hadn't seen the Thing because he wanted to watch her tongue pop out like her eyes when she realized what she was looking at. Thinking about Millie's surprise made it hard to listen to what his father was saying, although everyone was being ever so jolly.

"I'm glad you're here," Barry said to his father, beamingly. He wanted everyone to share the big moment. "I'm glad no one got sick in the night and called you out." Ordinarily it would be his mother who was more thrilled than anyone over a big surprise, but this was something dif-

ferent.   No doubt his father would even want to run the
Thing.   Well, he could.   It was plenty big if his father
didn't mind being squeezed up a bit.

After breakfast, Barry unwrapped the other presents.
There were more of them than usual and even nicer.   It
was great of Uncle Tom to send him the little kodak.   Ordinarily a kodak would have occupied him for a long time.
It was great of his father and mother to get him such a
swell set of tools, but he wished they hadn't.   Vaguely he
felt that they really couldn't afford the Thing and then all
these tools besides.   Anyway he wouldn't have much time
for tools now.   He hoped his father wouldn't mind car-
pentering alone in the hobby hour which they tried to spend
together just after dinner.

Pretty soon everything was unwrapped and Barry had
said all the " thank you's," folded all the papers, and stood
tremblingly beside the door which led into the garden.

" My stars, I never saw you so excited, Barry," said his
mother, patting the dark head.

" It's something to be seven years old, eh, son? " said father, starting for the living room.

" I'm ready now," said Barry.   The moment had come
and there was no use waiting longer.   In fact he couldn't
wait longer.   " I'm ready now."

" Ready for what? " asked mother, looking mystified.

" You know for what! " laughed Barry.   " Let's go together."

After that, Barry didn't know what was said.   It seemed
as if he had stood in the doorway for long dizzy hours trying to understand their words but never really believing
them at all.   At first it was a joke they were making . . .
the joke was too long . . . then it wasn't a joke at all . . .
they were surprised he had ever expected the Thing . . . it
hadn't even seriously entered their minds.   A toy automo-

bile the size of the one at the Fair, with an engine and all
those gadgets — why, the Thing cost hundreds of dollars.

"Hundreds of dollars?" cried Barry. "But hundreds
of dollars are nothing to God."

He had *prayed* for that automobile. He had prayed be-
lievingly. Not a shadow of doubt had crossed his mind.
He been good for weeks, even in little things his mother
would never know the difference about, such as brushing
his teeth after breakfast. He had been good and he had
prayed. And God — what had God done? He had paid
exactly no attention at all. What kind of God is that who
doesn't answer the prayers of the good and believing?

This proved to be one morning when father's patients
waited in the office and mother's painting waited in the
studio, and Millie had the same answer for all telephone
calls: "If you will call again at noon, please." Father and
mother knew a major crisis when they met it. Afterwards
they said to each other, "If we had only known he wanted
it so badly . . . if we had known he was praying and expecting." But Barry had had so much faith and such a
very special kind of excitement that he had never mentioned the automobile in the prayers he said aloud. And
now he was through with praying. Through with God,
too, for God the Almighty who could do anything he
wanted — make a world and raise the dead — God hadn't
even bothered to listen about the little car.

"Barry, I have a question to ask you," said father after
they had gone into the living room and were sitting before
the fire which mother had lighted on the hearth. Barry,
hunched on a footstool, waited. "If you were sick in bed
with a bad case of measles and asked me for a piece of mince
pie and I wouldn't give it to you, would you think I was
just being mean?"

"Nope," said Barry, shaking his head. That was a silly

question. He was not going to be led off the track by any
nonsense even though his father seemed as solemn as if he
were talking to another doctor. But he would be patient
with his father because he wanted him to understand now
and finally that he was through with God. "No, I
wouldn't," he repeated.

"You would believe that I knew more about the measles
than you did, wouldn't you? You'd believe that I knew
more about pie and about small boys."

"I'd know you didn't want to make me sicker. You
wouldn't want to hurt me. But I'm not sick and an automobile isn't like pie. An automobile would only make me
happy and not hurt anyone."

"You miss the point," said father gently. "And besides,
you know more than lots of children about what to eat
when you're sick. A lot of boys cry and holler for things
and if the doctor doesn't give them what they want, they
think he is being mean. They're too small to realize that
the doctor knows lots of things they never even heard of."

"I know it," said Barry dully.

"I think we are often quite a bit like the child who
wants mince pie when we are asking things of God. I
don't mean you and your automobile, particularly. But all
of us, asking for all sorts of things. We know what we
want and it seems a good thing to us. But we can't even
guess the other considerations which God has to think
over."

Barry nodded. What his father said was plain enough.

"Now take your automobile. You prayed for it, but
you didn't expect God to drop an automobile from the
clouds. He works pretty much through natural laws and
situations. If you were to get that automobile, I'm the one
who would have to pay for it. That particular car cost
close to a thousand dollars if it cost a cent. It was a show

car and a marvel of mechanics. I don't have a thousand dollars to spend. In order to buy that car I'd have to borrow money on my insurance, which would be a foolish thing to do, or we'd have to cancel our order for coal and live in a cold house all winter, and not buy any winter clothes. We couldn't even buy gas for the car we now have and I'd lose a great deal of time trying to reach my patients by streetcar. God knows all these things. When you ask for a car, he has to consider everybody who would be concerned with getting the car."

Barry stuck to the point about the money. " Supposing mother got sick," he said. " Supposing she had to be sent on a trip like Mrs. Perkins. You'd find the money fast enough. You'd ask God to help you find the money. We all would."

" You bet I'd ask him," father admitted. " I'd not only ask him but I'd expect him to send me patients who could pay me so that I'd get the money. I'd expect him to give me better ideas than I'd ever had before so that I would be worth more money. But that's different, Barry. Health matters more in the world than automobiles. Health seems to be part of God's plan. And when it comes to your mother's health, you and I would work harder than we would for all the automobiles in the country. We wouldn't even care what we had to do without. But to do without food or clothes to buy a toy might risk our health. There's a good deal of responsibility in handling money, you know. We aren't free to take money from a necessary thing just for our own pleasure."

" I know that," said Barry. " I wouldn't expect God to take the money that some sick person ought to use to go to the hospital. But some kids get those cars. Why couldn't I be one of them? "

" I don't know, Barry. No one knows the answer for

sure, but there are a lot of possible reasons. For instance, it's a lot easier to ride around in a little car, especially such a honey of a car, than to take your tools and go make a box for a wagon and learn how to put on the wheels by yourself. And yet in the end you might be much happier to know how to use the tools. You might really have more fun, although you can't believe that now. Or there may be some other reason why the car is not a good thing for you. Perhaps if you had the car, you couldn't put your mind on your school work which you really need to do after all you missed last spring. There are a great many possible reasons why it may not have been best for you to have that car. We don't know the reasons but since God didn't send the car, I believe the reasons are good ones which he knew about and considered."

Now mother spoke for the first time. "Barry, you never doubt your father's love for you, do you? Even when he cannot stay home to play with you, even when he punishes you, you never doubt he loves you, I know."

"I know he loves me," said Barry.

"Most of the time, you trust his wisdom, too, don't you?" Mother seemed to be caring a lot for what she was saying. "He's only human, we know, and he can make mistakes, but most of the time we think he acts wisely, don't we?"

"Yes, we do," said Barry.

"It seems to me it's the same with God. He cares about us. He loves us. And he is wise enough to see what is best. We have to believe that he knows best even when we cannot see or understand what was the matter with our own plan." Mother spoke as if she had tried out her idea and believed it with all her heart.

"Either we have to trust him," said father, "we have to believe that he cares for us and will send the thing that is best for us and withhold the things which are not best for us, or we must believe that we simply do not matter in the eyes of God."

"Maybe we don't," said Barry.

"My own experience indicates the other attitude," said father. "I think that the Maker of the universe is very much concerned with man. He has a plan for his children. If he forced us into that plan, then we wouldn't be the sons of God. We'd be merely puppets. No doubt his plan is all about us, plain enough. But we have to find it by using our own minds and hearts. We'll make ten thousand mistakes, just as men have made in the past, but we hope we are working a bit nearer to the plan with each generation of those who give themselves to finding the mind of God."

Barry looked at his father wonderingly. "Do you believe God has a plan for me?"

"Yes, I do, son. I believe that there is some task for you to do, something which perhaps no one else in the world could do quite so well in the place and manner he wants you to do it. I believe that if you listen closely enough and don't hurry and don't insist on the plan's being carried out your own way, then the plan will come plain to you."

"The queer thing is that you begin to know in your heart when you've found the plan," said mother. She moved nearer the fire and smiled at father as she spoke. "It's something like falling in love. Sometimes I used to wonder if I were in love when I met this nice boy or that one. But when I really fell in love, I didn't have to wonder about it at all. I just completely knew this was the man with whom I felt the most deeply contented and happy. Feeling that way, I could do my own work better. Much, much better. It was part of the plan for me, I think."

Barry felt that his mother and father had forgotten about

him for the moment, but he did not feel left out. The things they were saying to each other were important, too.

"I felt the same way about you," said father. "The only other time I ever felt so sure was when I stumbled into medicine. Somehow when I was growing up it never occurred to me to be a doctor. None of the men in our family went in for the medical profession. Being a well little tike without ailments, I'd never come into contact with doctors. During high school I concluded I'd go into the hardware business with my dad but I never was much elated over the idea. When I was a freshman I thought I'd be a lawyer. One summer I tried playground work in a settlement house. By the time I was a junior, I'd tried a lot of things. They all seemed o.k. but none of them interested me much. It began to worry me not to care more about what my profession might be. When I worried, I lost my appetite and got thin. Finally I was in such a miserable state that I went to a doctor. Old Dr. Hewitt. I went to him because my father always thought a lot of him. He wasn't even a general practitioner but a specialist on duodenal ulcers. After he had reassured me about my health, he talked to me. He took me over to the hospital and showed me around. By the end of that afternoon I was a full-fledged doctor — all except going to medical school and interning and a few such little things. . My mind was made up. Doctoring was *my* job. Simple as that."

Mother smiled. "You say you stumbled into your profession but I think you were led."

"I guess we're meaning the same thing," said father. "Something in me couldn't be satisfied until I found the place where I seemed to fit. I wanted to find that place a great deal. I wanted it so much that I didn't really need to pray for it in words. Although as a matter of fact I did pray. I not only prayed but I had almost decided that prayer was no use and that God couldn't be bothered about me — when I went to Dr. Hewitt."

"'Prayer is the soul's sincere desire, uttered or unexpressed.'" Barry knew that his mother was quoting poetry even if it didn't rhyme. "Probably the sensitive heart of the universe isn't so very dependent upon our words. I suspect our words are more useful to us than to God because when we put our ideas into words we think them more clearly, and the clearer our ideas get, the easier it is for us to understand God's answer."

His father turned back to Barry, speaking gravely. "There isn't a lot one person can say to another when it comes to this business of prayer. But it seems to me that you hardly want to discard it until you've given it a little more trial. It takes some time to learn to want wisely. I'd experiment a little more if I were you."

Barry had been thinking his own thoughts while he listened to his parents. "It's o.k. about the automobile," he said. "Prob'ly Jack and Raymond would feel kind of left out if they didn't have automobiles, too. Prob'ly we'll go racing our wagons some more. It's o.k." Thus pragmatically Barry disposed of the matter and reached for his new kodak.

Had the whole discussion been over his head? Not at all. Most of the ideas he understood — not well enough to put them back into words again, but well enough so that the matter of not having received his automobile seemed logical to him. More than that, he understood that his parents believed in the love of God and in the wisdom of God. He understood, too, that his parents thought it was important to know about God, to trust him, to find his will. But above all else, Barry had the feeling that God had never let his parents down and that they expected to go right on keeping as near to God as they could. They must have thought it was quite important for him to understand how they felt or his father would never have put off going to the office.

Barry wound the film into his new kodak, exactly the way he had seen Jack wind his. It really was all right about the automobile. It really was all right about God. He hoped God did have a plan for him. He hoped he'd find it. He hoped his father and mother would live until he himself was an old, old man, and that Millie would always be their cook. Having thus taken care of eventualities, he went out to play like the normal growing child he was. Years later he knew this had been a big day in his life, although he never remembered what his parents had said. It was the day which might have left him feeling cheated by life, defiant against his disappointment, finished with prayer and skeptical about the future. Instead, it left him — although he never put his feeling into words — ready for whatever came next.

Not all parents who believe in a personal God could have said to Barry that God sent him what was best, what was meant for him to have. Some, believing that God himself is limited by the imperfect, growing universe, would have said that human beings do not by any means receive what is " best " for them to have. The most they can hope for in this precarious world is strength to match their circumstances. They would say, for instance, that it would be impossible for God, being good, to send an attack of infantile paralysis to a careless but gifted youth in order to make him realize his ability as a painter. But they would go on to say that when the youth contracted infantile paralysis because mankind had not yet learned how to eliminate disease, then God might match the boy's pain with a new awareness of the flowers in his sickroom, a new comprehension of the world's need for beauty, a new desire to make that beauty manifest through pictures, and a stern new patience in developing the necessary technique for painting.

And still others would not admit a plan in the universe which includes a place for the contribution of each individual. They would say that "God" has nothing to do with the ordering of events, that the life of man is an evolution of law and circumstance, making itself as it progresses. Barry's receiving the automobile or not receiving it was merely a contributing circumstance to be woven into the fabric of events. But, they might add, long years of living in this world of nature, people and resulting circumstances have given a few pointers. Among them is the fact that it pays not to lose energy repining for what does not come one's way. They would say, "That's that," to Barry when he did not get the automobile, and then cheerfully point to the tools and the kodak he did get as being, if he cared to make them so, equally valuable and pleasurable.

Children, being also people, differ greatly in their acceptance of experience. Some, especially adolescents, having experienced through prayer a heightened awareness of the beauty and wonder in the world about them, a quickened sense of other people's needs, a wider perspective, an infilling of their own spirits, are content to accept the fact of prayer as one of God's provisions for their needs. They would put answers to prayer in a class with the water which satisfies their thirst and the food which satisfies their hunger. They do not press the question, How can this thing be so? They merely *use* the experience of prayer.

But other children, also particularly adolescents, are driven to hunt an explanation. " What is prayer? " they ask. " What really happens when I pray? I don't want to spend my time on something which isn't reasonable. Even if I grant the strengthening which comes to some people through prayer, where does it come from and how does it come about? "

For such questions it is not enough to say, " There are states of consciousness in which man's experience outruns his explanations." For these are the children who are likely to become the unravelers of the world's mysteries. Some among them are the men and women who will wrest out the secrets of astronomy, of medicine, of radiant energy, and push the limits of man's control of his universe one step farther. They have to know the how of things.

Mary stopped suddenly in the midst of a Chopin prelude which she had been playing with apparent absorption. She often played for a half-hour before dinner while her father sat in his favorite chair with the newspaper still unfolded on his knee, just listening.

"Father, it's a funny thing about Mr. Ryerson." She spoke quickly as if releasing thoughts long bottled up in her mind. "I've thought about it before but I never knew how odd it was until today."

"I don't know anything so funny about Mr. Ryerson," said her father with a smile which seemed as much for Mr. Ryerson as for Mary. "I've always thought he was a pretty grand old man. Prince of the city fathers."

"Yes, I know he's grand. They said out at the Home today that he has placed over twenty thousand children in the Home and that he's never let one leave without a real home or a job."

"I guess that's true all right."

"This afternoon he talked to all the high school seniors who go out there to help with the recreation and story hours. He said that for thirty years the Home had been run on prayer. Then we got to talking about prayer and John Addams came right out and said that he had heard that Mr. Ryerson didn't even believe in God. And Mr. Ryerson said he didn't believe in the kind of God most people believed in, but that he believed in prayer. He believed that when we pray in need, we do honestly receive answers but that our prayers are heard by human ears and our answers are delivered by human hands and feet. Does that make sense to you? "

" It makes quite a bit of sense to me," said her father slowly. " I know Mr. Ryerson's habit of contemplation and silence. He never thinks of starting or closing the day without a whole hour of silence. I've known him when he was faced with quite tremendous problems, when a mortgage was about to be foreclosed on his big farm back of the Home and his creditors literally waited at the door; when the scarlet fever epidemic swooped down on the place; when the near-by public school was about to refuse to take his orphans without tuition because so many of them came from out of the state. But I've never known him to miss that hour of silence and meditation no matter who was waiting to talk about what. I've asked him about it once or twice." Father stopped short.

Mary left the piano and came over to sit near him. " Go on."

" I'm not so good at explanations as he is. But the gist of what he says is that when he is completely quiet in body and mind, then the noise and petty problems of the day recede before the stillness of his deep desire, and help rises up from the recesses of his mind, probably from his memory."

"What on earth do you mean — help from his memory? "

" He means that during his life he has had many fine experiences with friends, with books, with people he has never met personally but has heard about and studied and admired. All of us have countless friends of this sort, in real life and in books, who have been our living companions and have stirred our imaginations. All these companions together have a rather tremendous amount of wisdom. We may have forgotten them, but deep in our minds they have made their imprint nevertheless. Now Mr. Ryerson says that when he sits in complete silence and spreads out his problems before all these wise and capable and generous people he has known, he feels just as if he were looking into the faces of a mighty audience before whom he wanted to lay a problem which they could decide and act upon. In an audience one doesn't see individual faces but the audience has personality none the less. It responds. And just as a reaction comes back from an audience so that a speaker is inspired to say things he never thought of before, and to use words he didn't realize were in his vocabulary, and to feel power surging in him which ordinarily he just does not have — so with these unseen friends of all his life, he also has the sense of dealing with a great reservoir of wisdom and common sense and power. He stands before them, so to speak, and be begins to get ideas. His mood begins to change. Anxiety gives way to peace, doubt to security, fear to confidence. He is more than his ordinary self."

" Maybe it's a kind of self-hypnosis."

" I think he is too practical for that. He just reminds himself quite objectively, he says, of the brave minds which have touched his, knowingly and unknowingly. Theirs was a human courage, nothing occult about it. But he feels his own tension relax, his perspective widen and his mind become inventive. Sometimes he sees the next step clearly. Sometimes he doesn't see the next step at once but he has insight into what really caused his difficulty and then he knows that a solution is going to be possible. He hasn't really talked to anyone. No one has been in the room with him, and he doesn't feel that he has reached out to anything supernatural. He has merely given his own resources a chance."

" Well, for goodness' sake, father, if that is as sound psychology as it sounds, you'd think hundreds of people would try it because Mr. Ryerson just about does perform miracles."

"Hundreds of people don't try it because it takes tremendous self-control to spend two hours out of every day in honest-to-goodness meditation. Most of us couldn't even bear two hours of complete silence without trying to think. And you must remember that he doesn't do this meditating only when he is stuck with a big problem. He does it every day. Usually at least one of the hours is in his room, but he often walks through his wood-track or down the river bank. All his boys and girls and his friends know about his need for silence and if he meets one of them and raises his hand in quiet salute, they pass on without speaking."

"I should think a person would feel silly to just sit down in a chair and start to meditate."

"Not silly so much as empty. A lot of us haven't cultivated very wise and resourceful friends, either in real life or in books. We don't have a lot to turn to or to meditate about."

"I know he reads an awful lot."

"He reads awfully well. He knows most of the men and women whose thoughts have outlasted the centuries. That's partly how he gets his sense of humor."

Mary sat silent for a moment or two and then asked, "Do you mean that Mr. Ryerson could get answers to all his problems if he just meditated and never mentioned them out loud to anyone?"

"I doubt it. And I don't think he'd claim to. Probably he would get more answers than most of us because he has this superb discipline of mind. But he lets people know his problems, too. He asks for money and he asks for help, just as he asked for twenty volunteers among the seniors of the high schools. He goes after what he has to have."

"*That* kind of prayer is heard by human ears and answered by human hands and feet and tongue, I'll admit myself."

"Asking other people directly is probably part of the praying process. I used to be amused by the stories of the great old man of Bristol who ran his scores of orphanages 'by direct reliance upon prayer.' He said that he had no other means of support for his vast number of dependents. He made many a speech and wrote many a letter about his direct and single-minded reliance upon prayer. But he never seemed to realize that every time he spoke he was letting people know about the need of those children and the fact that he had no regular support for them. In a sympathetic world, such faith does not go unrewarded. Of course he found checks in his mail, wagonloads of food at his door, orders for clothing to his credit just when his resources were exhausted."

"However you explain it, his prayers were answered, too, though."

Her father smiled. "Surely they were. Some will say that God, anticipating his need, planted the answer in human hearts so that it arrived right on time. Mr. Ryerson would say that there was nothing mysterious or supernatural about the prayer that ran those famous orphanages. People were told of a genuine need and they responded. And in both cases, it isn't beside the point that a man's consecrated, unpretentious life had something to do with the answers to his prayers."

"Mr. Ryerson's idea seems more reasonable to me, but harder."

"Why harder?" Her father looked quizzically at Mary.

"Why, if you have the old-time idea of God who is omnipotent and mighty and all that, you don't have to spend so much time reading great books and getting wise friends. You can just leave the ideas and the answers to God."

"I'm afraid you're mistaken, Mary. As far as I know all great men of prayer have also been men of disciplined lives. Read about St. Francis or any of his Little Brothers and you won't think that their unceasing cultivation of the friendship of every living thing — lepers, rich men, peasants, scholars, birds, donkeys — the greatest and the humblest of all who live — was any easier than Mr. Ryerson's habit of meditation, study and work."

"But, father, doesn't the other idea of prayer as a sort of mystical communication between man and God sound more — well, more wonderful to you?"

"To me, it doesn't happen to seem more wonderful," her father answered slowly. "Maybe it does to you, Mary, and if it does, then you go on your own way because for each of us the way that works best is best. But for me, answered prayer is no less wonderful because it can be explained by the laws of psychology. For me, it doesn't even lose its mystical quality because I think I understand something of its process. There isn't any short-cut to this human sort of prayer. There is no substitute for the silence in which such communion flourishes, and no substitute for the faith with which one waits an answer."

"We don't know everything yet," said Mary practically. "I guess if there is a God — I mean the kind of God most people have in mind when they say 'God' — why, he won't mind our trying to figure things out and explain them. And explain him, too, if we can."

"I don't think he would mind. After all, we are said to be made in his image."

The dinner bell rang and the conversation changed to other matters. Nor has it been resumed in the months which have followed. But Mary's father has noticed that ever since that conversation her alarm has been ringing a quarter of an hour earlier than was formerly its custom. Perhaps Mary is experimenting on her own theory of prayer but whether it is Mr. Ryerson's theory or some other, her father doesn't know. He does not intend to ask. In her own time Mary will probably make her own comments on her own conclusions.

There are a good many children, especially adolescents, who must figure out what seems to them to be a scientific explanation for prayer before they can use it. But to other children, as to many parents, the very idea of trying to explain prayer is sacrilege. The adage which holds that one man's meat is another man's poison fits very well the mystery of the seeking heart. One man's explanation is another man's confusion. It is this fact which makes the parent's answers to his child so difficult. The practical, insistent parent, who must have a reasonable explanation for his most ecstatic states, may go into a discourse on the hows and whys of prayer to a son who asks no other validation for the mystical experience than the fact that a certain uplift has come to him and may come again. But another parent, wishing no technical explanation for the success of her prayers, is shocked by her son's persistent, "How? How can these answers come?" To this parent, the fact that the answers come is enough. To the son, still new at finding his way in the complexity of life, there is no use trying to begin the habit of prayer if it just doesn't make sense.

Perhaps the best a parent can do, whatever his attitude toward prayer, is to say, "It seems to me," or "It has been my experience," and then to add quickly, "But others feel —" and "It may be different with you." For good or ill, the chances are that the child's experience is weighted in the direction of his parents' experience.

If A Man Die . . .

I never spoke with God,
Nor visited in heaven;
Yet certain am I of the spot
As if a chart were given.

EMILY DICKINSON

" If a man die, shall he live again? "

Old as the race, the question rises freshly to the mind of each child.   For him it is a new question and terrifically important.   He is fortunate, probably, when it comes to him first as a speculative, impersonal question written across a far horizon.   From the shelter of his family, it appears interesting but not threatening.   The years will give him plenty of time, he feels, for weighing the answers.   But other children run upon the question as upon the point of a sword which has already shattered their security.   It is against such a possibility, before death comes suddenly near, that a parent can fortify his child by sharing something of his own feeling for the further outreaches of life.

The answer to the question, " If a man die, shall he live again? " has always been one of the concerns of religion. In rite and ceremony, primitive man made manifest whatever answer he had figured out.   Civilized man does the same thing.   And if he refuses to take part in rite and ceremony, his refusal is his answer also.

Although the Christian tradition predicates a belief in life after death, there is plainly a growing tendency to be less concerned with the specifications for immortality. Whether there is a bodily resurrection, whether each sepa-

77

rate personality continues to exist, whether life is never lost entirely but only broken down into constituent chemical elements which are themselves " alive," whether the spirit wings free to be merged in some great Oversoul — all these things are today of secondary concern to much of Christendom which even one generation ago would have demanded an answer in the form of creedal statement.   Nevertheless, within or without the creed, most Christians answer the question of immortality in terms of their interpretation of Jesus' life and teaching.   They admit that he lived for his fellow men, he died for them and at their hands.   But what did his dying mean and was it the end?   For Christians the possibility of immortality for the rest of mankind focuses upon this dramatic personality.

If Alberta came willingly to set the table it was almost a sure sign there was something on the top of her mind which she wished to talk about.   Alberta is one of the seven-year-olds who give themselves completely to the interest of the moment.   This night being the night before Easter, she was excited about coloring Easter eggs.   Her mother expected an effervescence of chatter.   Instead, Alberta set the table with no word at all.   She moved quickly but she seemed absorbed in some inner contemplation.   When everything was ready, she called her brothers, Grant, who was nine, and Jim, who was eleven.   Her father was out of town.   The candles were lighted, the plates served, and Alberta spoke.

" Do you believe this talk about how Jesus rose from the dead? "

" Alberta! " came automatically from mother.

" Grandmother believes it," Alberta said with open skepticism.   " I asked her today.   She believes that Jesus got hung on a cross and then buried in a grave made like a cave with a rock for a door, and then after three days he just sat up and unwrapped the yards of cloth they had buried him in, and got up and walked out of the grave. She believes that he went around for forty days doing good and then he stepped on a cloud and waved good-by to his disciples and went on up to heaven."

The words did not sound like grandmother's, but the ideas were plainly enough those she shared with much of Christendom. Certainly Alberta had heard the Easter story often enough so that it should not sound like news to her now. But mother realized that children sometimes hear the same thing over and over a great many times before it finally lays hold on the imagination to the point where it must be accepted or rejected. Before she could reply to Alberta, Jim took up the argument.

"Yes, do you believe that story, mother? Brad says to me today, ' Why do church people make such a fuss about Easter? ' His folks don't go to church and they get along just as good."

" ' Just as well,' " mother corrected, still sorting her ideas for a convincing answer.

"Just as well. I told Brad that I don't know why we make such a fuss about Easter, except that it's a kind of a celebration left over from the days when everybody believed those things and now no one wants to hurt the feelings of those who still believe that way, so everyone keeps on acting as if they still believed that way, too. Now in our family, if you told grandmother you didn't believe her ideas about Easter, she'd cry a week. She'd think you didn't believe any of her ideas, and most of her ideas are o.k."

"Do you believe that Jesus rose from the dead? " The direct question was Grant's. He was given to direct questions, small argument, and simple " yes " or " no " answers. "Either you believe it or you don't believe it. Yes or no."

"It's this way — to me," said mother. "You remember when Jesus was living, he tried to help his disciples to understand things the way he saw them. He had a good many new ideas. Big ideas. For instance, the idea of doing good to your enemies. It's a pretty breath-taking idea if you never thought of it before."

"Why, it really is, isn't it?" interrupted Alberta, as if it were new to her that very minute.

Mother went on: "To Jesus' disciples, the idea of loving their enemies was entirely new. And that's the way it was with most of Jesus' ideas: they were new and they were amazing. They were hard to take in and very, very hard to act on. But his disciples were big enough men to realize that the ideas were worth trying. And they did try them. While they were trying, they kept very near to Jesus because they needed his explanations, his strength. You know how it is when someone has an idea that you feel you just have to understand. You feel very near to that person."

The children nodded. They were a family bent on finding out things. It was quite easy to understand how disciples would cling to a really good teacher.

Mother continued: "Then all of a sudden, before the disciples ever dreamed that such a thing could happen, along came the enemies of Jesus and worked up a mob that killed him. A mob who nailed him to the cross."

"They had a trial first." Grant liked his stories accurately told. "You remember about Pilate."

"They did have a trial but even after the disciples heard the sentence, they didn't quite believe that Jesus would be killed. He had talked so much of life. He had brought healing to so many. More than that, he was so very much alive himself. Probably he was one of the most 'alive' men who ever lived. Whenever he came among people, they felt more alive themselves. They laid aside their sick-

nesses and worries. Jesus seemed to love all sorts of growing things and was always talking about them — trees and
grain, birds and animals and certainly people. When he
was sentenced to be nailed to a cross, the disciples couldn't
take in the idea that he might soon be *dead*. And then
that unbelievable day came so quickly when he was crucified and was indeed dead. His disciples were stunned, just
as you and I would be if someone we loved were so tragi-
cally taken from us.

"For a while after that, the disciples couldn't do anything at all. They couldn't go back to their work. They
couldn't talk about him, and they couldn't talk about anything else. There wasn't any point to anything. Jesus had
furnished the ideas and the strength for all of them, and he
was gone. They had had such a good time with him too,
and now there wasn't anything to have a good time about.
Still, all of his best friends kept getting together and talking.

"And then one day when they were together, one of
them spoke up and said, 'We can't go on this way. He
gave us work to do and we said we'd do it.'

"Another one said, 'People are still hungry and sick and
unhappy. He'd be doing something about that.'

" 'But now he's gone,' said someone else. It seemed as
if they couldn't get past that fact.

"Then the disciple who knew him best spoke up, 'If he
were here, he'd say, "Don't be so cast down. God lives,
doesn't he? The world is green and beautiful. The sun
shines. Birds sing. If these things are true, it isn't fair to
weep as if you'd come to the end of the world." I can
almost hear him say such words.'

"Another disciple said, 'If he were here, he'd tell us to
empty our pocketbooks onto the table, count out our
money, and plan a trip for teaching.'

" 'By the way,' said a third disciple, 'where did I put

that scroll of mine? The one I wrote his words on the day he talked to the crowd of five thousand people. I can't lose that.'

" ' He told us not to bother about writing down what he said,' someone else reminded him. ' He told me to remember as much as my heart could hold and that would be enough. And if he were here today, he'd say the same thing. Why, if he were standing there by that door — can't you see him? — he'd tell us that we didn't need any more of his words until we had used up the ones he had already given us. " Sufficient unto the day." Remember how he was always saying that? '

" The disciples chuckled out loud — the first time they'd laughed for days. ' You simply could not make him worry. " Sufficient unto the day," he'd say, and then whittle away as if he didn't have a care.'

" ' I must say he did plenty of planning, though.' This remark from someone else. ' When he and I made that last trip across country, every time we sat down by the roadside to rest, he'd begin drawing a map in the dust with a stick and pointing out villages where he wanted to teach, and trying to decide which of us should go to which place.'

" ' And that's what he'd be doing this minute, if he were here.'

" ' If he were here, he'd make a plan. He'd send Andrew and Peter south again, probably, and James and John to the northwest.'

" Then I think John's face shone. ' I know exactly how he'd walk around this table giving one of us a set of directions, making a list of provisions for another, telling a third a new parable which any man would surely get the point of.'

" ' He'd stand right there and look at all of us and — '

" And then — or at least this is the way it seems to me — it seemed as if he *did* stand there. They remembered him so plainly. They heard his voice. They knew what he would say to them. They'd worked together so often before. Suddenly they knew they would always work together! You couldn't call a man like Jesus 'dead.' Not when his voice rang in your ears and his words rang in your heart. Not when you meant to spend all of your days to the end of them trying to make people understand what he meant by love for everyone. Probably he was the livest person in the room that minute."

Mother stopped abruptly. She brushed back her hair with her hand the way she always did when she was excited.

"That's it! " said Jim, standing right up at the table. " I see you do that — " he repeated her gesture — " I see you do that when you aren't here. 'When you go away I can't always remember what you look like if I just think, ' What does my mother look like? ' But if I think of you in a special place saying some particular thing, then I can see you as plainly as if you were here. I can always remember the day you and I wired the back doorbell ourselves and you stood on a ladder brushing your hair out of your eyes just that same way."

"What I do when you go away — " Alberta spoke slowly — " is to go to sleep as if you had hold of my hand. If you're in the house, I can go to sleep by myself. But if you're gone, I can't bear to. I have to pretend you're in the room."

Grant picked up his fork and started on his cold potatoes. "What I do," he said, with his mouth too full, " is to try not to think of you at all. Because if I think of you, then I can't forget to bring in the wood for the fireplace and clean my fingernails, and things. But when you're gone I really remember you better than if you were here."

For Jim, the argument was not finished. "I guess you could say that Jesus in that way did rise from the dead."

"I'd say he never died," contributed Alberta cheerfully. "I'd say he just seemed dead for a while when his disciples were in the dumps."

"I'd say somebody ought to tell grandmother the truth about it." This from Grant.

Mother hastened to protest. "But you can't say that any one person's ideas are more true than another's. This happens to be *my* idea. But it makes him more real to grandmother to think about his rising from a tomb and being caught up into heaven. As indeed it must have done for the man who wrote the story which was finally put into the Bible."

"Probably it doesn't make a lot of difference," said Grant, "just so it works for you."

"Oh, no," cried Alberta in alarm. "I don't want to have the wrong idea about something and go on thinking it's the right idea. That's dreadful. Supposing I thought the world was flat."

"Try out your ideas. That's what Columbus did." Jim was triumphant. "Columbus thought the world was round, and he knew that if it was round then he could reach the east by sailing west. If he'd been wrong, he would have fallen off into space and then he'd know he had the wrong idea."

Grant protested. "That's a good way to try out ideas about sailing or ideas about keeping your airplane up in the air, but you can't try out an idea about will you live after you're dead. You can't come back and tell anyone else and no one can tell you. Now with some ideas, you just take 'em or leave 'em."

Alberta also protested. "Still I don't want the wrong idea. If it's true like grandmother says, then I don't want to believe mother's way. Mother's idea makes more sense to me, though."

Jim spoke slowly. "Well, there are some things you can't find an answer for in a book." He hesitated. "Although, of course, it's grandmother's story that got written in about the best book there's supposed to be." Then he smiled. "Even if it's in a book, you've got to figure it out for yourself: was it that way or was someone trying to explain something which maybe he didn't completely understand himself?"

This conversation took place in an old white house on Eleventh avenue in Ashland, Wisconsin. It was written down almost verbatim by the mother before the children's voices had died away for that night.

Some persons sum up the possibility of the soul's continuation after death with the pragmatic conclusion that one loses nothing — and probably gains — in living his life *as if* immortality were an accepted fact.

It is more than two generations since Pete Peterson was ten years old and put his birthday pennies in the collection at Sunday school. Then he came home announcing, "I don't want immortal life."

"What do you mean, you don't want immortal life?" asked his Aunt Anna in astonishment.

"I mean that when I'm dead, I want to be dead. I want to live to be about as old as Grandpa Neilson and then when I die, I don't want to live forever."

His sister Hilda looked up with surprise. "All through eternity, don't you want to remember things, or to think, or to know about your family, or *anything?*"

Pete shook his head. "When I'm dead, I don't care what happens. They can chuck me to the wolves if they want to. Everybody can get drunk if they want to. Everybody can murder everybody if they want to. When I'm dead, I'm dead."

Then spoke Grandma Peterson. Her blue eyes snapped and she clicked off her words with precision made more emphatic by her accent. "It's just for people like you that God Almighty gave us immortality! So that you *have* to care what happens after you're dead. You never saw a drunk man, Pete Peterson, but you know it's a dreadful thing and you're right. You never want to see one, not now nor after you're an immortal soul in glory. I don't hold traffic with the idea of leaning out of heaven to watch the wicked burn in hell, but I must say I'd do a lot of work in my day to keep from seeing the sons of men drunk after I've gone to my reward."

Pete Peterson is an old man himself now but he remembers his grandmother's words "as if they were yesterday." He says: "I never figured out to this day just what kind of immortality I believe in, but still I never got over the feeling Grandma Peterson put in me that if there might be the kind of immortality which allows for seeing how things are after death, then I want to be sure that the deeds of my living life won't rise up to wreck my immortal eyesight."

Ian is seventeen, a tall, slender lad, dark of hair, dark of eyes, somber of mood. In school he is a quiet student, but he becomes animated into a different person when any recitation turns upon the question, Why are these things so?

One day he came, as is seldom his custom, into his father's office at the college where his father teaches. Without preamble he spoke to his father. "It seems to me that the idea of immortality would be a very important idea if I could have faith enough to believe that one man's life matters in so vast a universe. But one life is so little, so less than nothing against the ages, that its significance doesn't seem worth considering either now or after death."

His father, taken by surprise, had no words ready, although his own philosophy was clear-cut enough for himself. He reached for a book and read to his son these paragraphs:

And Isaiah answered: One night while men slept I stood on the housetop; and looking upon the stars I measured my life against the life of the nations of men who had lived and perished before me. I thought on those who had scattered the seeds of hope and had gathered therefrom the fruitage of despair, and on them that had labored well, whom death found naked at the end of their days.

And while I considered these matters there came a voice thinly crying: What of the life of man, O son of man, whose days are like a vapor that bloweth across the moon? Yea, what of the life of man that breaketh off like the thread of a weaver's shuttle? Hath it no continuance when his breath ceaseth, and is its meaning then gone forever?

And a voice from within me made answer: The just shall endure, even the upright man until the end of the years of time, and his faithful deeds until the last generation. Yea, though he is slain by the sword; yea, though he be consumed by fire; yea, though his ashes be scattered over the sea, yet shall he abide forever and by his doing shall all the families of the earth be blessed. Since that night I do speak of faith to every man who will hearken.

"I believe this thing," said Ian's father. "I believe that justice and uprightness are imperishable and that those who give them reality shall live forever. The form of their immortality I do not know, but I believe they are not lost."

"I believe that, too," said Ian slowly.

"It gives meaning to life," said his father. "After all one has to choose his philosophy of immortality, and why not choose the one which has the most meaning for you?"

Ian hesitated. "It's only partly true that we are free to choose. It seems to me that regarding any speculative matter we have to accept the hypothesis which seems most reasonable to us. We owe it to our intellectual integrity to do so."

His father met the boy's precise vocabulary and earnest voice in kind. "Then let me say that my reading and observation lead me to conclude that justice and uprightness are tremendous forces moving through the world to shape humanity's well-being. Perhaps a just man may appear to die defeated, if he has never achieved any personal success or well-being. But he has added something to the total store of justice in the world and his contribution — which is indeed his very self — goes on forever."

"That's enough for me," said Ian, taking a deep breath as if a heavy weight of responsibility were lifted from his chest. "As long as I know what I'm doing — what I'm living *for* — then I think I won't mind how hard my work may be." Then he added shyly, "I'd like to contribute something to the immortal store of justice."

Ronald and Rachel were twins, tall for twelve years, and as full of energy as an east wind. If they had not been quick at their lessons there would never have been any school work because neither of them had time to waste indoors. Then suddenly an epidemic of scarlet fever caught them both and the quarantine sign on the door spoke weeks of confinement.

At first they were very ill. Except in their concern for each other, they scarcely seemed aware of what went on. "How's Ronnie?" Rachel would ask the nurse or her mother. "Tell me about Rachel," Ronald would beg of them.

On the night when Ronald grew rapidly worse, Rachel seemed to sense the fact, although through her closed door she could not hear the coming of the doctors nor the summoning of her father. At midnight she spoke up firmly to the nurse keeping vigil beside her, " Please ask my mother to come here right away."

" She's busy," said the nurse.   " Won't I do? "

" I know she's busy," said Rachel.   " She's watching Ronnie die.   Anyway, that's what you think she's doing. But she must come here now."

Her mother came.   Rachel looked up at her anxious face. She spoke quickly because talking hurt her throat.   " Listen, mother, if Ronnie dies, do you believe that's the end of everything for him? "

" Of course not, darling," said her mother, leaning near and taking Rachel's hand in hers.

" We believe that Ronnie's soul goes out to some other place, but he's still Ronnie, isn't he?   We believe that he keeps on growing, somehow.   Maybe not the way we grow here on earth, but in some other way which God understands.   We believe that, don't we? "

" Yes, we do," said her mother firmly.

" We believe that we'll go on living after we die, don't we?   Somehow, some place, you'll be you and father will be himself and Ronald will be Ronald.   God has a plan and a place for all of us and it won't be any time at all until we're all together again.   That's what we think, don't we? "

" Yes, we do," said mother again.

Rachel looked up into her mother's tired, drawn face and spoke sharply.   " Then act your age.   Act like God was God and his plan was best.   I bet it gives Ronnie fits to see all of you looking so worried.   If I could go in there, I'd laugh at the idea that dying could make any difference between Ronnie and me.   Ronnie'd laugh, too."

Whereupon Rachel turned over and went to sleep.

Her mother returned to Ronald's room.   As she came in, everyone looked at her.   Her face was serene.   She spoke in a natural voice.   " Constance," she said to one of the nurses, " I wonder if you'd scurry up some sandwiches and coffee."

" My dear," said father in bewilderment, " this is no time — "

" Yes, it is," said mother quietly. " We haven't eaten all day and that's not right. We need our strength." She stood at the foot of the bed looking down at the boy.

Ronald opened his eyes and smiled faintly. " I feel better now. I'm not so smothered now." He drew a deep breath and fell into a natural sleep.

Afterwards one doctor said, " I didn't think he could possibly open that throat to speak again."

The other doctor said, " It doesn't make sense, with that racing heart."

Mother said — with what seemed to the doctors considerable irrelevance — " Bless her heart, she *believes* her beliefs."

Still later, in their own room, father said, " How is Rachel? What did she want with you? "

" She's asleep," said mother, beginning to brush her hair. " She just wanted to tell me that immortality isn't merely a doctrine. She said it was a fact to act upon. She said that if we believed the soul was immortal and had ages ahead for its perfecting, why then it was selfish to grieve when it merely passed from one state to another. She said there was something grand and triumphant about some of the family's going ahead and others of us coming on. She said it made us think in longer terms than our little lifetimes and that we gathered a kind of cosmic courage into ourselves when we made room for the death which is only transition. She said it must be terribly hard for God when faith gives way to apprehension, and that a Christian ought to act like a Christian because it wasn't as if no one had gone before to show us the way."

Father interrupted. " It doesn't sound like Rachel to say all that."

" She used other words. But that was her idea: immortality is a fact to act on."

Some parents prefer to dismiss the matter of immortality more summarily. Life, they feel, is finished by death; that is the sum of the matter. The fact is a stark one or a comforting one according to each man's temperament. But, being a fact, it cannot be evaded. In dealing with their children they do not try to temper the fact, as they see it, to the child's wistful questions.

" Will we ever see mummy again? " begged little Marie, wiping her swollen eyes and clutching her father's hand.

" No, we won't see her again, Marie," her father answered through tight lips. " She is dead and she cannot come back."

" But can't we go where she is? "

" We don't know where she is, except that she is gone. Some day we will be gone, too."

" To some place we don't know about? " asked Marie hopefully.

" No, not gone to any other place. Just gone. When our bodies have finished their usefulness, they slowly turn into dust and are mixed with the earth. And that's the end, as far as we know." Her father felt that he should say something more and added, " Perhaps some of the dust which was once ourselves is used by the plants and trees which grow in the earth. I like to think so. Perhaps, as some scientists say, living matter is never completely lost. It just changes its form, the way hydrogen and oxygen may sometimes be water and sometimes steam and sometimes ice."

" But we won't see mummy." The one stark fact obliterated all explanations for Marie. For her father, also, the fact blotted out every lesser matter. He had no words to ease the child's heart, but he held her closely.

Years later Marie remarks on that day: " My father gave

me something then, when we clung to one another in our grief, that has comforted me more than any assurance of immortality. I think it was a kind of assurance of one human being's understanding of another, a thing so rare and wonderful that it makes all the rest of life worth living."

Edith Worley at fourteen seemed•at once the most care-free and the most thoughtful youngster in her high school class. She was always aware of other people's needs, always — as her classmates said — "doing something for some-body." And yet she had plenty of time for her own very active life. Her favorite pastime was riding a horse. Al-most every Saturday morning found her dashing cross-country on Midnight, dark hair streaming in the wind. A fence was nothing to Midnight, or to Edith. If anyone remonstrated with her father over the girl's feats, he would say, "Life is sweet. Sweet and hard. Edith's equal to all of it. Let her ride."

Then one day when Midnight was trotting down a peace-ful lane, his foot slipped on a rock and for no accountable reason he stumbled, reared back, and flung Edith — expect-ing nothing and unprepared — upon a pile of fence rails. Her back was broken.

For ten days in spite of the best care of a modern hospital staff she gasped for breath. Pain continually drove her into unconsciousness from which she seemed to emerge with in-creasing reluctance. One morning, at the doctor's request, her father stood beside her bed and spoke to her sternly. "Edith! Edith, you've got to hang on to consciousness. Do you hear me? The doctors can't fight for you unless you fight, too."

With an effort she looked up at him. "Will I ride again, father? Some day will I ride again? "

Her father did not hesitate. "No, Edith. As far as the doctors can tell, you will never ride again."

"Will I walk?"

"No, you will not walk, either. Not unless a miracle happens."

There was a faint smile on her face as she spoke. "We don't believe in miracles, do we?"

"Not that kind." Then as she seemed slipping away again, his voice became stern. "Edith, listen to me. You have to take hold."

"Why? There's nothing to live for." Then she made an effort to raise her head. "There's nothing to die for, either, is there? We don't believe in life after death. I like living, you know."

Her father took the two limp hands firmly in his own. "Edith, listen to me. We have to live to the end of our strength — the strength of our bodies and the strength of our spirits. It's our compact with the people who come after us. There's no other way to pass on the courage that came to us from our forebears. Your great-great-grandmother was blind from her childhood but they say that a gayer, finer spirit never lived. You can't let her down. We Worleys stand up to life. Whatever comes after death — we let the future take care of that. We dare to let the future take care of itself because we live up to the present." He felt unhappily that his words sounded like quotations but he had to find some way to make the child understand. "Listen, Edith. I don't understand about dying and what comes after. But I've got a sure hunch that it matters a lot *how we live*."

Then Edith looked straight up at him, her young brown eyes searching the older eyes so like her own. "I understand you without any talk. It's all right. I'm living."

And Edith lived, long and merrily, as the neighbors for three counties around can testify. She never rode again. But one day there was a miracle of knife and bone and she did walk again.   Walking, as she says, is a thrill her friends can never quite get the flavor of.   The surgeon who performed the operation was astounded at its success.   " I thought she'd walk, all right, but I never thought she'd stride! "   Her stride is long and certain, free and firm.   Like her life.

Some people, such as Edith and her father, find life condensed into an essence.   For them, present responsibility has a quality which those who think in eons sometimes miss. Pleasure too — each day's joy — is tasted for its full flavor. And who shall say that their views are wrong and some other views are right?   Each parent hunts the kernel of the matter for himself.   He passes on his secret to his sons and daughters.

" ' If a man die, shall he live again? ' "

" My child, it seems to me — this way — but others feel — "

Immortality, in the mind of the small child, is not concerned with human beings alone.   There is the important question of their pets.   What of the dog poisoned through someone's carelessness?   The kitten who wanders away and never comes back?   The canary, the pony, the rabbit?

Edwin and his spaniel Bridget were born on the same day and so, as Edwin would gravely explain, " it's different than with most boys and dogs."   For more than five years they had been inseparable companions indoors and out.

One week end mother and father both went away on a trip and Great-aunt Hester came to look after Edwin and Bridget.   Aunt Hester did not know a great deal about small boys but anything she lacked in imagination she made up in good will and meticulous care.   Edwin had never been so promptly dressed and fed and read to.   Bridget, too, had exactly the right food at exactly the hour mother had

marked on her schedule. Aunt Hester remembered everything except Bridget's fondness for open gates and the fact
that even a shut gate did not keep her in unless the latch were
tightly snapped. So on Saturday afternoon Bridget got
out into the alley. A coal truck . . . the driver did not see
Bridget . . . and the next thing Aunt Hester knew she
was standing in the back yard looking into the contorted
face of a small boy who, in turn, looked down incredulously
at his dead dog.

After the first dreadful hour when the veterinary had
taken Bridget away and Aunt Hester had telephoned the
news to father, the questions began. " Where did Bridget's
soul go, auntie? Has she gone to heaven? "

" My goodness, no, child. Dogs don't go to heaven."

" Where do they go, then? Auntie! You don't mean
that Bridget's dead forever? You don't mean we'll never
see her again? "

" There, there, child. Your daddy will get you another
dog."

Small comfort to a boy of five. Another dog? As well
another world entirely. " I don't want another dog.
Bridget was my dog. Where is she now? "

" She's dead, darling. There, there. Dogs have to die."

" So do people die but then they go to heaven. Why
isn't Bridget in heaven? "

" The Bible doesn't say anything about animals in heaven.
There wouldn't be room in heaven for all the animals. You
can see that."

Edwin stood squarely before his aunt, feet spread apart,
hands behind him, a look of stubborn bewilderment on his
face. " Then I'm not going, either."

" Edwin! When you get there, everything will be so
nice that you won't mind about not having Bridget."

" I'll always mind about not having Bridget." His chin quivered again. " And if God hasn't got room for dogs, I'll be bad all my life so he won't let me in."

" You mustn't say things like that." She tried to draw Edwin into her lap. " There's a difference between humans and dogs."

Edwin maintained his stance. " I know there's a difference. Dogs have four legs and people have two legs. People sleep in beds and dogs sleep in baskets. But dogs can play and have fun, can't they? Dogs can love you and stick by you. Why Bridget — " He stopped. There wasn't any use.

It was nearly midnight when father drove in. Edwin, sleeping fitfully, heard the car on the driveway. He might have known his father would come back. He scrambled out of bed and by that time his father was coming through the bedroom door followed by Aunt Hester. Edwin jumped into his father's arms and neither of them said anything. They just hugged each other. Finally Edwin slid down from his father's arms. " It's tough, isn't it? " he said. " It's tough that nobody could bark when you drove in."

" You bet it's tough, son."

" Father, she didn't go to heaven." Edwin reached desperately for his father's hand when he heard himself saying the words. " She's dead but God didn't want her."

" Who says she didn't go to heaven? " asked father sternly.

" Auntie says that heaven is no place for animals. It doesn't say a thing about them in the Bible."

" Oh, that — " Father dismissed the matter with a gesture. " It doesn't have to say anything about them in the Bible because it says that God is our Father and we expect a father to look after his children's dogs and other pets."

" Edwin! " Aunt Hester was speaking to the senior Edwin now and her tone was severe. "You're talking about Holy Writ."

"Nonsense," said father, patting Aunt Hester's shoulder. "You'd look after a puppy in need any time one came your way, my dear. I'm just allowing God to be as friendly as we humans are."

Then father turned to Edwin, speaking seriously. "I don't understand a lot about heaven, son, except that I believe that whatever happens after we're dead is all right. Do you know what I mean? It may be all different from anything we know now. But whatever it is, God will do the right thing by all of us. Men, women, boys, girls, babies, dogs — everybody. After all, if God is love, we don't have to be anxious about his taking care of us. That's the way I see it."

"Oh." Edwin looked at his father's face intently. Evidently he was satisfied with what he saw there for he climbed into his bed again.

His father tucked the covers under his chin. "Tomorrow we'll talk about it some more. We're sure going to miss little Bridget, but wherever she is, it's o.k. with her."

"O.k.," said Edwin, drawing a long breath which was both a spent sob and a yawn. He could go to sleep now, really to sleep, and figure out the rest in the morning. Tomorrow he'd miss Bridget just as much, but he could stand missing her if everything was o.k. with Bridget.

It would seem unnecessary that so many children must wait until calamity forces their parents to some sort of declaration on a philosophy of life after death. After all, the fact is always at hand and it might as well be accepted with serenity and dignity and common sense as left to an emotional crisis. Not so many years ago, a great many people refused to speak of life insurance in tones above a whisper.   Husbands, in broaching the subject to their wives, were met with a frantic, " Don't talk about it, darling.   I can't even bear to think of such a thing."   Pedagogical salesmanship has helped to recondition thousands into a more sensible attitude.   A little more pedagogy is in order on the whole subject of helping children to meet the fact of death.   Certainly those who believe that death is only an incident in the long life of the soul should be able to speak not only triumphantly but, in a sense, casually.   And those who hold that death is life's supreme adventure can share their courage and curiosity in conversations by the way. Fear of death probably saps more of the world's creative energy than any other fear, and those who have achieved a philosophy which dissipates that fear have something important to share with their fellows.

Children like to speculate.   The future looms so large before them, the years from eight to eighty stretch so endlessly into the future, that they feel a genuine impersonality in their speculations.   Many a parent has been momentarily startled to hear his small son's cheerful question, " Now when you die, daddy, what kind of a funeral do you think you'll have? "   Or his daughter's hopeful demand, " After you're dead, can this picture be mine to keep? "   Such offhand questions are a ready-made lead into common-sense family discussion of the practical considerations involved in funerals, in burial, in customs of mourning, as well as in the immortality of the soul.

The parent who can " condition " his child so that death appears at least as a door ajar through which honest questions dare peer into the future has probably rendered his child a larger service than the parent who writes any kind of final answer to placard upon a door tightly closed.

Making His Own Bible

Hard texts are nuts (I will not call them cheaters),
Whose shells do keep their kernels from the eaters.
Ope then the shells, and you shall have the meat;
They here are brought for you to crack and eat.

JOHN BUNYAN (*Pilgrim's Progress*)

There was a day, not so long since as the Christian era is reckoned, when a man was either a believer in the Bible as the word of God divinely revealed, or an "unbeliever." The distinction was clear. One came into the fold or remained outside. There was no loitering at the gates, and children pretty much walked in with their parents. Certainly in those days children were not inclined to ask questions about the authenticity of the written Word of God as final authority in matters of conduct. But after some thousand-odd years of practical unanimity of opinion about the Bible, along came a new light called "the spirit of scientific inquiry," turning its beams in all directions and counting no shadows too sacred for its investigation. It peered into the outer universe and laid bare the materials of the physical sciences, and then, in due time, the materials of the biological and social sciences. Man began to feel that he understood his world. So much new understanding of the universe and of man's place in it did something to the common interpretation of history, including "sacred" history. People began to ask how and what and why and whence of the Holy Scripture.

Today there is no "accepted" theory about the Bible and its place in the affairs of men. There are good men and true

who hold to sharply divergent points of view. There is
the view which accepts the Bible as divine revelation, different in kind from any other document ever written and
peculiarly ordained to be a standard of human conduct.
There is also the view which accepts the Bible as a great
historical and ethical document, written and compiled by
much the same sort of honest and sometimes scholarly men
who write great books today, a document which has significance in whatever degree men may find use for it.
There is, again, the view which accepts the Bible as one of
the outgrown superstitions of the Western world, interesting perhaps for its historical or literary significance but no
longer relevant to modern life. Some parents know exactly
which view they hold and consequently they know how
they will answer their children's questions. Other parents
have a degree of sympathy for all three attitudes, and are
not exactly sure what they themselves think about the Bible,
and still less sure what they should say to their children.

If difference of belief were more sharply reflected in
conduct, it would be easier to advise a new generation, " By
all odds, *this* interpretation seems to make better men." But
to date people of all degrees of goodness seem to be found
in all groups. An average child leading a busy life of school
and play will run into many of the varieties of conduct and
many of the varieties of belief about the Bible. To him
there may not seem to be much relationship between the
conduct and the beliefs. He will ask questions about all of
them, the slant and tone of his questions depending upon
his family experiences. Naturally his parents will answer
the questions about the Bible in terms of their own understanding of it.

" Do you believe things are true just because they are
written in the Bible? " Dorothy, aged ten, has seldom taken
any authority unquestioningly.

"No, I don't," says her mother promptly. "But I think they are written in the Bible because they are true."

"What's the difference?" asks Dorothy, squinting her eyes together as she does whenever she feels a good answer coming her way.

"It's the difference between my telling you that you will be severely punished if I ever catch you cheating and my telling you that I've found out through years of rather difficult living that it simply does not pay to try to cheat. Knowing me as you do, you probably have some respect for my conclusion because I arrived at it out of my own experience."

Dorothy catches on. "You mean that some things are so true that somebody decided they were important enough to write down in a book, and the book is important because what it says is so true."

Her mother laughs. "That's about it. In generations of living together, men found out certain basic things about life: justice *is* more important than might; it *is* harder to keep the tongue than to take a city; loving one's neighbor *is* vastly more effective than tithing of mint and anise. Fathers who had experienced these 'truths' told them to their sons who told them to *their* sons."

"Until finally someone wrote them down."

"That's it, I suppose. And in passing on these true things, parents also passed on the stories about the great men who had discovered them. Sometimes they also passed on stories which made the point of their experiences more plain. Large or small, only important things are treasured from one generation to the next. Gradually these truths which we sometimes call race experience were written down. Finally they were collected into a library of sixty-six volumes which were later put together in one large volume called the Bible."

"I think that does make them more important than if

God just sat on a cloud and said them off," says Dorothy comfortably.

"Maybe it's about the same thing in the end," her mother suggests. "The kind of God who is a father to his children would admonish them only for their own good. He'd tell them the things they are bound to find true."

"You mean the way you tell me I'll be sorry if I'm selfish about the playhouse?" Dorothy is always willing to take a lesson home.

Her mother smiles. "I mean the way we all try to save other people from making mistakes which will cost them grief and trouble. Whether you think of the Bible as a sort of great letter from God to his children or as a bundle of letters from our ancestors to us, the book is full of things which people have found to be *true*. No matter who said them first, man or God, they probably wouldn't have lasted so long if they didn't stand the test of our living by them."

"It's kind of an important book, isn't it?" Dorothy decides.

"That's what a good many people have concluded."

Lucilla and Maud are next-door neighbors and have been playmates from babyhood. Both are twelve, both are in the eighth grade, both are Girl Scouts, and both go to the same Sunday school in a church which is neither conspicuously conservative nor strikingly radical. In fact, the church, like the town, could be duplicated for friendliness and contentment in many parts of this country. Lucilla's father is a doctor, a family doctor who knows and cares for half the countryside. Maud's father is a hardware merchant by trade and an ornithologist by avocation. Both fathers read rather more widely than most of their fellow townsmen. Both of them pay their taxes, vote thoughtfully at each election, and do their bit for better roads, better schools, better sanitation.

One Sunday Lucilla comes home from Sunday school and goes at once to her father who is picking peonies in the garden. "Father, listen! Do you know what our new teacher, Miss Snyder, said today at Sunday school? She said she thought that the men who wrote the books of the Bible sometimes were just as likely to be mistaken in what they thought as the men who write histories of the United States. She said in an age when everyone believed in miracles, it was just natural for the disciples to believe that Jesus performed miracles when he had such a wonderful effect on sick people. And she said that the story about Jonah and the whale was never meant to be taken as fact. It was a story told to make a point, just like a fable makes a point without having to be a true story at all." Lucilla stops for a breath but her silence shouts, "Now what do you think of that?" And her father answers the unspoken question.

"I'll tell you what I think, Lucilla. I think that the Bible is the word of God, different from anything else that was ever written. I think the Almighty decided what should go into his Book. Many other deeds were done by the Israelites than those which were recorded in such books as Exodus and Kings, but God directed the recording of only such events as he thought would have meaning for people who came after. In the same way, when he reports a miracle, I believe that it was a miracle which occurred just as the story tells it."

Lucilla slips into a garden chair. "But, father, Miss Snyder says that the Bible went through a lot of translations before it ever got into English. She says that there is bound to be human error in any translation, and that the original stories of things like the tower of Babel or feeding the five thousand may have been quite a bit different from the stories we know now."

"The Bible has gone through a great many translations,"

her father agrees. "Most of the Old Testament was probably first written in Hebrew. Some of the New Testament was certainly handed down in Aramaic and then translated into Greek and later into Latin and then into English. But I believe that God cared enough about his Word to have a hand in all of those translations. I believe that he moved in the minds of the translators, that he called the best men for the task and then guided their hands so that they were able to use the exact word and even the exact punctuation which best suited his purposes. It seems to me not too much to expect of a God who could create the world, the sun and moon and planets, of a God who could make man in his own likeness, that he might also be able to supervise the rendering of his Word."

Lucilla looks at her father with admiration. She decides that he is a good deal like one of the prophets himself; he and God seem to understand each other, both about saving the sick and about the Bible. "It seems too bad for Miss Snyder to be so mistaken," she says sympathetically.

Maud likewise finds her father in the garden but all she can see of him is his feet protruding from under a blue spruce whose lower branches rest upon the ground. She judges from the feet that some place under that tree is the rest of her father and that he must have located the nest for which he has been looking these many days. Finally he emerges, dishevelled but triumphant, and Maud begins eagerly, "Listen, father, you know quite a bit about the Bible, don't you?"

"Well, I've read it," her father admits, as he makes an entry in his notebook. "I've read it between its own covers and I've read pieces of it, in one form or another, in most of the volumes we call English literature. What's the matter with the Bible now?"

"This is no time to be funny, father. We had a dreadful time at Sunday school."

"About the Bible?" They walk towards the side veranda.

Maud nods excitedly. "We have a new teacher named Miss Snyder and everybody in our grade is supposed to learn the books of the Bible. You know — 'Five books of law: Genesis, Exodus, Leviticus, Numbers, Deuteronomy; twelve books of history: Joshua, Judges, Ruth, First Samuel, Second Samuel, First Kings, Second —'"

Her father interrupts the flow of words. "I know. I learned them once, too."

"But instead of drilling us on the names, Miss Snyder told us about how the Bible got together. You see the thirty-nine books of the Old Testament weren't all written at the same time. And Genesis didn't come first! At least that's what she said. Genesis was one of the last books gathered up out of folklore, but when they went to make the Bible —"

"Just who is 'they'?" Her father stretches out on the porch swing and motions his animated young daughter to a chair. "I wonder now if you mean the seventy scholars who were appointed to gather up the various versions of the various sacred books and decide which should be included in the official Jewish scriptures?"

"That's it, I guess. But who appointed the Seventy? And where was the New Testament all that time?"

Whereupon her father launches into what he calls the world's best detective story — the sleuthing down of the old manuscripts upon which the first full "publication" of the entire Bible was based.

"My! I wonder if Miss Snyder knows all that," says Maud admiringly. "You wouldn't think so much work had gone into the Bible, would you? I thought God had just sort of dictated it to somebody a long time ago."

" I think we could say that human experience dictated the books of the Bible. The writers of the books of history wrote from the point of view of Hebrews who had forged a nation out of scattered tribes and all the while kept raising their ethical standards as they struggled against their foes within and without. The compilers of the books of poetry brought together the poems which best reflected the national mood and the longing of human beings who had been through great tribulation. The stories of the heroes — Moses, Joseph, Joshua, Ruth, Samuel, David, and all the others — probably grew as they were told by father to son for generations, but the heroes themselves were real enough in the beginning. Altogether the Old Testament is probably one of the greatest collections of human experience, and interpretations of experience, ever written in the world."

In her usual fashion, Maud has two questions for every explanation her father makes so that it is dinner time before her curiosity is satisfied. After dinner she goes to Lucilla's house, according to their Sunday custom. After they have settled the urgent matter of whether they shall first take a walk or read the next installment of a continued story, Lucilla says, " Did you tell your father about Miss Snyder and the Bible? "

" I should say so," Maud admits. " Wasn't it exciting? He knew all about how the books got written and about the Seventy and everything. You know, I felt entirely different about the Bible after he told me all those things, didn't you? I felt that it was kind of important."

" Important? Why I should hope it's important. It's the very word of God. My father said — "

Whereupon the two girls compare stories, first with considerable asperity because each feels that she must defend her father's authority, then with growing conciliation. Finally Maud suggests, " Maybe it isn't so important how you think about the Bible just so long as you get good out of reading it."

But Lucilla looks doubtfully toward the porch where her mother is reading. " I wouldn't exactly say it doesn't matter. My mother thinks it matters so much that Miss Snyder ought to be asked to quit teaching a Sunday school class. But of course the important thing probably is whether the Bible helps you to be good or not."

As the weeks go by and Miss Snyder does not give up the Sunday school class, the home conversations become more animated.

" How do you suppose they ever happened to collect all of Paul's letters to the churches? " Lucilla asks her father one day.

" It was part of God's purpose that they should not be lost," he answers firmly. " So when it was time to gather together the books of the New Testament, these letters came forth from their various hiding places."

Maud asks the same question.

" I suppose we'll never know just how many letters Paul did write," her father answers. " No doubt some of them were destroyed or lost by people or churches who never thought of their being specially important. But it seems to me that the most likely theory of their collection is that when the dramatic story of Luke-Acts was written some time toward the end of the first century, the groups of Christians in various places were suddenly aware what a tremendous figure Paul was, how largely he was responsible for the spread of the gospel, and so they hunted out their letters from him and began to read them again and to exchange copies. Probably these sets of copies of Paul's letters were treasured in many places before there was any thought of gathering together the books about Jesus into a canon."

Another day the girls come home with the inevitable question, " Why are there differences in the way Matthew, Mark, Luke and John tell the same stories about Jesus? They can't all be right."

" Oh, yes, they can," says Lucilla's father. " Moreover, they may not be exactly the same stories but different incidents which were much alike. At any rate, God doesn't contradict himself. If there's a difficult statement in the Bible, you can rest assured it is there for a purpose."

Maud's father says, " Use your common sense. Did you ever try to get the story of an automobile accident from a dozen different witnesses? Or the description of a wedding? Or the report of a lecture? Send a lawyer and a doctor and a teacher and a milliner to the same county fair or the same play or the same riot and each will come home with a different tale because he saw the event through his own experience and training. Each of them tells the truth as he saw it."

The questions pile up. " Father, did you know that a part of the New Testament was originally written in Greek and part in Hebrew? " " Why were the apocryphal books first included in the canon and later excluded from the Protestant version? " " How did the western and eastern texts come to differ? " " Did you know that for hundreds of years all the Bibles were written in Latin and that everybody had forgotten how to read Greek until scholars like Grotius and Erasmus dug out the Greek language and tried to find old, old copies of the Bible which were written in Greek? "

From Maud's father come the exciting stories of the guarding of the Vaticanus, one of the oldest Greek manuscripts in the world, at the Vatican; and then the finding of

another ancient parchment manuscript, in an old abbey on
Mount Sinai, by a German scholar named Tischendorf; the
rush of scholars to consult this new-old manuscript for its
rendering of doubtful passages; its sale to England and its
later comparison with the famous Vatican manuscript; the
consequent revisions of the "accepted" text. From
Maud's father, too, the story of the way the Bible was divided into verses for convenience' sake, as late as the sixteenth century, by an energetic publisher who marked
them off as he jogged along on horseback on his way to the
printer. Also the story of Tyndale, the sixteenth century
Englishman who demanded that the New Testament be
translated into English so that the common man who knew
no Latin might have access to its teachings; of Tyndale's
consequent imprisonment in Holland where he continued
his translations by candlelight in his dungeon until he was
brought forth to be burned at the stake. Maud's favorite
is the story about the Bishops' Bonfire which was supposed
to deliver England forever from all English translations of
the Bible, when in reality unknown to the bishops the
money from the sale of these Bibles to be burned was being
sent over to Holland so that more and better English Bibles
might be printed. There seems no end to these tales which
Maud begins to call "Bible stories about the Bible." She
likes to hear about the Great Bible, a copy of which was
chained to the pulpit in each parish church. And she likes
to hear about the present-day translations, in preparation
for which great scholars are able to use papyrus fragments
in colloquial Greek, photostatic copies of old Greek uncial
texts, and a wealth of other relevant data never before available.

But if Maud's father furnishes the most exciting tales
about the Bible, it is Lucilla's doctor-father who comes to
the Sunday school and talks about the meaning of some of

the passages in the Bible. When he talks he leaves no doubt in the children's minds as to what it means to be a Pharisee and pass by on the other side of the road when someone is in trouble. In fact, it seems to Maud as if Lucilla's father could almost have written the New Testament himself because he understands it so well. She tries to explain her feeling to Lucilla one day: " Nobody makes me feel the way your father makes me feel about — about its being important how we live and terribly important how other people get a chance to live, too."

Probably, as the years go by, it will matter less and less to Lucilla and Maud whose father taught which, and they may forget the names of the other pupils in Miss Snyder's Sunday school class, but there will remain a heritage of understanding and conviction without which they both might have been the poorer. With the Bible, as with other matters of religious significance, it is the actual sharing of knowledge and experience which matters — sharing of experience plus the grace to understand that in the end the child must do his own experiencing.

Of course, many children never have access to the Bible, or are delayed in learning to know it, because their parents have so long considered it a " religious " book, an outgrown volume full of odd moral teachings, that it never occurs to them to read it for its dramatic human tales nor to come freshly to its ethical perceptions. Sometimes it takes the child to discover the book to his parents.

Warren is a gangling fourteen when he goes off to prep school. His letters home come regularly enough but are exceedingly sketchy on the subject of his studies. The only teacher he comments on is a " Prof " Harney. " Boy, does he know the swell stuff! " says one letter. And another, " Prof Harney was sure up and at 'em today. He's the hardest teacher the school's got but nobody cares if he is."

At Thanksgiving time, Warren comes home, more gangling, more enthusiastic than ever. After making the rounds
of the house, garage and refrigerator, he opens his suitcase
of books in the middle of the living room floor. His algebra
goes under the davenport in one scoot. "Don't know why
I brought it because it doesn't give me any trouble." *Nineteenth Century Poets* goes onto the table with a sigh. "The
man who wrote that book's a dope and don't you forget it.
Names, places, dates, and poems; lot of tripe." American
history, general science, first year Latin, all have their pedi-
grees read aloud. Then with a flourish, out comes a bright
red book which Warren promptly designates as "a honey
if there ever was one. That's Prof Harney's class and say,
does he know his way around!" Warren's father reaches
for the book. *The Bible: An American Translation.*

"Here, I'll read you a piece," says Warren, taking the
book from his father and flipping it open to a well marked·
page. Then, long legs apart and red head thrown back, he
reads aloud the sixth chapter of Matthew. He reads as one
who likes the crisp, determined words for their own sake;
but he reads also as one who dares to handle large truths.
Somehow, his father thinks, the words, coming from the
boy, are not so incongruous as one might have expected.
His father has a quick feeling that the boy has reached into
a hidden cache of racial treasure and brought forth something magnificent to make his own. He listens to the end —
and then he has nothing to say. It would sound foolish to
remark to his own son, "But I never knew the Bible was like
that." As a matter of fact, he isn't quite sure whose words
the boy has been reading. Sayings of Jesus, probably, but if
so they are as grand as Confucius at his best. He knows
Confucius. He reads the Chinese master often, charmed by
his insight into the qualities of "the superior man."

Warren closes the book with a flourish. "Sometime I'll

read you the book of Job. Sometime I'll read the fortieth of Isaiah in the King James Version, and the fifty-fifth. And I'll read you the nineteenth psalm. Oh, yes, and the thirteenth of Corinthians the way Moffatt has it."

His father still has no fitting comment. He says, " Good going. You must have a first-class teacher."

" Prof Harney? Yep. He knows about people."

That night after the boy is in bed, his father goes back to the living room for the red-covered volume. He takes it to bed with him and reads the whole of the Sermon on the Mount. The margin is full of notes in Warren's almost illegible script. " Blessed are the meek," reads the text, and in the margin is a note, " He means the teachable." " Blessed are the pure in heart " — and in the margin " Single-minded; one purpose; don't clutter up your mind." His father closes the book and turns off the light. Maybe it is a good thing he has never taught the boy anything about the book because now the boy comes to it freshly. It isn't merely a historic document to him. He is really getting something, something his own dad had passed by. If the boy could get all that out of the Bible, tomorrow he'd try a bit of Confucius on him. What should it be? Suddenly he finds himself sitting up, with the lights on again. He is hunting through the Analects. He'd like to make a good showing for the sage. Amazing the way those old teachers — Confucius, Jesus, Buddha, Lao-tze — all had a way of cutting to the simple heart of this business of living with such fearless precision and a way of stating their findings with such pure persuasion. He turns off the light once more. Maybe he's missed out on the Bible because in his day it had a black leather binding, and the text was chopped into chapters and verses. Anyhow he's glad the boy thinks it's a " swell book."

Obviously, Warren's father, like any other parent or

teacher, could pass on only what he himself had found in the
Bible. In that respect the Bible is like any other masterpiece
of literature. Even a Scotchman cannot make Robert
Burns seem intriguing to his son if he himself has never been
able to read the dialect. No child was ever stirred to read
Shakespeare by his parent's remarking, " He's a great writer;
everybody ought to know something of Shakespeare." And
probably few boys have picked up *The Critique of Pure
Reason* because some parent remarked, " They say Kant has
had a tremendous influence on ethical standards of conduct." Parents pass on what they have experienced: no
more, no less. They pass on their own Bible. After that,
the Bible, like any other experience, has to become the
child's own.

Do I Have To Go To Church?

My wife could not help wishing we had some place like a church for the worship of the Sabbath, till I said to her, " There is no place in the world that may not serve for a church, because we may entertain pious sentiments everywhere, and this majestic arch of Heaven, the immediate work of the Almighty, ought more effectually to raise the soul and touch the heart, than an edifice of stone made by the hand of man."
JOHANN D. WYSS (*Swiss Family Robinson*)

" Mother, do I have to go to church today? " " Why does our family go to church, dad, when Ted's family never does? " " Do you think that going to church is so awfully important if a person feels he can live just as good a life without going to church? " " Church is kind of an outgrown idea, don't you think? " " I never saw a better man than Dr. Peters and he never goes to church. He's too busy doing good. Don't you think that doing good is more important than going to church? " " I don't want to join a church, mother, because I can't live up to all that. Isn't it better to do the best you can without joining anything? "

These are among the questions which parents have to answer. To be sure, there are still communities in which practically everyone who " is anyone " goes to church and asks no questions. Sometimes these communities are Protestant, sometimes Roman Catholic. There are more of them in the south than in the north. In such places children are likely to go to church without much comment, at least until they go away to school. But most American communities,

in these days, are pretty well divided as to churchgoers and
nonchurchgoers. There is no longer an inner circle of respectable church-attending citizens who set the community's standards of conduct. If one were forced to a generalization he would probably be safe in saying that there
are far more highly intelligent, cultured, socially significant
(meaning useful to society) persons outside the church than
was the case two generations ago. Some critical commenta-
tors on the current scene hold that the church is going
through one of its periodic cultural lags, that there are fewer
great preachers, fewer prophet-priests, less genuine minis-
tration to spiritual need than in any other period since our
country began. Others hold that there has never been a day
since our nation became a republic when the church — both
Catholic and Protestant — has been so aware of its task, so
resourceful in leading the way in social reform, so much a
spiritual leaven in a needy world. The difference in opinion
is itself a commentary on the place of the church in modern
society.

For the practical purposes of answering children's questions about the church and their relation to it, it must be
acknowledged that an increasing number of those who set
the ethical standards of our day do not find need of any
identification with a church. It must also be acknowledged,
after a sampling of a great many local churches of many
denominations in widely scattered localities, that many
church services (including the sermons) are a waste of time
for a vigorous-minded child.

The Sherman family have moved into a new community
and for six successive Sundays they have gone to six different
churches. The church of their own denomination came
first, but the minister was what John, the fifteen-year-old
Sherman, called "a monotone monologist." John's father
had pointed out the good aspects of the service but had too

much common sense to insist that the hour and a half had been well spent. And so the family had cheerfully gone from church to church, quite frank to admit to such callers as asked, that they were looking for the place where they felt most at home. Now the rounds have been made.

"If you ask me," volunteers John, since no one has asked him, "not a minister said a thing worth staying awake for except a couple of good illustrations that white-haired man used, and he talked the rest of his forty-five minutes about nothing."

"If you ask me," says Helen, two years younger, "I was bored all the time. The music was good at the brick church, but we can get just as good music or better by turning on the radio."

"If you ask me," offers Charles, a contemplative nine-year-old, "I'd rather read a book."

Father clears his throat. He knows he must make some kind of defense of the churches because the Shermans have always been churchgoing people. He begins cheerfully: "I think there are two or three churches in this town which are really as good as our own church back in Austin City, only we are used to that church and we aren't used to any of these churches." As soon as the remark is made, he feels that it might be considered a little weak.

John thinks so, too. "Then I'd say it's a good thing we moved. If we've been spending our time listening to this same kind of palaver and didn't know it, it's lucky we came away."

Feeling the argument slipping, mother now wades out with an anchor. She is more than cheerful; she is brightly animated beyond her usual wont as befits this crucial matter. "It isn't very important whether the minister is brilliant or dull," she says emphatically. "It isn't important whether the music is good or mediocre — although, of course, our family does enjoy good music. After all, we don't go to church primarily for instruction and certainly not for amusement. The important thing is that we go to church to worship. I've always found that regardless of the service, one receives food for his soul in the very act of worshiping with other people."

No one says anything for a moment. Mother is like that; she does seem able to worship regardless of the service. She listens to the dullest minister and finds something to thank him for. She compliments the choir for their faithful attendance if for nothing else.

At last John speaks, slowly. "Maybe *you* feel worshipful, mother, but *I* don't. I don't feel uplifted; I don't feel like being better. I can't think with all that chatter going on and I can't even sleep."

"Oh, I can think," Helen breaks in. "I never hear a thing the minister says, after I've listened to see if he is going to say anything. I plan out clothes and make up valentine verses and think of all kinds of things just as well as if I were sitting there alone."

"For that we get up and go to church," observes John pessimistically, "when we might as well be home in bed."

Mr. Sherman feels restive. The children seem to have the better of the argument but there are still family custom and his wife's convictions to reckon with. So the Sherman family keeps on going to church for the better part of a year. Then Mrs. Sherman finds herself going alone "to avoid an argument." She dreads Sundays. If she leaves the family, she feels guilty. And if she stays home with the family, she certainly feels guilty. When father sees that she is unhappy, then he is unhappy, too, although not so unhappy as if he went to church. The whole family now dreads Sundays. In theory, they still approve of churches; in fact, they find going to church a plain waste of time.

If the Shermans were alone in their dilemma, they might worry through without being considered a problem for Christendom. But there are many hundreds of families facing the same predicament. Statistics on church attendance and on benevolence receipts tell the same story: people no longer go to church on momentum. They have to feel that church attendance is worth while. The problem seems to be a personal one which each family has to work out in terms of its own ideals, its responsibility for those ideals, and its common-sense adjustment to personalities and situations.

In general the answers of parents who do not themselves go to church can be summed up under two points of view. There are those who say frankly that they can use their Sundays to better advantage than by going to church. Sunday is the day for the family to catch up on sleep, to have a leisurely, chatty breakfast, to get out in the open for golf or other exercise, to be at home to friends. The church has no place in the already full and satisfactory day. The family has no sense of loss in staying away. There are other parents who do not themselves go to church but who nevertheless encourage their children to do so, or at least to go to Sunday school. They say, "We would like to have the children go until they are old enough to decide for themselves whether or not they want to continue." Or perhaps they remark to the minister, "We don't want Nancy and John to grow up to be heathen like their father and mother." Or, "We don't know what to say to Dorothy when she asks about God and life after death and things like that. We hate to say we don't believe anything. It seems to us she ought to go to Sunday school and learn enough to satisfy her until she is older."

At first glance, it seems that these latter parents are not being fair to their children. Why give the children an-

swers which their parents have found invalid? Why try
to fill an assumed need? Why shirk the direct answer?
But final judgment is not so easy. Sometimes the parents
are honestly not sure whether they have chosen the wiser
part in making no place for the church in their lives, not
quite satisfied that the best they have to offer is sufficient for
the next generation's need. Perhaps, they feel, there may
be deeper springs than they have drunk from. Perhaps
their children may find such springs. At least they want
their children to loiter where such springs might rise, even
though their own experience in churches has not been helpful.

The answers of parents who do go to church also may
be divided into two general types. There are those who
have never questioned the value of the church in their own
lives and in the larger life of society. The church is the
polestar of their reckoning. They take their general direction and steady their course in its light. A week which
does not start with a Sunday service is for them just a head-
less procession of days. Their spirits are tuned to the
seventh day renewal, like clocks which stop if not wound.
Also their daily lives are likely to center around church
events. Monday is Women's Guild, Tuesday the Missionary Society, Wednesday all-day sewing for the poor,
Thursday — but every church is different, although to its
more ardent members its pattern seems eternal and inviolable, as anyone who has ever tried an innovation can testify.
Parents who belong to this group have a ready answer for
their children. In effect their answer is, "Come with us
and see."

In a sense this group of parents may have no more perspective on the actual place of the church in society than
has the group which never goes to church. Propped up
by conviction and pinned down by habit, their attitudes

form a roomy tent within which they order their lives. Being satisfied as they are, they accept the church, just as it is, as the center of the universe. (Conversely, the group which never goes to church are not very accurate judges of what the present-day church has to offer. They might be surprised to find that the church, in some places, has kept pace with their most advanced thinking and has a modern mood to meet their modern needs. Naturally, the perspective of either group is foreshortened by their own experience.)

There is a second group of those within the church who seem forever to be weighing its value to them, their value to the institution, and the place of both the church and the individual in society. With due appreciation for tradition, they nevertheless still have an appraising eye upon the needs of the day and are continually trying to keep the form of the church as elastic as its spirit. Naturally this is a small group compared with the total membership of the church. In proportion to its size it makes more than its share of mistakes and carries more than its share of the burden. From it have come the innovators — Francis, Savonarola, Luther, Huss, Knox, Wesley, Calvin, Carey, Gladden, and others who make the new ways possible. Today in the humbler ranks of this group are a growing number of parents who use their intelligence in trying to conserve the church's sense of mission without circumscribing whatever their children may feel that mission to be.

Talking to children, small or large, about " the church " is a good deal like talking about " government," " education " or " the profit motive." The words mean different things to different people. Frequently when children ask questions about the church, they have a specific organization or instance in mind, but because they state their question in general terms their parents answer with generalities.

"Mother, our church is prob'ly the best church in the world, isn't it?" asks eight-year-old Ann, fresh from a heated argument with her chum who goes to a different church.

"We think it is, dear," answers her mother complacently. "We think that no other fellowship offers such a workable plan for church union as the simple New Testament ideas we have always stood for."

Ann's expression betrays surprise and amazement. She didn't know that "we" were as important as that. What she had in mind was the fact that the particular church she attends has the largest stained-glass windows and the highest steeple she has ever seen in her whole life.

In another home Edwin's confusion is no less genuine although he is a high school senior and a leader in the young people's group of his own church. One night at dinner he presents his problem. "We had a big argument over at Marian's about churches. Sam said he was through with churches because nine out of ten churches he'd ever been in had such sappy ministers. Katy — she's a Catholic, you know — said she didn't think you could judge the church by any one congregation or priest or minister because it was the church universal which Jesus had established and you have to keep the whole thing in mind."

His mother looks up quickly. "I think she's right. I think the church is one institution in which the whole is actually greater than the sum of its parts. The best and most elaborate individual institution in the country, or the best denomination — if we could be sure which one that is — couldn't speak *for the church*. At least not to me. When I say the church I think of the whole of Protestantism."

"The whole of Protestantism?" Grandfather Wainwright's bright blue eyes twinkle as they often do when he is enjoying some idea all by himself.

"The whole of Protestantism," repeats his daughter firmly.

"I don't think it's very practical to talk about the whole of Protestantism," says Edwin. "After all, in our daily lives we don't deal with the whole of Protestantism. We deal with one individual church, one group of people who worship in one church building."

"Let us thank the fates for that," says his father fervently. His father is treasurer of the church of their choice. "If we had to carry the burdens of the whole church, the church universal as you call it, we'd be paralyzed. One individual congregation is enough to think about."

"Not for me," says Grandfather Wainwright blithely. "Even the whole of Protestantism is too small for me. When I think of the church I think of that vast body of believers who assemble all over the world for common worship, for praise and supplication, for acknowledgment of sin and hope of pardon, for renewal of spirit through sacrament or silence, for dedication to the service of God."

"Why, grandfather!" says Edwin proudly. "That's a better statement than the creed any day."

"I'm not sure it means such a lot, though," says Edwin's father. He directs his remarks to his father-in-law, for the two men like to spar — and the family likes to sit in at the sparring. "It seems to me that this body of believers who make up the church universal differ in so many ways — so *many* ways — that they really have little in common, except perhaps the desire to lead more godly lives."

"But in having that much in common, they have everything," says his wife. "Everything that really matters."

"That's the way it seems to me," says Grandfather Wainwright. "Once you feel this oneness, the differences no longer seem important. They're merely interesting. They're merely commentaries on human nature which has so many ways of expressing its longing and striving. Do you know where I got an understanding for this oneness of the church? I got it when I stood before the Buddha of Kamakura. There it stands beside the sea — you remember, Mary — this great calm figure in bronze. One of the largest figures ever cast in bronze, they say. Eyes of pure gold looking out above the trees, across the valley, to the sea. Once Kamakura was a great city and once a temple stood over the statue, but the temple was carried away by a typhoon about the time Columbus was discovering America. There is a room inside the statue where a hundred people may stand to worship. I stood among them, those men and women who were making it the event of a lifetime to see the Dai-Butsu. And then I stood outdoors among other hundreds of pilgrims who were there to receive the strength which comes of beauty. I thought of the religious ardor of the sculptor of that Buddha and of those who had cast the statue — the same sort of devotion that the old masters put into their paintings of Jesus. And I thought — no, I *felt* — devotion, longing, the search for the thing which Buddha called enlightenment and Jesus called the way — *that's* the search which makes mankind all one. I suppose I was having what might be called a religious experience. For a few moments I really sensed the brotherhood of man, and I sensed it so deeply that the insight has never left me. After that I had a different feeling about the institution we call the church. It's part of something larger than itself, old as time, I suppose, more real than any tangible evidence in buildings or images or clergy or ritual."

After Grandfather Wainwright finishes speaking, no one says anything for a moment. Then Edwin speaks out in amazement. "But grandfather! You're making churches and temples — heathen temples — all seem part of the same thing."

"Maybe I am," admits his grandfather slowly.

"I don't think you can quite lump them all together," says Edwin's father, also speaking slowly. "After all, the church was founded on a totally different concept of life from anything that has ever grown out of any other religion. It's built upon a personality. You can't lump churches and temples and mosques all together any more than you can put Buddha and Confucius and Mohammed and Moses and Jesus into the same category."

"Maybe not," says Grandfather Wainwright. "But I don't think they'd mind. They'd probably have a great time comparing notes, comparing insights, and if Jesus had the most light to offer I think the others would be filled with appreciation."

"I'm afraid your theology doesn't hold water, sir," says Edwin's father in a kind but regretful tone.

"Maybe not," grandfather admits indifferently. "Anyhow I didn't mean to get myself so far out on a theological limb. I just meant to say that I feel at home with all sorts of Christians in all sorts of churches."

"You really do, don't you, father?" His daughter looks over at him in surprise as if she had never really noticed the fact before.

"I sort of like to go to church no matter where I am," says the old gentleman. "Edwin here and I, we're alike that way. And I don't give a continental whether the church happens to be some plain little meetinghouse which prides itself on its bare and unimaginative interior, or whether it happens to be some high-vaulted cathedral which offers the worshiper every aid of beauty and aesthetic appeal. In fact, it doesn't matter to me whether the ritual is in English or Latin or some other tongue. I don't even care a lot whether the preacher is bigoted or the priest ignorant, whether a particular congregation seems to exist for its own glory or for the service of man. The ideal is so much more beautiful than any of its facets and the task is so much larger than any accomplishment that the church seems to stand out grandly above any single sect or group."

" I know what you mean — I think," says Edwin. " I sort of feel that same thing myself, sometimes. But I almost hate to feel the greatness of the whole idea, grandfather, because then when I go to my own special church, or any other individual church, I see all the imperfections. I see what a long ways we are from the main idea and it makes a person kind of discouraged."

" It's a healthy thing to be discouraged now and then," says his father.

" It's a healthy thing if you can train yourself to let encouragement flow in with the discouragement," says his grandfather. " You have to make room for both digressions and advancements, reforms and counter-reforms, failures and achievements. Insist, in your own heart, on being part of the whole church, past and present."

Edwin's mother speaks up, somewhat hesitatingly. " Sometimes, I have this feeling for the whole thing, a sort of pride and participation in the church universal. Maybe we all have it at times. But I must admit that I still like my own church best. I believe in the tenets of my own denomination; I like our way of administering the sacraments. I'd go to a good deal of trouble to find a church which sings the hymn I like to sing and uses the ritual I like to follow. Not to mention feeling it is important for Christians really to be of use in the world — as our church, it seems to me, tends to make them."

" That's fair enough, mother," says Edwin. " Different people prefer different kinds of a home and yet we all believe in the home. And we like our education served up differently — in my school the profs spend half their time making sure they're different — and yet we all believe in education and work for it. I guess it's only natural to like different ways and methods in churches. I admit I like the way our minister stands while he talks, just firmly on his two feet without striding up and down. And I like the way our choir sings; you never feel they're putting on. But even if I do like our ways best, still I've got enough sense to know they're not so awful important."

" ' Awfully important,' " his mother corrects.

" ' Very important,' " says his father. The corrections are automatic and in no wise detract from the family's interest in what Edwin has been saying. Nor do the corrections bother him in the least; he doesn't hear them. But grandfather begins to chuckle aloud.

"Tell you what," he offers, " I'll take you all to a church next Sunday where you have to stretch your imagination to feel at home. It belongs to the Pentecostal Assemblies of Jesus Christ, one of the Holy Roller group, and the congregation ' speaks with tongues ' when the meeting gets under way." Grandfather rises from his chair, then stops short and says seriously: "But before you leave you'll feel a part of even that group. I think you will. I did. A lot of people who have been pretty much lost, one way and another, during the depression feel that they are finding something they need right there. It's a wonderful thing the way this being a part of a group of like-minded seekers after truth does bring people together."

Perhaps it is worth noting that in a family such as Edwin's, where conversation about the church flows freely, although such discussion may not be frequent, the interest of the debate comes out of the fact that the family has had experience with more than one kind of church. They happen to be a family which has traveled rather widely. And when they are living in their own city, they go now and then to other churches. Father comes home and announces, " The choir at St. Agnes' is singing three Gregorian chants next Sunday. It might be pretty nice to hear them." Or maybe it is mother who says, " I'd like to see the confirmation service at the First Lutheran Church. Would any of you like to go with me? " Or Edwin announces, " Vine Street Methodist has the best young people's work in town and I'm going over there next Sunday. How'd some of you like to trip along? "

Their neighbors, the Rockwells, have caught the spirit of adventure in worship. One day Mrs. Rockwell says to the children: " I've never seen the windows of the Bethel Presbyterian from the inside of the church. It seems to me they are the loveliest in town and I'd like to sit where I can see them for a whole service." The family goes to Bethel Church. The windows do, as mother anticipated, provide a spirit of worship which pleases even the smallest of the children. He does not know why he feels so much at peace and at the same time so joyous. He only says, " This is an awfully very beautiful church."

On the way home one of the older children remarks, " Their minister says ' um-ah ' and ' so-ah ' until he just about spoils what he's saying. I like our minister better."

" But they have more better windows and more better steps," the youngest persists.

" Did you notice, though " — this from a third child — " they sing the same hymns we sing? I didn't even need to look at the book."

" The hymns aren't the only things they have and we have the same," says the older child. " They took up a collection for missionary hospitals and we do that, too. They said the Lord's Prayer in unison just as we do." The child hesitates a moment. " I thought they seemed to feel the same way we do about trying to be better people."

"Prob'ly they are just as good," the second child observes, "or maybe even better. You can't tell by looking at people, even in church, how good they may be. I felt as if they might all be friends of ours."

"I wonder how they'd like our church. I bet they'd think our minister was nicer than theirs. He has more hair," observes the youngest child.

And so, weighing the essentials and nonessentials, the differences and likenesses, the children have widened their sense of at-homeness in churches of different sorts. Once they are emotionally comfortable in a new atmosphere, once they no longer feel the strangeness of a different way of worshiping, their minds are open for entertaining the possibility of different beliefs, for deepened understanding.

The Protestant child's first visit to a Catholic church is likely to bring forth more questions than usual and he is fortunate if his parents can answer his questions with understanding, with historical explanations and genuine appreciation. Understanding and appreciation of their Catholic friends rises in many Protestant homes from happy childhood visits to Catholic churches. Emotional prejudice, habit prejudice, is harder to break down than intellectual prejudice.

In helping the child to become acquainted with forms of worship and tenets of belief other than his own, parents will not want to overlook the Jewish synagogue. Here again, sinking his roots into the rich soil of generations of religious thinking, the child draws up nutriment for his own religious growth. The prophets of the Old Testament will come to life for him, their impassioned words ringing against a sounding-board of present racial injustice. The "heritage of the godly" belongs to the Christian child as well as to the Jewish child. And when he learns to say, *Shema Yisrael Adonai Elohenu Adonai ehad* ("Hear, O

Israel, the Lord our God, the Lord is one ") in the very accents of those who pledged their lives by those words perhaps three thousand years ago, he has learned more of the history of religion than he can get from books.

But there is, of course, a point at which one guards against his child's becoming an experience-collector in churches, just as he would guard against the child's insistence upon continually changing grade schools. The church, like the home, is a place for steady growth, for carrying responsibility, for pride in improvements and genuine sympathetic criticism of shortcomings.

There is always the possibility that the child, as he grows older and continues attending the services of various creeds, may find a church which suits his needs better than the one to which his parents belong. He may have a nature which responds to ritual and feel that the more informal service of his home church has left him cold without his knowing why. Or if he is used to intricate ritual, he may turn to the simple quiet of worship in a Friends' meetinghouse. The preferences for certain forms of worship are more likely to become apparent in the adolescent than in the younger child because the adolescent has a new self-awareness which makes him conscious of his moods. Whatever gives him peace and integration, through the years when so much new emotion is pulling at him, is deeply valuable to him. He may decide that he wants to join a different church from the one to which his parents belong. If so, his parents may have to call forth in themselves a large measure of understanding. For while it makes no difference to some parents to what variety of church their sons and daughters go and the children are given their teen-age freedom and allowed to follow their preferences, other parents feel their children's preference for another church as keenly as if the children had expressed a preference for another home.

"Alan Lee!" says his mother in great distress. "You can't mean that you want to join an Episcopal church. Why we've been Methodists on both sides of the family ever since Wesley. My grandfather and two of your father's uncles were Methodist ministers. You know that."

Of course Alan knows but he feels that it has about as much relation to his present life as the fact that Jefferson was the father of the Democratic party. In the Episcopal church on the corner of Tenth and Harper, he has found the spirit and the ritual he needs. Maybe he has also found a gray-eyed girl who carries her prayer book demurely and enters into the service, kneeling and rising and kneeling again, with a grace which Alan does not feel his hearty sisters possess. Maybe in his mind the girl is mixed up with the question of ritual and Alan doesn't know it. Whatever the reason, if the new church meets Alan's needs it is the church for him. In it he may grow to maturity without disillusionment and find, as the years add responsibilities, that he has a place for the continual renewal of his spirit. No parent wants to risk cutting his child off from the food upon which he best thrives.

Nevertheless, it is true that families become identified with certain congregations and with particular denominations until a sense of heritage is built up, and naturally a parent does not want his child to cut himself off from that heritage too casually. The parent feels that the family carries responsibility within this group and that the children, growing up, may better serve the whole cause of religion by standing by the family faith. Children who are old enough to feel strongly about a choice of churches are old enough to weigh the imponderables. But having considered the matter as their parents present it, they must make their own choice. Moreover, a mother who may once have felt that she could never go back to a half-empty pew in the

Baptist church after John turned Congregationalist and Mary turned Dutch Reformed, may later find herself quite happy in the feeling that she has furnished young leadership for sister churches. She can lean back upon the realization that the church exists for the nourishment of human hearts and for the service of mankind, and that sooner or later each individual member of the church has to make his own decision as to how much and what kind of nourishment he needs, how much and what kind of service he will render.

These are only a few of the questions which children, young and older, are asking about the church. But no matter how many or how demanding their questions may be, it is true in the end as in the beginning that both the kind of question they ask and the kind of answer they receive depend upon the family experience. Children ask in the light of their own experience; they ask the people from whom they expect to get the most satisfactory answers. Parents answer out of their own experience; they give the answers they expect to be most useful in the long run. In some communities children are bound to ask, " Why so many churches? " In others, " Why no church at all? " In some families children ask: " Why should we join the church just because we agree that it is probably a worthy institution? And if we do join, why all the ceremonial? Why baptism or confirmation or formal reception into membership? We've outgrown the symbolic paraphernalia." Or they may ask: " Why join something we don't feel the need of? Our lives are full of useful pursuits; we get our inspiration elsewhere. Then why continue with an organization which we feel to be outmoded in present-day society? "

Categorical answers do not seem to be answers today. Parents speak out of genuine thought and experience — or they keep still.

To Me He Means . . .

> *But Thee, but Thee, O sovereign Seer of time,*
> *But Thee, O poets' Poet, Wisdom's Tongue,*
> *But Thee, O man's best Man, O love's best Love,*
> *O perfect life in perfect labor writ,*
> *O all men's Comrade, Servant, King, or Priest, . . .*
>
> SIDNEY LANIER (*The Crystal*)

Was Jesus a real man who truly lived or did someone just make him up like King Arthur? How can you prove he really lived? Do you believe that Jesus never had any father except God? What do they mean when they say he was born perfect and couldn't sin? But if he couldn't sin, why does he get so much credit for being good? Do you believe that he performed miracles like changing water into wine, and feeding five thousand people with those tiny loaves and fishes, and walking on the water? And if he did perform miracles, what help is that to us?

If Jesus was so good, why did God make him suffer on a cross and die? But if he was divine, how could he feel any pain? Did he truly rise from the dead? Do you believe that Jesus really meant to start a church? Doesn't it make him sound awfully conceited to be going around telling people to worship him? Or did someone else think up the idea of worshiping him after he was dead?

Anyhow, why should Jesus matter so much to *us?* What do *you* think of him?

Probably four observations can safely be made about the answers that parents will make to these customary questions of their children. First, there is a group of parents who can answer wholeheartedly within the framework of traditional Christian theology. Second, there is an increasing group of parents who would like to give authoritative answers to their children but have no adequate theology from which to draw answers satisfying both to themselves and to the children. Third, there is a not inconsiderable number of parents who will say, in effect, " I don't know the answers " or " Do you think it really matters? " Fourth, there is a growing number of parents who will speak in warm friendly terms of Jesus as one of the world's great teachers who seems to have lived with unusual clarity the principles he taught. Perhaps a fifth classification should be added: the parents whose answers fall now in one category and now in another as they flounder in a sea of inherited ideas, mixed emotions, and unconscious reflections of current thought.

Loyalty to a personality, like loyalty to a cause, finds expression in so many more ways than spoken statements that a child is half-answered before he puts his questions into words. If his parents see in Jesus a supernatural figure who transcended natural law in being born into this world as the Son of God, who lived a life of miraculous deeds and died only to rise from his tomb and be caught up into heaven where he now sits on the right hand of God, then they probably also believe that he established the church through Peter and that the church sets forth the rules for worshiping him and amplifying his teaching as necessity demands. And if his parents believe these things wholeheartedly they probably act upon them, in which case the child is inoculated from infancy with both their beliefs and practices. He does not need to ask questions of persons who have already taught their answers. And if he doubts their answers, he will probably address his questions to someone else.

Or perhaps another child's parents are never heard discussing the ideas which Jesus advanced. They do not refer to the book which tells his story; they find no special reason to attend the church which has grown up in his name. In this case the child knows from the beginning that the personality of Jesus is not a great factor in his parents' lives and that his questions are not so very important, else his parents would have broached the matter themselves at some time.

In another home, perhaps the parents happen to be the sort who are interested in the personalities who have set the ethical standards and moral values for society. These parents have a habit of appraising the current scene in the light of such ideals. Probably the child in that home will have heard the name of Jesus mentioned often enough so that he will have built up from the family talk some picture of the man and of his teachings.

But obviously, children's questions do not spring entirely from the context of their family life. Play with other children, visits to other homes, the books they read, the movies they see, all sorts of experiences precipitate questions. The more speculative the child, the wider the range of his questions. Almost every child living in a so-called Christian culture sooner or later asks questions about the place of Jesus in world thought. The chances are that he asks his questions casually or speculatively without emotional coloring. But let him try to get an unemotional answer! It is the unusual parent who can use the name of Jesus easily in conversation. On the one hand, the name calls forth a tone of devotion, genuine or forced; on the other hand, a tone of skepticism or disbelief or restrained boredom. Only occasionally does a parent manage to hold up his end of an objective, animated conversation which leaves the child intellectually informed and emotionally open-minded.

The Danforths are not a churchgoing household but they might, nevertheless, be called a religious household because of their unusual sensitivity to the ennobling things in life and because of their unflagging interest in human welfare. One Christmas Eve, Donald, an energetic eighth-grader, comes into the library where his father is surreptitiously wrapping presents.

"It's a funny thing, dad, but I never really heard the Christmas story until yesterday when Dick Beach read it at our school program. Yesterday I thought, 'Well, good-night, this is a real story about a real person who once lived just like we live.' It seems queer, doesn't it, that one person should have so much written and said about him for such a long time. I bet he never thought that people would talk about him this way every time Christmas came around."

His father sits down by the desk and settles back comfortably. "You can be right sure he didn't think of Christmas any more than George Washington thought of the cherry tree's becoming a national symbol of honesty. Those things come after a man has lived significantly and died without being forgotten."

"I bet he never thought people would make a religion about him." Donald sits down and crosses his legs in his most grownup manner. "I bet he was just a plain good man, and a smart one, and he went around being useful. I bet if he'd lived today he'd been a doctor or a labor leader or a teacher or something more useful than a model for church windows like we think of him."

"I think you could call him more than just a plain good man and a smart one," says the father contemplatively. "He must have been unusually discerning when it came to reading human nature and unusually resourceful in putting his finger on human needs. That's what impressed the people he lived among."

" Most likely he was a swell teacher, the kind that always gets to the point and makes you want to do something about it."

" He must have been a great teacher, as you say, or his illustrations and parables and stories and arguments wouldn't have been so faithfully treasured as they have been. But it isn't his teaching which has made him famous, really. It isn't his teaching which matters most."

" But it's the things he said that people today are always talking about. ' Jesus said this ' and ' Jesus said that.' "

" What he. said is largely important because of what he did. Most of what he taught had been said before by the rabbis and other wise men. Jesus could have talked like a combined Demosthenes and Savonarola and never have been crucified — or remembered. His trouble, and his greatness, began when he got into action. He and his disciples picked the ears of corn and ate them on the Sabbath. He went about curing the sick who gathered at the sacred pools and were supposed to be incurable. Finally he drove the money-changers out of the temple. That was the piece of civic reform that the city fathers couldn't take. That's when they really got busy to find something they could pin on him so that the law could deal with him. It seems to me that it's the combination of insight and action which gave him what we call immortality. Most great men achieve only one of the two."

" What about the other men who started new religions? Were they about the same kind of people? " Evidently the idea just occurs to Donald and his face shines with the excitement of a new thought. " Mohammed and Zoroaster and Buddha and all those."

" Tell you what," says his father, walking over to the bookshelves. " There are two or three pretty interesting books here which tell how other religions got started. I'll mark some chapters for you and you might like to go after them during vacation."

So Donald does go after them. With his flair for biography and a more than ordinarily curious mind, he reads not only the chapters his father has marked but hunts out some more material for himself. He becomes particularly interested in Buddhism, and for two or three days goes about the house with a preoccupied air. Finally one night he comes to his father.

" There's something I want to tell you, dad. I've become a Buddhist." He speaks as if he were announcing to polite society, " I've become a cannibal."

His father lays down the book he is reading. " Is that so? Well, sir, it's a grand thing to find a philosophy of life which really suits you, and to find it when you're young. Just what do you like most about the teaching of the Buddha? "

Then father and son are off on an animated conversation in which the father's questions reveal somewhat more knowledge of Buddhism than the boy's answers, but nevertheless it is a two-way exchange of thought. His father ends with a friendly admonition, " Even if you have discovered ' the enlightened one ' I'd keep my mind open for further enlightenment if it came my way."

Now of course the next ten years of Donald's life should have shown a growing understanding of the religion of his choice and a staunch devotion to his ideals in spite of the disapproval of his friends. But as a matter of fact before a year had rolled around, Donald developed a violent interest in photography, an avocation in which he forgot most of his devotion to the Buddha. Then in his sophomore year in high school he met a girl who went to church every Sunday and Donald began to go to church himself. At Easter he joined the church, thoughtfully and earnestly, and he began to read his Bible with considerable discrimination and devotion. Two years later he went off to college and stopped going to church. At the moment he seems headed toward a life work in biological research, maintaining on the side a lively interest in economic and labor problems.

And so what? What did his father contribute to his son's appreciation of the character of Jesus? He contributed an open mind, an understanding of the needs of the human spirit and of the way in which these needs are met in part by valiant, intrepid souls around whose ideas and actions systems of religion grow up. He contributed what is likely to be a life-long enthusiasm, intelligent and effectual, for the man Jesus and his way of life. His was one kind of answer.

Jessie Holsman has been what her father fondly designates " a snub-nosed enigma " since she was four and was noticed stopping stock-still in the middle of a game of tag because she had suddenly " thought a poem." Ever since, her young life to the age of twelve has been a combination of outdoor games, at which she excels, and rapt reading and inventing of poetry. One day she comes to her mother and asks, " What do people mean when they say, ' Do you believe in Jesus? ' "

Her mother puts down the sock she is darning and looks at her daughter earnestly for a moment while she hunts for words. " People mean different things, I think. But usually the question means, Do you believe that Jesus was the son of God and that he suffered for our sins and died for us, that he was raised from the dead and ascended to heaven, that he will come again some day to judge the living and the dead, and that all who believe in him will have everlasting life? "

" My, that's a lot," says Jessie thoughtfully. " Do you

believe all that?   If someone asked you if you believed in
Jesus, would you say yes?"   She looks directly into her
mother's eyes as she speaks.

Her mother looks back at her, serenely, confidently.
"Yes, I do believe all that."

"But I don't exactly understand it all," says Jessie.

"Neither do I," her mother acknowledges, "but I believe
it.   The story as I read it in the Bible is so simple and direct
that I see no reason to doubt it.   And the beliefs which the
church has long held about Jesus seem to me reasonable
and secure.   So I believe in him even when I don't understand exactly how he could have ascended into heaven or
how he will come again."

Jessie starts out of the room slowly as if the conversation
were finished, gets as far as the dining room door and turns
back.   "Well, but mother, what difference does it make
if you do believe in Jesus?   Maybe you may get everlasting
life, but what difference does it make now?"

"It makes a difference every day of my life, every hour
of the day.   I'm always thinking to myself, 'Jesus wouldn't
make that cross answer I'm about to make.   He would hold
his peace, or say something helpful.'   Or I say to myself,
'Jesus wouldn't sit contentedly at home when people along
the river flats live in hovels and have no fires to keep out
the cold.   He'd be doing something about their needs.'"

"You do something about their needs; you're always
gathering up clothes for them and all sorts of things."

"I try to do things, but the reason I do them is because
I know Jesus would want me to."   Her mother speaks
simply and surely.

"Does he really matter that much to you, mother?"

"He matters much more than that.   When I walk in
the woods on grandfather's farm, I think to myself, God
made a beautiful world for his children but it's Jesus who

puts meaning into it all because he showed us the love of God. He loved us so much that he could give up his life for us."

"I'll tell you, mother, he doesn't mean that much to me. But I'm going to get him to." The shy, earnest look in her eyes says, "I want to be like you, mother, and if he's the one who makes you the way you are, then I want to know him the way you do."

Jessie starts from the room again, humming happily. She realizes that she doesn't understand everything her mother has said but she feels secure and at the same time rather heroic. She hopes she will have a very hard life full of sacrifices because she feels that she not only wants to do something worthy of this one who died for her but that somehow he will give her the strength to do it. That night she writes a little poem which begins,

> I know not why I trust him so
> Except he trusted me.

As the months go by, and then the years, Jessie maintains her feeling of close relationship to Jesus. Her poems grow and she grows. There is no doubt in the minds of her friends what she will say to her own little daughter when the child is old enough to ask, " Do you believe in Jesus? " That is another parent's answer.

William Mateer is also twelve when he asks his father, "What do you say when people ask you if you believe in Jesus? "

His father happens to be fixing a broken ironing-cord at the moment. " I say yes," he answers promptly.

" You say yes but what do you mean? I know you don't believe that he had no earthly father, and I know you don't believe he rose from the dead, and I know you don't believe he performed the kind of miracles the Bible talks about. So what do you mean? "

"Maybe it would be easier to state the things I don't believe, just as you have done. But there are certain things I do believe — pretty strongly." He puts down the screw driver and contemplates the young questioner.

"Such as what? "

"I believe he understood the deep needs of the human heart, and that the principles of living which he figured out are the best that have ever been presented to mankind. If we could live according to his ideal of brotherhood, the world would be transformed. 'In honor preferring one another'. . . 'Let each one bear his brother's burdens'. . . 'Do unto others as you would have them do unto you.' It's an amazing concept of living. It works. At least, as far as the human race has tried it, it has worked. So I say that I believe in him. And when I say that, I mean that I honestly do try to live according to his ideas." And that is a third parent's answer.

Which is right? Three parents have passed on to their children their particular appreciation of a personality and have led their children into intimate acquaintance with that personality so that Jesus means something definite and real in their lives. But beyond these three there are many, many more parents with many other answers. If the parent when he answers is mouthing words, then his answers merely fail to register or they register negatively. But if he is expressing genuine appreciation of some sort, then his appreciation is likely to be contagious. Appreciation, gratitude, honor, devotion have been expressed in exquisite phrases, as in Lanier's " The Crystal "; in brush and canvas, as in Da Vinci's " The Last Supper "; in music, as in Handel's *Messiah;* in humanitarian service such as Livingstone's journey into the heart of Africa. But it is also expressed — perhaps with

just as great consequence — in the honest answers of ordinary parents who pass on nothing they have not actually
thought through for themselves.

" What do you think of Jesus, father? "

" Some people say . . . the church teaches . . . to me he
means. . . ."   The first two phrases may be important, but
the last one is sure to be so.

About Babies

Where did you come from baby dear?
Out of the everywhere into the here.
GEORGE MACDONALD

" Where did I come from, mummy? " Anita has been playing with her building blocks, talking to herself in the animated fashion of a four-year-old who is forever acting out stories. " The fairy brought the baby princess to the castle " — she points to the work of her hands — " but who brought me? "

Mother, absorbed in letting down the hem of one of Anita's dresses, is taken by surprise although she has known that of course Anita would ask the question some day. But she had imagined it would arise logically from some such event as their dog's having puppies, instead of popping out of the child's irrelevant play. She looks at Anita for a moment and then answers, " Where did you come from? God sent you, dear." It is a beautiful answer, she thinks to herself, never having grown used to the wonder of having a child. But it does not satisfy Anita.

" How did he send me? In an airplane? "

Mother hesitates. After all, four years is young to try to understand the problem of sex, and she doesn't know how much or how little she should explain to the child. There is the stork answer and the answer about the doctor's bag, but it seems to her as if those are lazy answers which lead to further embarrassment. By this time Anita is standing by her mother's knee, drawn by the very fact that her question is not answered so quickly as usual. Mother snaps

143

off a basting thread, as if her sewing had been absorbing her attention, and turns to the child.

"You grew from a seed, darling. Practically everything that lives grew from some kind of seed."

"Did I grow in the ground like a radish?" Anita is incredulous.

"Gracious, no. Different kinds of seeds grow differently. The seeds of plants and trees grow in the ground. The seeds of chickens and birds are hidden in their eggs which grow in the mother hen's body. Then when the hen lays the egg, she has to keep it warm for quite a while until the little chicken is strong enough to break through the shell."

Anita smiles delightedly. She has seen baby chickens. "So you just laid an egg," she says, patting her mother's hand proudly. "I never knew you could do that."

"Oh, no, you didn't grow from that kind of seed, either," mother hastens to explain. "Animals don't lay eggs the way chickens do. Their babies remain inside the mother until they are big enough to be born alive. So a mother dog has puppies and a mother cat has kittens. And human mothers have baby girls and baby boys."

"Hum," comments Anita thoughtfully. "So it's different with all the different kinds of things." Then she looks up brightly into her mother's face. "I'd much rather be a baby than an egg! Thank you very much for not having me be an egg."

And then, whirling around to her toys, she is absorbed in pretending that she is a baby again.

Thus it happens that Anita's mother does fairly well with her little daughter's first questions, but she could have saved herself that moment's hesitation and every bit of her incipient embarrassment if she had realized that she and Anita were really talking about different subjects. The mother was thinking of sex with all its adult connotations. In her mind were the jumbled emotions of love and courtship, of mating and fear and ecstasy and childbirth and social opinion — a thousand impressions too intimate, and probably too unconscious, ever to be caught into words. She felt uncertainly that no matter how little she said, she was really initiating her small daughter into all those things, without warning and certainly without adequate vocabulary. But she was mistaken. Anita merely wanted to have herself accounted for: how did she get here?

Most of the questions our children first ask about " sex " are just such mechanical questions largely summed up in the simple phrase, How did I get here? Such a question springs from the same curiosity which makes them ask: " Where did my sled come from? " " How did the world get made? " " How did the stars get in the sky? " If the answers call forth from the child any emotional reaction, it is the emotion of wonder. And the child's world is so full of wonders that he easily makes room for another.

If the parent could remember that the small child's questions are to be taken at face value — no more — then he would find himself emotionally free to give quick, plain, complete answers. He would find not only that the next questions come more readily but also that the succeeding answers are more objective and forthright. A parent all aflutter with candidness is just as much of an emotional liability to the child as is a parent swathed in secrecy. The trick is to see the questions in the simple framework of the child's curiosity and to answer them from the point of view of the child's need.

When a very young child asks about his beginning, he is likely to ask only two or three casual questions which, if answered plainly, satisfy his curiosity. It is the fantastic answer that lingers to perplex the child. If he is satisfied, he may forget both his questions and their answers and come back a year or two later to ask the same questions again. Indeed, this questioning process may occur two or three times before the information makes enough impression to remain in his mind.

But not all children, even as young as Anita, are so quickly satisfied as she with their first conversation on the subject. Some will push their questions until the entire process of birth seems plain to them. The most insistent question seems to be, " But if I grew inside of you, mother, how was I born? " Sooner or later, that question becomes uppermost and then the answer must be given.

An increasing number of parents turn for help to books written especially for the child. In any one of several excellent books on the subject, pictures help to make the story plain. The book may begin by presenting a black page with a tiny white pin point in the middle of it under which is the caption, " This is how small you were when you began." And then will follow the stories, simply told, of the reproductive processes of plants and animals. There will be a short chapter on the fertilization of seeds, another on the fertilization of the hen's egg and the development of the baby chick. The story of the way in which animals carry their young is likely to have illustrations of a mother cow with her calf, a mother sow feeding her piglets, a mother bunny with her large family. Then comes the story of the human baby, and this story probably has diagrams that show the location of the uterus in the mother's body and the relative size of the baby at different stages in its development.

Usually a young child will not be interested enough to listen to the reading of the whole book at one sitting. He will follow along for some pages and then either wander off to his play or return to his original question, " How was

I born? " But his parent can answer, " I want you to know the whole story because it's quite an important story and we will read some more tomorrow."

Naturally it is sometimes easier for the parent when dealing with a young child to sketch the contents of the book in his own words, using the pictures by way of outline and illustration. Naturally, too, different children ask different sorts of questions, and whether the parent reads the story or tells it he has to be ready for interruptions.

One advantage in answering the child's questions with the aid of a book is the fact that the book can be left on his bookshelf for further reference. He will occasionally pick it up to look at the pictures which are likely, in time, to lead to further questions. Thus, between the book and the questions, the parents have a fairly secure feeling that the child is getting information as fast as he needs it.

It is soon after Leonard's seventh birthday that he climbs up on his mother's bed one morning with the request he has used since babyhood, " Tell me another story, won't you? "

" What shall I tell you today? "

" Tell me about when I was born." He snuggles under the covers ready for a good time.

His mother has told him on other occasions some of the facts about birth, but for some reason he has not mentioned the subject now for more than a year. Today she senses that this time he will want more information. She says, " Downstairs on the third shelf of the bookcase by the door is a little book called *How You Grew*. You trot down and get the book."

Leonard goes. He comes back, climbs into bed with the book and is at once absorbed in the pictures, turning the pages rapidly.

" Slow down," suggests his mother, " and I will read

you about them." A half-hour passes quickly and she says, "We will read some more tomorrow."

"Tonight," begs Leonard. "Tonight when I go to bed."

When night comes he appears with the book and his mother begins to read again. When she comes to the word "spermatozoön," Leonard halts her with a squeal of delight. "Let me see that word," he cries.

Mother points it out, wondering to herself as the child spells it aloud over and over whether he has some pornographic tendency she was never aware of. Finally he exclaims: "Well, sir, that's the longest word we know. It has twelve letters. Prob'ly it's the longest word in the dictionary."

His mother smiles as she realizes anew that curiosity counts everything grist for its mill, and the reading goes on. Leonard makes matter-of-fact comments now and then, and appears moderately interested. When the book is finished and mother sits waiting for additional questions, he merely yawns widely and kisses her good-night. It is a good story finished and that's that.

The next day is Saturday and the two little boys from next door, who are rather new neighbors, arrive to play before Leonard is awake. But he hears them downstairs and hops out of bed. Then mother hears him calling over the banister: "Hey, Buddie! Walter! Come on up. Do you know how long it takes an elephant to have a baby elephant? Come here and I'll show you a picture of ten little pigs all born at the same time."

A few minutes later mother goes into Leonard's room and finds all three boys lying on the floor looking at the pictures in the new book while Leonard explains the subject matter. She stops aghast. It is one thing to tell her own child what he wants to know when he wants to know it, but it is something different to educate her neighbor's children. From the conversation it is plain that Buddie and Walter know nothing at all on the subject of babies. Indeed they know less than nothing for they have a lot of misinformation.

"It's a funny thing," says Walter, "that my mother didn't know about this."

Buddie's long clear laugh rings out. "She must have been asleep when I was born because she thinks that the doctor brought me in a bag."

"She found me under a bush in the garden," says Walter, turning to Leonard's mother. "Now how did she suppose I got there?"

Mother has an inspiration. "Lots of people make up fairy stories about how their babies came, just the same as they make up jolly tales about the way Santa Claus comes. We all like the Santa Claus stories even when we know they aren't exactly facts."

"That's o. k. for little kids," says Walter, "but I was really asking her what I wanted to know. I'm no baby." He is disgusted.

"Bless your heart," says mother, "all of us mothers go right on thinking our children are little kids even when they grow taller than we are."

Mother feels she is doing rather well by her neighbor, but her apprehension is none the less real when she thinks of going next door and having to announce, "Pardon me, but I have just told your offspring the facts of life." She is fond of the mother of Walter and Buddie and most certainly does not want to hurt her.

However, at the moment she cannot take the book away from the children without filling Leonard's mind with a new set of questions. So she does the common-sense thing and sees the incident through, answering the boys' animated questions with offhand explanations as she makes Leonard's bed. When they have fully satisfied their interest in the subject, the boys go off to play. Mother goes off to think.

Later in the morning she goes to her neighbor's house. Unfortunately she happens in at a time when her young neighbor is in a bit of a temper over the maid's carelessness, but mother snatches the opportunity to talk about maids instead of small boys. The moment comes, however, when she must state her errand. She begins by telling about Leonard's questions, and then edges in the fact that in her experience with Leonard's two older brothers she finally decided it was easiest to tell them the full truth from the beginning. She comes to the place in her recital where she must tell how Buddie and Walter arrived on the scene and were met by Leonard's enthusiastic offer to share his book.

" Oh my goodness! " cries the neighbor. Mentally mother reaches for the doorknob to escape. But her neighbor is beside her, radiating gratitude. " I'm so grateful! I'm so much obliged! You've no idea how you've helped me. The boys have asked so many embarrassing questions lately, and I've told them so many jumbled answers that I just didn't know what they might come out with in public. I've been hoping that some boy at school might tell Walter the truth and then he'd tell Buddie and they'd keep still."

This is no time for comments on pedagogical procedure. Besides, the mother of Leonard feels that the mother of Buddie and Walter has probably already got the point of anything she might have to say. Instead, she offers to lend the book. The conversation turns to children's books in general. And finally mother goes home greatly relieved.

But she might not have met with such a cordial reception from her neighbor, for some mothers still believe that ignorance is the best guarantee of virtue and they resent bitterly any attempt on the part of school or mothers' club to impart sex information scientifically. Nevertheless, the best approach to such mothers is probably the indirect one of suggestion through the Parent-Teachers Association or the Woman's Club that one of the excellent films on the subject be bought and presented to the school.

Whenever and however the small child is listening to the story of the birth process, his questions and comments are certain to be very explicit. Almost every child makes more or less the same remarks. " It would take such a big opening for a baby to come through, mother! I should think that everything inside of you would fall right out too." And then the mother explains the elasticity of muscles which can, when necessary, let the tiniest of openings stretch to considerable size. The child has had some experience through which to understand this explanation because he knows the use of the rectal muscles and realizes that de-fecation is a normal and usually painless process. It seems reasonable that nature should provide another scheme of the same general sort for letting babies be born.

Most children also comment, " But didn't it hurt awfully to born such a big thing as a baby? "

" Very new babies aren't so awfully big, and their bones are soft. Even the bones of the head are soft enough so that being squeezed a bit doesn't harm the baby at all. Nevertheless it's true that having a baby does hurt a good deal. That's one reason a doctor comes to look after the mother and baby. Sometimes he gives the mother some medicine which makes the pain easier. And the nice thing is that as soon as the baby is born, the pain is all gone. The mother is usually so thrilled over the baby that she forgets all about its hurting her."

Many children pause to comment, " I didn't want to hurt you, mother," or, " I hope I didn't hurt you too much." And then, their curiosity satisfied over the mechanics of birth, they want the rest of the tale immediately. " Were you glad I was a girl (or a boy)? Was daddy glad? What did I look like? Did I cry? What did I do first? " It seems important for the child to know all the little things about his becoming *himself* and he will call for that part of the story over and over.

The ideal time to explain to a child the process of a baby's prenatal development is when the family is expecting a new little brother or sister. Then the child feels that something tremendously interesting is happening to *his* family; the baby will be *his* brother or sister; it is *his* mother who is helping the baby to grow. His interest is personal and his healthy curiosity has a logical focus.

Arthur is a rough-and-tumble little boy, inventor of the neighborhood's most hazardous games, and unusually fond of babies. No matter how fast he may be dashing down the sidewalk on his roller skates, he comes to a halt by every strange baby carriage and takes an appreciative look at the occupant. When he is nine years old his mother tells him that their own family is going to have a new baby. At once he is elated and proprietary. He knows, from earlier conversations, that a baby grows inside its mother until the time comes for it to be born. But he has never had any special interest in the subject before.

" How long will it be before it comes? " he asks.

" Six more months," his mother answers. " It takes nine months for a baby to grow strong enough to be born, and it is now three months since the baby started growing."

" You couldn't hurry it up, could you? Eat more or something? "

" Not very well. Nature can't be hurried."

" It doesn't take a rabbit nine months," Arthur observes. "Fred's rabbits can have bunnies in six weeks. Fred's father says that you can just about count on six weeks after the father comes to visit the mother rabbit. He has to borrow a father rabbit from Ernie." Arthur has never questioned the father's place in human procreation, nor does he do so now. He merely adds, "You'd think a person could have babies as quick as a rabbit."

"The time depends somewhat upon the size of the baby, although not altogether. It takes a mother elephant nearly three years to have a baby elephant."

"But look what she gets! Oh, boy!" Arthur's eyes shine. In a way a baby elephant appeals to him more than a mere brother or sister.

For some days thereafter, Arthur asks questions about the forthcoming baby. He may be playing hilariously and suddenly be reminded of something he wants to know. As happens in regard to his other interests, there seems to be a certain fomenting of ideas deep within him. He speaks when the ideas come bubbling to the surface.

"What does the baby eat? It has to grow. Does it nibble like a fish inside of you?"

Mother, who is writing a letter at the time, takes a sheet of paper and begins to draw a picture. She has drawn so many pictures — of stomachs and livers and hearts and brains and all the things which Arthur calls "the inside works." Arthur likes these impromptu lessons on paper. He stands beside her now, watching with interest. She draws a somewhat pear-shaped figure.

"This is a kind of sack called the uterus," she explains. "The uterus is an organ a woman always has in her abdomen, although she uses it only when she is going to have a baby. It is the baby's cradle, you might say, because the baby lies snugly inside it for the whole nine months. It is one of the most interesting organs in the body because it can grow many times its ordinary size without hurting the other organs around it, such as the stomach and spleen and liver."

Arthur nods. He knows something about the other organs. "But how can the baby get food? It can't grow on nothing, can it?"

"While the baby is being carried inside the uterus" — mother uses her pencil again — "the uterus grows a special lining called the placenta. This placenta is filled with little blood vessels not directly connected with blood vessels of the uterus but so near that there is an interchange of tiny substances of nutrition. The process is called diffusion and you'll learn more about it when you study botany. But the main thing is that the food does get from the mother's uterus to the placenta, and then the placenta is connected to the baby's abdomen by a special cord called the umbilical cord."

"Do you mean a cord like a string? How funny."

"I mean a cord about as big around as your finger and maybe twenty inches long. One end of the cord is fastened to the placenta, as I said, and the other end to the baby's abdomen. Inside the cord are two arteries and a vein to carry the blood back and forth from the placenta to the baby. So you see the baby does have a blood supply of its own, in a way, but still it depends on its mother's body for every single thing which makes it grow — for the minerals for its bones and the food for its muscles and blood."

"Well, I never," is Arthur's old-fashioned exclamation. He chuckles to himself. "The baby can't get anything to eat different from what you eat. If it wants an ice cream soda, you will have to eat it for him." Then he has another thought. "If the baby is fastened to the placenta by a cord, how can the baby ever get born? Does it break the cord?"

"Nature has a better way than that," his mother explains. "The cord is rather long — almost two feet long — so the baby can be born easily enough, and then the first thing the doctor does is to take a sterile pair of scissors and snip off the cord close to the baby's abdomen."

"Doesn't it hurt?"

"Not a bit. The navel in the middle of your own abdomen is the place where the cord once fastened you to the placenta."

"Think of that! And everybody has one to prove that he got born. But what good is the cord after that? Does the mother's next baby use it?"

"No. Each baby has its own cord and its own placenta. A few minutes after the baby is born, the placenta comes out, too, just like a worn-out lining which the uterus doesn't need any more. The doctor disposes of it, cord and all. Then the uterus takes a rest and slowly shrinks to its former size."

"Did all of that happen to me?" Arthur is feeling rather important.

"It certainly did. Just about the same thing happens to every baby. Some day our new baby will grow up and ask questions about the way *it* came to be born."

Some weeks go by before Arthur makes another observation. He is in the living room with his parents after breakfast. His father is reading the paper and his mother is standing before the mirror putting on her hat ready to go shopping.

"I see our baby is growing," he observes. "If it keeps on, you'll have a tummy as big as the milkman's, I guess."

"But more important," comments father.

"Mother's more important than you are," says Arthur suddenly. "A person might think a man's more important because he can lift so much and run engines and be an explorer. But he can't have a baby." He stops. "Or could he, if he wanted to badly enough?"

"No, he couldn't," father agrees. "That's one place where nature has put the responsibility on the woman."

"Then listen here," says Arthur. "You're really no relation to me at all, are you, dad? Why should people say I've got your eyes and chin? Everything I've got came from my mother."

In this offhand manner arises the question whose answer will determine much of Arthur's future attitude toward relations between men and women. His father and mother have known that the question might come any day now. They have planned to be casual and forthright. Father recalls the method his father used, which was to take him into the library for a solemn but vague discussion that left him impressed but confused by the inadequacy of the facts presented. Mother, too, recalls how she was taken upstairs and told a long story beginning with the sacred precincts of the Garden of Eden.

Now father says in a matter-of-fact tone: "What do you mean, your mother gave you everything? She's smart but she isn't that smart. It takes a mother *and* a father to have a baby." Father puts down his paper. "You see human beings are very much like other animals in the way their bodies work. They all eat and they all digest and assimilate on about the same principle. Likewise they have their young on about the same principle. The mother develops the egg. If she's a mother chicken, she lays the egg and then keeps it warm until the baby chick hatches. If she's a higher type of animal, all the way from a rabbit to a human, the egg develops inside her body until the little new creature is ready to be born. But no egg would ever start to grow, not in a thousand years, unless the father gave it the living spark which makes it grow. It's a good deal the same principle as having a fire laid but nothing happens until you touch the lighted match to it."

Arthur is listening raptly. "What's the spark like? And how does the father give it to the egg?"

"The spark is called a sperm or spermatozoön," his father begins.

"What a long word," says Arthur. "Spell it."

His father spells it. "It's a long word for a tiny organism too small to see without a microscope. The spermatozoa are developed in the testicles of the father. The testicles are two bag-like structures connected with the penis. In a boy, they are small and unimportant because they aren't used. But when a boy becomes a man old enough to be a father, then the testicles grow larger and begin to secrete a fluid called semen. It's a heavier fluid than water and although there is not much of it, it contains a great number of these tiny spermatozoa any one of which can fertilize the egg and make it grow."

"Is that what fertilize means? Make it grow?"

"That's it. The eggs are formed in two little sacks called ovaries inside the mother's body. About once a month, one of these eggs makes its way into the uterus so that a baby can start to grow there if the egg is fertilized by a spermatozoön. So then, if the mother and father decide they would like to have a baby start to grow, the father must see that the spermatozoön is sent to the egg. The way he gets the spermatozoön to the egg is to insert his penis into the mother's vagina and let the semen from his testicles flow through the penis into the vagina. You remember that the vagina leads right into the uterus. It's really the hallway to the uterus and these tiny spermatozoa, too small to see, swim into the uterus until one of them finds the egg and unites with it. Then the egg starts to grow. So the new baby is literally made by both the father and the mother.

Although the spermatozoön is much smaller than the egg —
and the egg is scarcely as big as the head of a pin — still
it carries half the baby's characteristics. So the baby has
just as much chance to look like his father as to look like
his mother."

"Fair enough," says Arthur. "And so we all get started
the same way. Famous people and poor people and everybody. You'd think — " But he doesn't pursue the subject now. He seems contemplative for a moment, as if
about to ask further questions. Then his eye sees something under the davenport. He dives under and comes
forth with his catcher's mitt. "Fred told me I'd find the
good old mitt right here at home. I thought all the time
we'd left it on the field."

Five minutes later he is bounding down the front steps,
and his parents hear him shriek, "Hi, Fred! Spitzy! Hi!
I found the mitt. Lookutit."

Mother looks at father. "He was so explicit, wasn't he?
And so were our answers. Do you suppose he'll remember
all that?"

"Probably not. But he'll remember the general idea.
And the next time he has a question, he'll remember that he
was interested in what he learned today and he'll come back
to ask some more."

"Do you think that maybe — perhaps — we should have
said something about just one man and just one woman and
all that?"

"I do not," says father emphatically. "The boy hasn't
any experience to comprehend the emotional coloring.
Wait until adolescence begins to tug at him. Wait until
he knows the difference between girl and girls. I'd like
to make a wager that when Arthur grows up he won't be
able to remember when or where or from whom he learned
the baby lore. It will come out of the storehouse of things

he's 'always known' just as he now claims he's always known how his digestion works."

Naturally, Arthur's questions might have gone on for some time and might have turned in any one of a dozen directions. How many spermatozoa does the semen contain? What happens to the ones which do not unite with the egg? Is the semen ready whenever the father needs it? What happens to the egg if no spermatozoön comes to fertilize it? The only sure thing about such questions is that they will reflect curiosity about the mechanics of fertilization and will be as unemotional as questions about a cross-cut saw or an automobile engine — if there is no emotional coloring in the parents' explanation. And, of course, if the child's previous questions have been answered in a straightforward manner.

During the remaining weeks before the baby is born, Arthur's interest is in the mechanics of its development: "What keeps the baby from sticking tight to the placenta?" "Does it lie straight out or curled up?" "Does it turn over?" "If the mother died, would the baby die too?" "How does it finally know when it's time to get born?" All of which are answered as completely as seems necessary for the satisfaction of his own honest curiosity.

Only once does Arthur broach the subject of the baby in the presence of anyone else. One night there is a guest for dinner. Chloe, the maid, is pouring drinking water. Suddenly Arthur speaks up: "Give my mother plenty of water, Chloe, because the baby floats in water. The water sort of cushions it so that if my mother bumped into a door or something, the baby wouldn't get hurt so easy."

No one makes a comment. The conversation goes on as before. Later, when he is undressing for bed, mother says: "By the way, Arthur, don't you remember that there is a custom that we don't talk about our physiological workings while we are at the table? We don't talk about the details of digestion or circulation or — "

" Or bloody noses," contributes Arthur.

Mother agrees. " Or the mechanics of the baby. Some things we keep among the family affairs to be discussed when the family is alone."

" It's a sissy idea," scorns Arthur. " I can eat just as well if people talk about blood and wrecks with a hundred people killed. But I'll remember."

Some weeks later when his mother is taken to the hospital Arthur's concern is very real. So is his intelligent comprehension — to the limits, of course, of a well informed, interested nine-year-old. He asks whether the baby came head-first, whether its head was " squashed " badly, whether his mother suffered much. But after he has seen the baby (who proves to be a little sister, of more use as an ornament than as a future member of the ball team), after she has been brought home and he has assisted at her bath and commented on how complete she is while yet so tiny, he seems to have no further interest in the general subject of sex for several years.

Arthur just happens to be among the lucky children who ask questions freely. He has always been given forthright answers, casual when the question was obviously of no special importance, thorough and complete when the answer might supply part of his working equipment for life. For instance, once, at the age of four, he had an experience which might have been harmful. At a summer hotel he made friends with some older children who were secretively curious and experimental about their sexual organs. One morning Arthur came in from play flushed and irritable, not at all like his direct self. A few questions from his mother brought out the difficulty. She expressed no horror, no abject dismay. She merely made a firm statement that handling the sexual organs is as poor physiology and as poor taste as sucking the thumb, just one of the distressing habits a healthy boy doesn't want to cultivate. If his mother had threatened him with punishment or branded him as guilty of "a dreadful habit," the incident would probably have remained firmly fixed in his mind. But because she was resourceful and unemotional in this situation, as in others perhaps less alarming, Arthur has never known the barrier of embarrassment or guilt between himself and his parents. He could ask his questions about sex, about procreation and babies and birth, without hesitation.

Without doubt the successful answers to the young child's questions about sex, whether the questions are explicit in words or implicit in some experience, are the answers which add to his understanding of life without emotional bias.

Taking In The Teens

And yet there was the impressiveness of size about him, especially about his legs and chin. At seventeen and eighteen growth is still going on, sometimes in a sporadic way, several parts seeming to have sprouted faster than others. Often the features have not quite settled down together in harmony, a mouth, for instance, appearing to have gained such a lead over the rest of a face, that even a mother may fear it can never be overtaken. Voices, too, often seem misplaced; one hears, outside the door, the bass rumble of a sinister giant, and a mild boy, thin as a cricket, walks in.

BOOTH TARKINGTON (*Seventeen*)

It is in his second year in junior high that Arthur begins to go with the boys from across Davis street. The new boys come to the house freely. Sometimes they stay for lunch and Arthur's mother makes them feel at home. She tries to keep them from being embarrassed by the maid's careful service, and Arthur tries not to let on to her that he notices how they " guzzle their soup " and sprawl over the table. They are older than Arthur, all four of them, and obviously he covets their approval. Both father and mother decide that in this case it is better to supervise the friendship as best they can and let it wear itself out.

One day Arthur appears in the library where his father and mother are looking at a new book. He is embarrassed. His face is flushed; he twists his cap in his hands.

" What is it, Arthur? " asks his father easily, sensing the boy's apprehension.

" Oh, nothing," says Arthur. " I thought you were alone and I was just going to ask you something. But it isn't important." He turns away.

" I'm leaving anyway," says his mother quickly. " We're cleaning the pantry." As she goes through the door, she tousles his hair just the way she sometimes does to father's.

As soon as he is alone with his father, Arthur speaks in one gulp. " Those kids — Lem and Pinky and Toots and them — they say it's the bunk about one man and one woman and the baby business. They say somebody's fed me a lot of baby talk. They say every man has a lot of women and that he doesn't have them because the girls want babies either. They say there never was a man that didn't have his women a long time before he got married, too. Lem, he's tried it and Pinky's aiming to soon. They say you don't know a thing about fun until you find out what a girl's really for. They say there's a special way you do with girls so they won't get babies but they won't tell me what it is because you got to pay to get it."

Arthur stops, pale and shaken, emptied of these things he has been unable to digest.

" Sit down," says his father seriously. The boy sits, and for a moment neither speaks. Then his father's words come deliberately, sternly. But Arthur does not feel that the sternness is for him. Rather for the facts of which he speaks.

" Some of the things the boys have said are true. But those things have the same relationship to normal sexual relations that anarchy has to government." Father pauses for a moment. " It is true that sexual relations have other importance besides the desire for procreation, and having a family isn't the only reason that a man and a woman live together although most men and women do want to have children. When a man loves a woman more than anyone else in the world — even more than himself — he naturally wants to express his profound and particular respect for her. He provides a home for her. He provides food and fuel and the other necessities. He likes to be doing things for her, exercising his brain and muscle. But he also likes to come home to her in quiet moments and to feel by the very nearness of her presence that she belongs to him. He holds her in his arms. He sleeps with her. Being able to reach out and touch someone you love is often more important than any words you can say to them, or they to you. And probably the highest point of this wordless understanding which flows between two human individuals is reached by a man and a woman who love each other. The sex relation is the culmination of this feeling of oneness. It is a moment of complete fulfillment — to be treasured for its own sake, for the security and elation and peace it brings to the spirit, as well as for the fact that it may provide the physical basis of new life.

"Of course, there are cheap counterparts for most of life's rare gifts, this among the others. You realize, for instance, that a surgeon has it in his power to know a tremendous sort of exhilaration when he invents and performs a difficult operation — or he can find a degree of cheap exhilaration in a bottle of whiskey. He rates the value of each kind of exhilaration by the results, by the way he feels about the experience afterwards, by what it does for him. In something of the same fashion, there is a cheap counterpart for the full experience of the sexual relationship as it exists between a man and a woman who love each other a great deal. It is true that a man may perform the same act with any other woman, no matter what her color or class or quality, and it will provide a physical thrill. The woman may be a stranger for whom he cares nothing at all. No affection enters into the deal; she doesn't matter to him, and it may make no slightest difference to her who he is or what his real need may be. That's one kind of sexual experience. It seems to me that you pretty much have to choose in life which you will have — one woman or many. You can't have both. If, as these boys said to you, a man wants to go from woman to woman hunting a momentary thrill, he can get it. But if he does that, then he will never know the fullness of the peculiar bond which exists between a man and woman who belong exclusively to each other."

All the while his father is speaking, Arthur sits very still, intently watching his father's face. He seems to be taking in more than the words. He feels, without having words for the feeling, that there is a quality about his father which demands the best things from life. He feels there is an integrity in his father which puts the best back into life, a *noblesse oblige* of the human spirit to give and to take only the best. He wants to be like his father. When Arthur stands up to leave he feels taller. He also feels as if he has had a violent sickness and suddenly got well but is still weak — weak and strong, stronger than he ever felt before. All he says is, " Well, I guess I see now how it is," and then he goes upstairs to get ready for school.

In helping the adolescent to find his way among the problems of sex, the parent surely cannot overlook the immediate physical manifestations of maturity with which the child has to deal. The sex urge may come so swiftly and disturbingly upon a boy or girl as to be overwhelming. Or it may upset his emotional balance without his knowing what is making him so irritable, so tired, so careless, so — any one of a dozen things.

Here again the parent can find much help for the child, and for himself, in books written with the particular purpose of explaining the physical and psychological changes of adolescence to the one having the experience. The parent need not be mysterious or heavy-handed about offering such books to the boy or girl. A mother, for instance, may meet an unwonted burst of irritability on the part of her daughter with the cheerful remark: " My stars, you must be sailing into the stormy waters of adolescence. Well, you may find some help for charting your course in a book that has helped me." (It is to be hoped that her words will sound less like a line learned from the book.) Or a father may say to his son: " You are growing so fast that I can't keep track of you. Growing up has its special problems. I can't remember them all, and those I do remember may not be your problems. But there's a pretty good book on the whole business which will give you some pointers."

Each family has its own vocabulary, its own camaraderie, its own way of sharing confidences. But whatever the family characteristics, one thing the present-day parent can be sure of: his sons and daughters are likely to be flippant when they are in earnest, and very, very offhand about a thing in which they have deep concern. If the parent can come somewhere near to matching the child's mood, he stands a better chance of holding the child's confidence.

Both boys and girls need some explicit instruction on the matter of menstruation. Gone are the days when boys from " good families " frequently grew to maturity without any knowledge of this part of nature's preparation for parent-hood. National advertising has taken care of part of the instruction, and the frankness with which many girls refuse a swimming date, for instance, with a casual, " Sorry, but not today," makes it impossible for a growing boy not to be aware of the problem.

It is probably more important that a mother anticipate the problem for her daughter. There have been, and still are, too many serious emotional consequences when a girl is suddenly overtaken by the menstrual flow and thinks she is the victim of some mysterious disorder or is dying of hemorrhage. Gone are the days — one hopes — when a mother takes her daughter into the darkened guest room and offers to talk to her " as one woman to another about a certain time of month when a lady doesn't do some things." Today, although some girls still suffer extreme discomfort during a menstrual period, most girls take it in their stride and are able to go right on with their daily routine of work and play. A mother can best treat the subject in that spirit.

When Effie is eleven, her mother decides that it is time she know the facts of menstruation. The child is maturing, and also beginning to go about with girls older than herself; she should be saved the embarrassment of being the uninformed one. Her mother has no dread of explaining the matter to Effie but she does wish that a logical moment would present itself. She hates to say, while Effie is practicing the piano or washing her neck, " Oh, by the way, there is something you need to know." But as always the child makes her own opportunity. Effie in her snow suit, dripping melted snow, drops down on the rug in front of the fire. " Gretchen's getting to be an awful sissy. This is about the fourth time this winter that we've started off skating or sliding or something and she's said, ' I can't chase around today. Tomorrow maybe.' I hope I never get like that."

" You may, though," says mother. " If she feels the way I do today, she has a perfectly good reason for not chasing around, and if you'll take off that wet snow suit before it makes puddles on the rug, I'll tell you about it."

Effie dispenses with the wet suit and comes back to the fire. " O. k.," she says. " The story of Gretchen's pain in the neck."

" She's probably beginning to experience nature's preparedness program," says mother. " Nature begins quite early to get a woman ready for the business of having a family. You remember that when a woman is carrying a baby, she has to furnish the food for the growing foetus, indirectly but surely, from her own blood stream. It takes a good deal of food, too, which is another way of saying it takes a good deal of blood and strength. If the mother's body had that drain put on it all at once, she would lose more energy than she could afford to part with. So nature has a way of beginning, when a girl is about twelve or thirteen, to store up extra blood every month. It collects in the uterus which, you remember, is the organ the baby lives in during the nine months of pregnancy. But when there is no baby, the uterus has no need of this extra food supply of blood. So it empties itself about once in twenty-eight days."

" Good night! " says Effie with more interest than alarm, " I hope it gives some warning. What if you were at school or out playing? "

" It doesn't happen all at once, but flows slowly for three or four days. Usually a girl knows by watching the calendar which day it will begin and she protects herself by wearing a sanitary pad."

" I wondered what those were," says Effie. " I keep seeing ads about them and I was going to ask you."

" I'll show you when we go upstairs. In fact, I'll give you some so that you'll have them handy if you should begin to menstruate when I'm not around."

" Does it hurt? I mean do you feel like you'd had an awful cut or something? "

" Gracious, no. Nature is a better engineer than that. The whole process is as mechanical as digestion and when a girl lives a healthy normal life, she is not much more conscious of it than of her digestion. But if she is nervously tired or under some tension — such as examinations at school — she may be aware of some discomfort. That is, she may feel irritable the day before the flow begins and wonder why nothing suits her, and she may be vaguely miserable or unusually tired during the first day of the period."

"If you don't have pain," says Effie, "then I think it is a slick idea that nature figured out."

"When a girl does have some discomfort, it is up to the doctor to discover what causes it. In these days when so much is known about the endocrine glands, something can usually be done. Perhaps Gretchen is one of the girls who feel a bit seedy during their periods. At least you might give her the benefit of the doubt when she says she doesn't feel like too much exercise."

"Then she should have said what ailed her. It's nothing to be so mysterious about."

"It's nothing to shout about, either. It's what you call 'one of those things.' But the whole process of the monthly cycle and the parts played by the uterus, the ovaries, the Fallopian tubes and various glands is much more complicated and amazing than I've made it sound. I'll look up a good book for you. In fact, I'd like to read one again myself."

The conversation terminates with Effie's feeling a little more grown up and a little better acquainted with her mother. Being forearmed with knowledge, she has the security which she does not even need to be conscious of.

The physiological problems of growing up are not the only problems the adolescent faces. There are also new problems of social adjustment. The boy not only is awkward; he knows he is awkward. Also he hears his voice performing strange antics. The girl frequently realizes that she is neither a child nor a woman. She feels rather grown up — at least part of the time — but as surely as she acts grown up, someone calls attention to the fact that she is only " a little girl." But it is irritating for either boy or girl to feel that his or her growing-up process is the center of family comment.

A thoughtful parent can save his child some of these embarrassments. He can anticipate the child's needs and help to ease him into the grownup status. It is difficult, for instance, for a boy to ask for his first razor. If there are younger brothers and sisters, they are likely to shout, "Ernie's learning to shave! Isn't it funny!" As if Ernie doesn't feel conspicuous enough in the very fact that he needs to shave. Fortunately, in the actual case of Ernie, his mother sensed his embarrassment over the heavy down appearing on his face and spared him possible annoyance from his younger brothers by saying, in their hearing, "Ernie, I do wish you'd shave and not go around looking like a stubble field." She put some asperity into her voice. "You always used to take more trouble with your looks."

The next day she brought home the shaving equipment and said, again in the presence of the younger children: "You can't put off shaving indefinitely. It's just one of the things men have to do, and if you need to begin younger than some, that's merely your hard luck." Still grumbling a bit, she left Ernie to examine this implement for which he had been waiting. And when he went off to use it, there were no comments from the rest of the family.

Likewise a gentle scolding may help a daughter over her first self-consciousness about powder and rouge on her dressing table. When Ann is fifteen her mother begins to notice touches of red, rather sketchy and surreptitious, on her cheeks and lips. Since Ann is a particularly sensitive girl, it would annoy her considerably to have the two younger sisters twit her about her aids to beauty. So mother speaks first. "You're old enough to be more careful about your rouge and lipstick, Ann. Tomorrow when

you go to have your hair shampooed, I wish to goodness
you'd get some things that match. Let Marcella try out
different shades on you, and then don't go around looking
so haphazard."

The next day Ann comes home properly decked out,
never knowing that mother has had a talk with Marcella
and cautioned her as to how much, or how little, a fifteen-
year-old should wear. Ann feels herself to be the height
of restrained sophistication. Mother sees her putting the
powder, lipstick and rouge into her dresser drawer and scolds
a little more. " I hope you'll take care to use them regularly and not have lily cheeks one day and apple cheeks
the next." She realizes that of course Ann will favor the
lily one day and apples and cherries the next, because Ann
is an adolescent and nothing satisfies the budding ego like
dressing to suit its various moods. But the little sisters poke
no jibes at Ann. Instead, one of them remarks, " Mother
is going to be cross with you if you don't take more care."

The same method seldom works for two members of
the same family. When Ann's sister Bernice comes to the
lipstick age, she sits down by the living room window with
her mother's largest hand mirror and a whole beauty kit.
Then she proceeds to try different effects, calling on the
family to witness the results. Ann would have " passed
out " with humiliation at such publicity but Bernice really
wants these comments, from which she chooses the advice
she likes best. Lillian approaches the matter from still a
different angle. Although she is a year younger, she slides
into maturity without anyone's appearing to notice the
fact, least of all herself. She becomes " one of the girls "
and begins her life as an adult with none of the self-consciousness which is almost inevitable for an oldest child.

There is no single " right " way to meet the make-up
problem. Ann is one kind of child, Bernice another. Their

mother has to be aware of their separate needs — and probably even more aware of Lillian's needs because the child seems to be so completely unself-conscious.

Sometimes it is hard to say which are the more difficult aspects, for the child, of the many-faceted sex problem: the actual physical development, the psychological stress or the social adjustments. But whatever the problem, the adolescent is fortunate when he is articulate enough to put his difficulties into the form of questions, and most fortunate when he has parents who will answer his questions with the wholehearted attention they deserve. The parent, for his part, may be a successful answerer and never know what made him successful, but the parent who fails with the answers is almost sure to know at some time that it was himself who failed his child.

What's In A Marriage

And stand together yet not too near together;
For the pillars of the temple stand apart,
And the oak tree and the cypress grow not in each
  other's shadow.   KAHLIL GIBRAN (*The Prophet*)

For many modern boys and girls there comes a time when they need an answer to the question what their attitude shall be toward sexual relations before marriage. A generation ago the problem did not greatly trouble the average girl because she accepted virginity as one of the qualifications for marriage. A generation ago, boys of " good families " might have their " affairs " before marriage but they expected the girls whom they married to have a stainless past. Statistics on sexual conduct were not so available twenty-five and thirty years ago as they are today, but it seems a safe judgment to say that at least the majority of girls refrained from sexual experience before marriage. Today, however, there are available a number of studies on the sex attitudes and habits of college boys and girls and of young people in various occupational groups. They make plain three things: that there is no single accepted code of sexual conduct; that the proportion of young people having sexual experience before marriage runs from one-fifth to three-quarters in the localities where the studies have been made; that a high proportion of young people put other qualifications ahead of virginity as most desirable in a marriage partner.

The parent who wants to give his child a wise and useful answer to this question of sex relations before marriage has to bear in mind these statistical findings and to realize that they speak for the generation of which his child is a part. Obviously, the standards have changed and it is to be expected that practically the entire age-group of fifteen to twenty-five are in some way affected by the change. The fact that young people ask the question what their attitude shall be toward sexual experience before marriage is proof that they are not sure of the answer; they are weighing the evidence. They know from their sociological studies, and perhaps from personal observation, that a great many marriages go by the board because of sexual incompatibility. From their reading and conversation they have a fairly accurate understanding of the biological and psychological disaster of such incompatibility. They realize, for instance, that a man may find his sweetheart's indifference to his caresses rather charming and exciting before marriage, but feel completely frustrated by what proves to be frigidity after marriage; or that a girl, before marriage, may feel that her sweetheart's constant desire to be near her and to touch her is an endearing trait, only to discover after marriage that his sexual appetite is overwhelming. They know that these are very real situations and by no means exceptional. They realize, too, that an even more common occurrence is the situation in which both the man and the girl have for each other tremendous physical attraction which may be maintained at high pitch for weeks, but later, when it wears thin or other interests demand part of their attention, there seems to be practically nothing else they hold in common. Perhaps the girl's incessant chatter annoys the boy, who is a rather quiet person, or the boy's preoccupation with books or photography bores the girl to tears. "Is it not much better then," the boys and girls ask, "that young people should find out these impossible barriers to happiness before they are married?"

Perhaps the parent's first answer is to make sure that the questioner is clear in his own mind whether he is debating on merits of promiscuity versus virginity, or hunting the wisest procedure in his relation to the one whom he hopes eventually to marry. The parent may turn questioner and ask his son: " At what point in your friendship with a girl do you feel it is necessary to know her sexual qualifications before you continue the friendship? Before there is any danger that you will actually fall in love with her and thereby lose perspective? Or after you have come to the conclusion that she is among the two or three girls who attract you most? Or when you feel certain that she is the one girl you want to marry? "

Stating the problem as clearly as possible is in itself a help, for the average healthy, busy young person is not drawn toward promiscuity as a way of life and is likely to hesitate before choosing a course which seems to point in that direction. But if he should be advocating wide sex experience regardless of intentions to marry, the parent has two general points of view from which to choose his answer.

He may say: " There is always a proportion of the population in every generation and in every land who feel that the variety of their experiences with members of the opposite sex is a mark of virility and conducive to general broad-mindedness. Among this number are some creative thinkers and thoughtful social experimenters. But among this number who practice promiscuous sex relations is also the social group which rates the lowest intelligence quotient, the border-line cases whom the medical profession designates as 'moron.' Look well at the advocates of your theory and then decide whether promiscuous sex experience will promote or destroy your growth as a creative individual. The final decision is your own." Parents who answer in this general fashion are content to state their position and then to leave the decision with the individual, feeling that each generation must meet the problem in its own way, must work out its own success or pay its own price for failure.

But another parent may feel that this answer does not sufficiently recognize the fact that promiscuity easily becomes sexual indulgence and as such drains the creative energy which is needed in other directions; also that the promiscuity which appears harmless to one of the partners in the sex adventure may prove disastrous to the other. This parent may feel that it is impossible for a young person to judge the long-time consequences of his own course of action. Therefore, the parent may decide to speak sternly, with or without explanation, offering his judgment that promiscuity is not conducive to later contentment in marriage. " It is my experience," he may say, " that the boy who boasts about the number of his conquests and the girl who maintains that heavy petting is the price of popularity are not likely to be conspicuously successful in their marriage ventures." The usefulness to the young questioner of this sort of a priori judgment depends largely upon his degree of respect for the parent who makes answer. If he feels the parent's judgment is sound in other respects and believes that the parent does indeed know a good deal about living, then the answer is useful to him.

But a more difficult problem than promiscuity for most young people is their decision as to what shall be their attitude toward the individual whom they honestly expect to marry. " When a young man concludes that he has found the girl whose qualities and interests and outlook seem to guarantee that their chance for married happiness is very good indeed *if* they also have a satisfactory sex life in common, is it not then better to give the sex relationship a trial before they enter into the more complicated state of lawful marriage? "

Here again the parent may prefer the absolute answer. He may say crisply, "Leave it alone," and substantiate his dictum with the authority of the law, of the church, of the Bible, or of experience. He feels that the question is not a debatable one and states his decision in as strong terms as possible. At the other extreme is the parent who says: "Go ahead and experiment. All of life is a process of trial and error. If the errors swamp you, perhaps you are better lost. I tried my way and now you are free to try yours."

In between these rather extreme points of view are a great many parents who do not feel that society has found the final answer. They admit that perhaps it is true that long-time marriage might meet the problems of adjustment more readily if both partners to it had previously had sufficient sex experience so that they started out on their married life with perspective. They admit the possibility that the permanent relationship between husband and wife may be enhanced by the knowledge that each has had enough previous experience to make the final choice a matter of genuine choice. They admit that someone must do the experimenting with forms of marriage if the institution is to be kept as elastic as the changing needs of each new generation demand, and that experimentation is probably safest in the hands of honest young people who are thinking in terms of the good of society as well as in terms of personal expediency.

"And yet — and yet," say these parents, " society being as it is, there are certain restraining factors to give a person pause. Long and thoughtful pause." Among these restraining considerations may be mentioned the fact that trial marriage, a term used to include engagements with full sex privileges, starts off with a handicap in the very secrecy necessary to the extra-marital relationship because secrecy precludes the full and spontaneous companionship which is necessary to successful marriage. Secrecy puts a strain on both parties. The chances are that they cannot be together regularly enough to fall into that contenting rhythm in which quiet companionship has as much place as the satisfaction of desire. They are unlikely to have a place of their own in which favorite books and personal belongings augment both personality and companionship. An unexpected knock at the door of their hotel room, or the ringing of the telephone in a week-end apartment, even the call of a peddler at a borrowed cottage or the call of a porter in the compartment of a train, fills them with panic. And panic is not conducive to the inner peace which cushions the bumps in an above-board marriage. Furthermore, there is disadvantage in not being able to speak aloud of the places they have been together, in having to garble reports of interesting experiences. The sense of having to be on guard all the time develops a nervous tension which breeds anything but security. For one or the other the tension is likely to snap, and then the girl begins to make excuses for not going with this man whom she had planned to marry, or the man finds himself hunting reasons for breaking a date which entails so much risk of unpleasantness if they are discovered together.

The parent may also want to point out that the " extra-curricular " sex relationship has another almost insurmountable handicap in the fact that both participants are aware that it is only a trial. At the first misunderstanding the girl exclaims, " I guess John is plenty glad we aren't really married. If he was disappointed in the week end, what would he be if he knew it were permanent? As if I could help it that the cottage roof leaked and the stove wouldn't burn." Or John says, "It's a good thing I found out that Rachel has such a quick little temper before I married her." Now any old salt who has sailed the sea of matrimony through years of bad weather, smooth seas or the doldrums, could tell the young couple that their annoyances are probably temporary. John's grumbling may have been caused largely by his having muffed an examination so that he was irritated primarily with himself, not with Rachel. It might be a year before he'd have another such spell of fault-finding. And Rachel's quick temper may have been largely due to a nagging pain in a shoulder which she had wrenched in trying to get the cottage windows open to surprise John. After a season or two of sailing together John and Rachel would know the ropes, and would realize so many advantages in having signed on together that they would only laugh at such trivialities as variations in the emotional barometer. But the trial marriage doesn't think in terms of the recurring seasons. However honest, the relationship is only a trial. Therefore it is almost impossible for either the man or the girl to exert the tact and forbearance, the enthusiasm and ingenuity, which go into building a long-time marriage program. Moreover, in a trial relationship it is too easy for them to escape their hopes and responsibilities. When a crisis comes, they are not surrounded by the household reminders of happiness which often stay the too-quick parting. Since they need not take time to arrange a separation which at least looks dignified, they do not have the additional hours together which ease the tension and fill the heart with premonitions of loneliness. They merely walk out on a bad deal.

The parent who is trying to set forth the whole argument against trial marriage will probably also call attention to the psychological difficulty arising from the fact that the trial may not be a first one for both parties. At least one of them may face the thought, " I was mistaken the last time." Confidence is shaken in his own ability to make good. Accompanying that lingering although often unconscious sense of defeat are the pangs of jealousy which even the staunchest heart is heir to. The girl thinks, " He said these things before to someone else. She lay in his arms as I am lying, his lips were against her cheek." Or it may be even more difficult for the man to accept the fact that this girl he means to love forever, once acquiesced as confidently to someone else as now she turns to him. Strangely enough, it is frequently harder to accept the failure of a trial marriage than to accept the failure of a lawful marriage.

There is at least one further consideration which the parent may try to explain, namely, that if the temporary marital relationship fails, there will be a subsequent deprivation which is difficult to adjust to. Both physiologically and psychologically the sexual rhythm is a habit which cannot casually be laid aside and forgotten about. The whole personality comes to depend upon it for physical and psychological support. It is the loss of psychological support, of close companionship, which may be the harder for the sensitive young person to sustain. In the breakup of the extra-marital relationship there is often a peculiarly tragic bewilderment in the mind of one or both the parties concerned. It is as if, having given their best under difficult circumstances and then finding that even their best was not good enough, life is scarcely worth taking too seriously again. In a disillusioned mood, the young person may either turn indifferently toward the next venture or steel himself against any further close relationship with the opposite sex. To be sure, any marriage carries the risk that it may not prove a workable partnership, and the breakup of any marriage entails physiological and psychological readjustment.

But that is all the more reason for not subjecting the relationship to avoidable risks.

The parent who has thus taken stock of the difficulties involved in the extra-marital sexual relationship will probably summarize by saying: "The ledger appears in the red. The argument is not about society as it ought to be, but about society as it is. And any two young people who take exception to the accepted standards are fighting for their happiness against odds. Against greater odds, altogether, than if they incurred the risks of making a mistake in their marriage."

In the final reckoning of this problem as of others, parents are pretty much driven back to the position that the best they can do for their children is to give them a fine sense of the value of personality so that they cannot — literally cannot — accept or give a shoddy substitute in any of the human relationships.

Relative to the larger question of sex experience before marriage is the question of the degree of familiarity which is advisable between boys and girls. Where does one draw the line between the normal, hearty give-and-take of boys and girls who share their tennis, swimming, picnics, dancing, school life and other interests, and the personal familiarities between one boy and one girl? In its far reaches the question is, perhaps, a moral one if society takes into account the possible results of unlimited familiarity, but for many young people — and their parents — the question is largely one of conforming to the current mores in a given locality and of respect for the personalities involved. Hence there is a variety of answers from parents of different points of view.

One parent says to a daughter: "Familiarity is pretty much a matter of taste. Aristocratic personalities which set high value on their own worth are not likely to permit actions which seem common. One fair standard is: do not do the thing which makes you feel shop-worn afterward. And by all means trust your first negative reactions; the thing which goes against the grain is not for you."

Another parent says to a son: "When it comes to petting, look at the situation as if you were seeing someone else — someone you admire very much — in your place. Does the action then seem a bit cheap? Does it seem to fit this other personality whom you know to be fine? If the action doesn't seem in keeping with this other young person whom you admire, then it is probably not in keeping with your own personality."

Another parent, attempting to take a long view, may say: "If your actions became the social standard, do you think that society would be distinctly benefited? Or if they did not become the accepted standard, do you think that young people would be deprived of useful experience? Considering the fact that there are so many kinds of human nature, would you say that your standards are 'best for the most in the long run'?"

And still another parent says: "Do the natural, spontaneous thing which rises from the situation. There is a time, no doubt, when any girl should be free to weep on the shoulder of the boy who understands her best. And there is a time when a boy expresses more spontaneous appreciation with a kiss than with all the vocabulary he can command. But either action ceases to be a tribute when it becomes routine procedure."

Probably the sum of the matter is that the rules and restrictions are made for the boys and girls, and not the boys and girls for the rules. Therefore the parent helps his child most when he teaches him to bear in mind the kind of person the child wants to become, rather than hedging him about with specific do's and don't's.

Taking A Flyer On Happiness

> *Ice cream is a very strange thing,*
> *And so is a codfish ball,*
> *But the people people marry*
> *Is the strangest thing of all.*

Quite apart from considerations of sex, children and young people have a good many questions to ask about the institution of marriage. Certainly they realize long before they are out of their teens that while the basic matter of sexual compatibility is complicated enough — what with its ups and downs of intensity, its promptings of jealousy, its monopolizing of the center of interest — the rearing of a family with the necessary adjustment to the economic and social responsibilities involved is even more complicated. Naturally, younger children do not sense these complications in such definite terms. But they do begin to feel their way toward an attitude on marriage by asking incidental and personal questions.

"Why did you marry daddy? What did he say when he asked you? . . . Why is Johnny's mother going to get a divorce from his father? What does divorce mean? Why is it wrong if they don't like each other any more? . . . Who cares how many times he's been married just so he's a good ball player? . . . If you don't get married, could you get wedding presents anyway? Why does a bachelor have to pay a tax when he already has to pay extra for so many things his wife would do if he had one? . . . Why couldn't everybody have two children apiece and then send all the children away to boarding school and after that they would all be people but not families? " The gamut of questions is wide and curious, and the answers might not be particularly important were it not that the child has a way of piecing together the comments of his parents into something of a pattern for living.

The adolescent's questions are more insistent, more immediate. He really needs to know the things he asks. Indeed, he needs to know even though he cannot find words for his questions. The parent may have to answer unasked questions, a feat which demands a high degree of sensitivity as well as some clear and serene thinking on the parent's part.

The adolescent, looking about with an interest newly personal, is probably sure of only one thing about marriage: he wants his own marriage to suit him exactly and to last forever. It is one of the marks of adolescence to insist upon rules and patterns and loyalties which will be good for all time, for the adolescent is busy putting his world together and he cannot go after the next building block unless his foundation shows a degree of reliability. Hence the avidity of youth in consuming outlines of history and of science and of philosophy. Hence his passion for the " everlasting ties " of a gang, a fraternity, a religious order. All the goods of life seem permanent to him, especially life itself. He cannot imagine a day when his college will be a second-rater. His town will always be different from other towns. His devotion to baseball or puppet shows or throwing the javelin is something to grow old with. His collection of phonograph records or stamps or matchboxes will be an enduring asset to civilization. Therefore it is not difficult for him, even when he is falling in and out of love every six months, to accept the doctrine of permanent affection between one man and one woman. Even when he is acquainted with unhappy marriages among his older friends or relatives, he still feels that love is forever and there merely

happen to be exceptions.   Whenever an individual adolescent is cynical about the durability of love and marriage,
his ideals are merely running in reverse for a time; the real
tendency of his age-group is to predicate permanency in
relationships.

To a youth of this age — roughly fourteen to twenty —
the parent may speak with especial helpfulness of the qualities to be desired in a marriage partner, and of the qualities
which that partner will expect of him.   General traits such
as honesty, tolerance, sympathy, loyalty, sincerity, become
yardsticks against which personality, including his own, is
measured.   Specific traits, such as neatness, promptness, ex-
actness, deftness, quickness, are among the qualities which
he wants, or does not want, in his scheme of things.

Somewhere in the late teens or early twenties, adolescence
gives way to young adulthood and then the questions about
marriage, which usually present themselves as comments
and observations, are even more personal and more important.   Of course, it is difficult for the young person
to know exactly when he is grown up.   Sometimes the
day of growing up is marked quite plainly by the acceptance
of some new responsibility.   Sometimes it comes by making
room for pain, or for sorrow, or for a new idea.   Then the
moment of its coming stands out starkly or grandly apart
from all the time which has gone before.   At other times
adolescence seems to flow into adulthood as the stream
flows into the ocean, unaware of a difference until it feels
the surging of high tide.   But no one needs to tell the young
man who knows that he is a man and loves a woman that
" this is different " from the sentimental promptings of
adolescence.   For one thing he measures his sweetheart not
against a possible " some day " but against the immediate
foreground of a home and its responsibilities.   He probably
knows what his work is to be, what his goals are, where

his interests lie. Either she fits into the picture or he changes the picture until she does fit.

It is at this time that he asks his most important question about marriage, about *his* marriage, about the whole, full, ecstatic content of his marriage: Will it last? He may not phrase the question in just these words; he may not address it to his father and mother explicitly. Nevertheless no one else can answer so well as his parents, or perhaps — no one else can have answered so well. It seems terrifically important to the young person about to undertake the responsibilities of a new home that his own marriage should endure. He knows that his life is intensified by his being in love. His energies are doubled, his potentialities quadrupled. Whether the reason is physiological or chemical or psychological, or all three and something more, no growing ego is willing to relinquish this surcharge of energy without terrific resistance. So he tries to give permanency to the relationship which seems to assure it.

For a long time society has tried to answer this demand for permanency. Society suggests the pledge and ring; it offers law and public ceremony. The church, too, has tried to answer this demand. It sanctions the "estate foreordained of God" and proclaims the "holy bonds of matrimony" inviolable. And still the son and daughter turn to their parents, in word or glance, to say, "You, you who are nearest to us, do *you* think it will last? *Can* it last?"

To the first question, "Will it last?" the parent has no reassuring answer. The only sure thing about the marriage relationship is that it will change, and the young fear change. Of course "Will it last?" really means, "Will it succeed? Will it maintain happiness?" And how shall a parent say to a son or a daughter: "Success . . . happiness . . . they are not the final measure of life. The measure of life is *life*. Disaster may hold as much of life as success. Pain, disappointment, regret — they too are the materials of life. Immortality has been known to hide in dregs of hemlock. So go right ahead. Your cup will be fuller and richer this way."

Actually, the parent probably says, frankly and objectively: "The odds might appear to be against you on the marriage risks. If you look at the brittle statistics — three marriages in five ending in divorce; if you look into the marriages of your friends — the petty bickerings, the edgy jealousies, the dull acceptance, and all the raveling of the fabric of their hopes — it seems that this marriage in which you invest so much has at best a fifty-fifty chance of paying dividends. But you are a part of a new generation and your generation has some advantages for building successful marriage." Then the parent may point out some of these advantages, leaving it to the young people to determine the meaning of the changed conditions in terms of their own lives. The new generation has, for instance, more help than was ever available before on the problem of birth control. Control of conception has long been a major difficulty in the marriage relationship. But now, unless they have religious scruples against deciding how many children they feel able to rear and when they shall have these children, the current generation of young people have available contraceptive knowledge which makes their adjustment easier to a wide range of the other problems of marriage, personal, economic and social.

Moreover medical science is not the only field of research which offers advantages to the marriages of the new generation. Beginnings have been made in various countries on basic studies of the whole personality. In time these studies should yield their measure of wisdom for marriage. Since the days of the Greeks society has recognized general classifications of temperaments and has noted that certain types seem complementary and certain types antagonistic. Katharine and Petruchio notwithstanding, the quick-tempered woman is popularly supposed to have a better chance for happiness when mated to a man of patience or humor than when mated to another quick temper, although the plodder and the speeder are said to be likely to get out of step. But only now is psychology on the edge of understanding why such things are true — if they are true — and what promises and warnings certain basic traits may signify, what qualities of personality predispose toward certain predictable behavior patterns. Although it will take the effort of many generations to wring the fullness of wisdom from such study, more help is available to the marriages of today than could have been found by the most earnest seekers of yesterday.

Marriage today has a still further advantage in the fact that the exigencies of the times seem to have brought about a state of affairs in which both members of the partnership, the woman as well as the man, have a better chance for personal development. Certainly the realization of personal growth is one of the prerequisites of happy marriage. Such growth may come through the individual's developing his own ability to obviously greater usefulness, or it may sometimes come through his investing his creative energy in the other partner's development. But in either case it must be genuine growth in order to yield the satisfaction which adult personality demands. Nowadays, economic conditions force both parents in an increasing proportion of marriages to become wage earners. Along with the disadvantages of such arrangement come distinct advantages in the form of varied contacts, the careful planning of time, new bases for companionship. In the rearing of children, also, the new economic necessity for two wage earners offers conditions which may be turned to advantage: the mother's heightened enjoyment of children whom she does not have on her hands twenty-four hours each day, the father's increased responsibility for the children, the children's greater opportunity for independence and initiative. The wife need not feel that she is crossing the accepted standards in going to work outside her home. Nor need the husband feel that he has failed in not supporting his wife adequately. For in creating the necessity for two wage earners, society has largely removed the odium. These psychological releases are of almost immeasurable value in promoting the respect and satisfaction necessary to contented marriage. When the ledger is drawn and the obvious disadvantages of the double-wage-earner setup are entered in bright red ink, there is still a long and comforting column of advantages to hearten the new marriage partners. And for the woman who is not a joint breadwinner, there is increasing opportunity for personal growth through social and civic service, through study groups, through club activities, through a dozen new devices of the modern inventive young matron. Every advantage may carry its particular hazard, but the advantage to modern marriage is nevertheless present.

But when a parent has totaled these and many other helps which modern society offers to modern marriage, he has still not said the most important thing. For while general tendencies in social attitudes and economic pressure do affect the institution of marriage as a whole, and while any individual marriage is a part of that whole, it is still true that any two people can make or mar their own particular marriage. At least it is fair for a parent to say that given all the help society can offer, a young couple must still put much individual effort into achieving their own happiness. Probably the most important thing a parent can do is to point up this fact.

One parent puts his conviction in this manner: "The chief guarantee of married happiness is your will to make the marriage succeed. You have a goal worth working for with all the imagination and ingenuity of which you are capable. If you succeed you will discover that a man and a woman in living happily together may each so augment the other that the resulting personality surpasses in awareness and enjoyment and usefulness anything that either could have attained alone."

There are plenty of examples of the kind of marriage this parent is speaking of. Sometimes in humble walks of life one sees a husband and wife who have been together through so many years that they have come to look alike and to speak alike. One speaks the other's thoughts. They need little conversation as they sit together of a winter evening, and yet they feel no lack of communication, no separateness, because they have achieved an active and abiding contentment together. The same sort of companionship may express itself differently in more articulate circles. There the man and woman who live happily together become one center for their circle of friends. Each brings out the other as the sun brings out a negative, and together they form one picture. Theirs is an achievement of super-personality, something distinctly finer, larger, happier than either of them might have attained alone.

However, the most optimistic of parents will have to admit that many marriages fall short of this complete, full-grown companionship. But nevertheless a marriage may furnish a measure of mutual understanding which neither partner would want to be without. Most humans live lonesomely enough at best. Their deep compulsions, their longings and defeats, their inward triumphs pass unshared and therefore are never fully realized. But the man and woman who feel their companionship deepening, who move toward the same achievement, who share the same creative ideas, who find the same delight in sun and wind and sea — this man and woman never know the meaning of drab insufficiency in themselves or in marriage.

When a parent has said all that he can about the possibilities for happiness in marriage, the young people have at least one more question: " But if a marriage proves not to have within it the elements of growth and happiness for either party, shall it be maintained, then, just for the sake of maintaining an accepted form? "

To which the parent may answer, " Perhaps. Perhaps the couple does just that — maintain a form. For it appears that to date society has found monogamy the most sure and useful way for the sexes to live together, and out of long, hard experience the present form of family life has been found best. An individual hesitates in breaking up his own marriage to throw his influence on what appears to be the anti-social side. One more broken home is one more loosening of a building stone in the citadel of civilization. Marriage as an institution appears larger than any single marriage, and as such is to be cherished. ' Best for the most in the long run ' is a relentless criterion, and the individual hesitates to call himself an exception."

But in saying so much, the honest parent has still not covered the matter. Account must be taken of the marriages in which both man and woman seem to defeat each other at every turn. If their interests not only pull the couple apart from each other but pull apart the integrity of their individual personalities, then society appears to have little to gain from their continued living together. It is difficult to make disintegrated individuals into socially constructive forces, no matter how rigidly they conform to pattern. Of course there are always some — lookers-on from the outside — to say that personality does not need to disintegrate no matter under what strain it lives out its days. There are resources, they would say, which enable the disciplined spirit to rise above any environment, no matter how difficult. But this is a matter for no outsider to judge. One person cannot measure for another the burden beneath whose weight an individual still goes on and sings, or at least goes on, or stops. If "good" were plain and "sins" were always overt, if contentment with things as they are were always virtue and the urge to live differently were always a vice, then a reckoning might be made.

Perhaps it might be better for society, the parent may admit, if priest or doctor or lawyer or some other outside authority could analyze each marital catastrophe and make the final decision. Frequently it would be easier for the parties concerned because burdens which must be borne usually can be borne. But a philosophy of democracy allows no such passing on of responsibility. It is the individual himself who must decide. Parents cannot answer for their children. Husband cannot answer for wife, nor wife for husband. An individual makes his own decision in terminating a marriage as in accepting it. Perhaps young people about to plunge into matrimony would take more thought to their own tomorrows if they could be made to understand the weight of the decision which must be theirs should they later decide to dissolve the marriage. They are near enough to their own receding childhood and near enough to their own approaching parenthood to comprehend something of the responsibility of one generation to the next.

Obviously, there is no final word which the wisest of parents can say to their grownup children on the subject of marriage. Here again attitude and example are probably more potent answers than anything contrived of words. And yet words may help tremendously. Almost every parent whose children are approaching maturity has faced moments when he might have said explicitly and without constraint, "This is the way I look at marriage." The timely moment may have risen from the tragedy of a friend's marriage, from the discussion of a book, from some college argument, or from tension within the home itself. However and whenever it rises, it is a moment to use.

Few marriages come to full maturity with the effortless blooming of a tree. Most success, or any degree of it, is bought at the price of discipline of both the personalities involved. Even when the discipline is self-imposed and gladly undertaken, it is none the less discipline. A husband who has learned to withhold judgment upon an impetuous wife, a wife who has learned to adapt her pace to the family gait — these parents have something of wisdom to impart to their children. And parents who have not made adjustment also have something to impart. Sometimes the sting is largely removed from an unhappy home situation by merely acknowledging and analyzing the state of affairs quite frankly with the children. In either case parents have the largest responsibility for the questions of their children, little or big.

The World Without

Twinkle, twinkle, little star,
How I wonder what you are,
Up above the world so high
Like a diamond in the sky.

                           JANE AND ANN TAYLOR

Every parent knows that no two children live in the same world. Even though they are born into the same family under relatively similar circumstances, their worlds may be as different as if they had been born centuries apart or lived on different continents. Some of the difference is no doubt accounted for by the physical make-up and the mental capacity with which the child is endowed. Some of it is accounted for by the child's opportunity to accumulate experience, to "interact with his environment," to see and hear and touch and otherwise try out the things among which he lives. But some of the difference between the worlds children live in is determined by the manner in which their parents answer their questions concerning the outer world.

"Daddy, how big is the world?" Almost every parent has been the answerer at the other end of that question.

"I don't know," says one father. He lifts his eyes from the newspaper for a moment feeling that perhaps he should say something more. But Billy is only three; certainly three is too young to deal with miles, or with oceans and continents. "I don't know," he repeats, "but pretty big. Maybe twice as big as the moon."

"Twice as big as the moon! It's a million times bigger than the moon," says the child.

"Then you tell me," says his father. And the conversation is either closed or whisked down another byway.

Other fathers are inclined to give factual answers — when they can remember the facts. "Well, sir," says one such father, "the world is twenty-five thousand miles around at the equator, which is about eight times as far as the distance from New York to San Francisco." Or he may say, "The world has about fifty-seven million square miles of land and approximately a hundred and thirty-nine million square miles of water. There are five continents and five oceans."

But of course such factual answers do not really answer unless the father is willing to meet a deluge of further questions. "Equator" is good for an hour if the child has any imagination and his father a fair supply of facts. "Square mile" has to be broken down into terms of experience — eight city blocks, north, east, south, west, or, for the country child, the size of Mr. Babson's potato field. But eventually the question about the size of the world can be answered with fair satisfaction to both father and son.

The same is true of questions about trees and stars and rocks and shells and birds and dogs and elephants and anteaters. There are factual answers of a noncontroversial sort. To be sure, the specialists may contend a bit; they may argue the nature of interstellar space and the learning capacity of the higher vertebrates and other important details in the world of nature. But the child's questions are not likely to go so far. There is enough accepted knowledge in most fields to satisfy his offhand curiosity. He may doubt the vastness of the skies or remain skeptical of the reported skill of the honeybee or in some other way express his wonder and bewilderment over the complicated universe, but for the most part he accepts, and to a degree assimilates, the facts about the universe — if he can get the facts.

If he cannot get facts, he builds his universe anyway. The only difference is that he rears a dizzy structure which will later have to be torn down and rebuilt. Obviously a waste of time and energy, for it is so much easier for a child to add to and undergird the simple framework of his early construction than to have to knock out whole sections of wall and foundation. Build he must. The only problem is what sort of materials he will have to use. Fortunately honest materials for building a reliable universe can now be had in book form keyed to any age-group and representing almost any field of inquiry. Less fortunately, parents may become parents without knowing a thing about such books or feeling any responsibility for making them available to the child through home, school or public library. We have not yet reached the day when the state requires minimum knowledge tests of parents-to-be. It seems ridiculous that a small child's questions about the world around him should customarily be met with such parental vagueness. Respect for and cooperation with natural law depends so directly upon understanding that the marvel is we dare to be indifferent about our ignorance and unashamed in acknowledging it.

"Mother, mother!" cries Ann Marie in glee. "Look at that star. It's the brightest star I ever saw. What is it?"

"I don't know," says her mother, likewise impressed by the star's brilliance. Then something echoes in her memory. "Maybe it's the evening star."

"What does that mean — the evening star? We have a lot of evenings but I never saw such a bright star."

"The evening star is the first star to come up in the evenings," says mother brightly.

"But it wasn't the first star. That one over there came first. It's a bright star, too, but not so bright as this one."

Then mother hears another echo in her memory. "It's probably a planet. That's the difference."

"A planet?" asks Ann Marie who likes new words. "What is a planet?"

"A planet is another world like ours." Mother feels herself on firmer ground now. "There are only six planets. Or is it eight? Some new ones have been discovered since I was in school. There's Mars and Venus and Jupiter and — others."

"But what's the difference between a planet and a star? If planets are worlds, what are the rest of the stars?"

Well, what *are* they? mother asks herself. She's heard the difference often enough. Are the planets supposed to support life or is it that they are nearer to the earth? Or do they move around our sun? While she is trying to compose an answer which sounds reasonable to herself as well as to Ann Marie, the child is asking more and faster questions. Mother gives up. "I don't know," she says. "We'll look it up sometime."

But she doesn't. Two or three times Ann Marie reminds her but there isn't any book around the house which seems to have that sort of information and when she goes to the library, she forgets about it. By and by Ann Marie gives up also. She continues to admire the stars occasionally. But she asks no more questions and soon becomes another hostage to dull acceptance.

Ann Marie's mother wouldn't think of giving the child a whack on her ears which might dull her hearing for life. She would be horrified if she thought that Ann Marie's eyesight might be permanently impaired by lack of glasses which she could provide. Yet she is serenely unaware that she is dulling the child's precious gift of curiosity — the gift that sets her apart from the dumber animals and allows her, now and then, to hobnob with the gods. Nice, kind, ignorant, stupid mother of Ann Marie! But then — when we listen in on ourselves, *we* do not sound so different.

OUR CHILD. Look, daddy, this stone shines like silver! Do you suppose it is silver?

OURSELVES (*shaking our head*). It's probably mica.

OUR CHILD. What's mica?

OURSELVES. Mica is a kind of metal — well, maybe not a metal but anyway an element or something which (*Which what? We've heard, but what did we hear?*) — which looks like silver but isn't very valuable.

OUR CHILD. If it looks like silver, why isn't it valuable? What makes silver so valuable? Who decided to make money out of silver? How does it get in the rocks? If you dug deep enough could you always find silver? Did you ever find any?

OURSELVES (*feeling suddenly inadequate*). I had an uncle who found some silver ore once. It was out in — (*And so we're off on a beautiful bypath which will never bring the child back to the main track but perhaps will divert him so thoroughly that he won't know the difference.*) Or —

OUR CHILD. Look, mother, what a beautiful tree! Its leaves are long and shiny. What is it?

OURSELVES (*looking closely . . . not a maple . . . not an oak . . . not a pine*). It *is* pretty. But I don't know what it is. I don't really know much about trees. Or —

OUR CHILD. This morning when I woke up, there was a bird singing outside my window. He sang like this — (*A*

sweet high call is whistled for us). What do you suppose
it was?

OURSELVES. A robin maybe. The robins must be coming
back by now.

OUR CHILD. It wasn't a robin because it didn't have any
red breast. I saw him and he was about as big as a robin
only more gray all over.

OURSELVES. I don't know just what it would be if it
wasn't a robin.
Or —

OUR CHILD. When we were walking down by the lake,
we heard something go " bang " out in the ice. Something
kind of like thunder only sharper. What was that?

OURSELVES. That? Oh, that's just the ice.

OUR CHILD. But what was the ice doing that could make
such a noise?

OURSELVES. It was — expanding. Or contracting, I forget which.

OUR CHILD. But why would contracting make a noise?

OURSELVES. I don't know exactly.

And so it goes. And so we go, and the child goes. And
time goes. Perhaps later the child will find the answers
some place else . . . and not be awfully interested by that
time . . . and forget them, the way we forgot them . . .
and grow up to be a good citizen and pay his taxes and
support his children and wish sometimes — but not aloud,
probably — that he were more interested in living.

Of course, there is a rosier side to this business of answering the child's questions about his world. Some parents do have the answers, or at least a respectable number
of them, and sometimes we ourselves are among those
respectable parents. Or sometimes our child has a scoutmaster or a favorite teacher or an adopted Aunt Judy
who knows the answers. Sometimes we send our child

off to camp among people who will "give him an interest in nature," or we take him on a trip hoping that in some magic way he will develop a passion for the wide open spaces and hunt his answers for himself.

In general, there are two honest solutions to this problem of answering the child's questions about the physical world he lives in. One: we can acknowledge the fact that we never have known much of anything about geology or astronomy or botany or physics (in other words, "the birds and bees and things") and still we feel that our lives have been perfectly full and happy. In fact we defy anyone to be happier than we are. It is a good answer, and probably a true one. Only — even we cannot be *sure* that our daily lives might not have been vastly enriched if we had assimilated a few more of the amazing facts about our universe. We *might* have found that some of the answers stimulated our creative capacities and steadied our uncertainties. Creativity and factual knowledge are not necessarily antagonistic forces, as even a cursory knowledge of Conrad or Shakespeare or Da Vinci or Michelangelo will disclose.

The other answer is: yes, we know that our "education" never included much real understanding of the universe about us, and what we did learn was so unrelated to our daily lives that we promptly forgot it, but we intend to keep at hand the materials for answering our children's questions. *Books.* Fascinating books, scientifically accurate, simply written, geared to the child's experience — which means our own — and amply illustrated.

Of course, in handling even the best books and the most recent information we have to remember that by tomorrow the facts of today will probably be branded as yesterday's opinions if not as its superstitions. During the past two generations the tiniest conceivable particles of matter have carried a pretty heavy weight of explanation and should almost have been pulled out of shape by opposed theories. The sound waves of one generation are the " wavicles " — packages of energy, the photons — of the next. Continually the lists have been closed for the basic chemical elements only to be opened again by new and amazing elements which have lain unnoticed before our eyes for centuries. Electricity and radiant energy pepper the ether with question marks so that the most didactic of parents, reading aloud to his five-year-old, is inclined to change simple declarative sentences to dependent clauses. But nevertheless, for all practical purposes there are plenty of materials with which to draw up honest, tenable answers about the outer universe.

The World Within

"It's very singular how hard it is to manage your mind," said Demi, clasping his hands round his knees, and looking up at the sky as if for information upon his favorite topic.... "I play that my mind is a round room, and my soul is a little sort of creature with wings that lives in it. The walls are full of shelves and drawers, and in them I keep my thoughts, and my goodness and badness, and all sorts of things. The goods I keep where I can see them, and the bads I lock up tight, but they get out, and I have to keep putting them in and squeezing them down, they are so strong."

LOUISA MAY ALCOTT (*Little Men*)

The child's questions about the physical world around him are usually easier to answer than his questions concerning the world of people, especially if among the people is included himself. Parents do not have to go into a huddle over the problem of what constitutes the " self " and how much of the outer world is an extension of the self and how much of the inner world is the product of experience with the outer world, to realize that it is easier to answer a straight " Where does rain come from? " than a wistful " What makes me naughty when I want to be good? " As soon as motivation must be dealt with, as soon as values must be set up and maintained, as soon as wishes and fears and loyalties enter the picture, then parents are inclined, if not forced, to deal with opinion instead of fact.

Handling opinion is dangerous business. Not having an opinion to handle is probably even more dangerous. Some way or other, the child has to find the reasons behind the

202

demands made upon him. The world, beginning with his parents, expects a great deal of conformity from him. He has a right to know *why* just as soon as he begins to question the demands because, after all, intelligent cooperation in social living is the first step toward individual freedom.

The rules of health, of work, of play which seem accepted facts to the parent may seem to the child to be merely the temperamental opinions of his parents. The child wants to eat and to play according to inclination, not according to rule. He does not understand the meaning of " proper food," " proper sleep " or " proper " anything, but he is almost certain to be curious about the how's and why's of his physiological habits. He may get a certain basis for understanding the intricate mechanism known as *himself* if his questions about his physiological processes are answered sensibly and practically.

"Where does my oatmeal go? " asks Marjorie, almost swallowing her spoon in her eagerness to give voice to the question which has just occurred to her. "Does it go clear down to my toes? "

" It goes to your tummy," says her mother, absently, with half her mind in the oven with the cake and the other half upstairs on a dress she means to make over. " Yum-yummy, yum, tummy, down to your tummy."

"How big is my tummy? Does it start at my neck? "

" Not quite. There's your esophagus and your heart and lungs and liver and a lot of other things which have to have room also."

Now Marjorie is all eyes and ears. " Tell me," she begs.

" Some other time," says mother. " It's time for your nap now."

" Oh tell me," begs Marjorie, who dearly loves a story in which she herself plays a part.

But mother tucks her in bed under a covering of wool

blankets, kisses and promises and goes down to take the cake out of the oven in a comfortable glow of motherhood. Actually, her child's question had never registered.

Twice after that Marjorie remembers to ask what else is inside besides her tummy but both times are the wrong time and then she forgets about the matter and drifts into the child's usual vague assent that it is important not to eat the wrong food although goodness knows why.

The truth is that although Marjorie's mother is one of the most energetic women in the neighborhood, she is also lazy. It just seems like too much work for her to explain the use and function of a stomach. Also, although she is known for her charming fairy stories, she really does not have a lick of imagination. She once learned the fairy stories in a class at summer school and they are accepted as coin of the realm among the other young mothers of her age. To tell the wonder tales of digestion in terms which her child could understand would take some genuine creativity. She finds it easier to wait for the schools to teach Marjorie at some later time. Of course she misses a chance to help furnish a first-class little mind which could have been utilizing during the important pre-school years some of the information it asked for.

Macie's grandfather goes to the other extreme. He thinks that knowledge of the body is the *sine qua non* of common sense. It is his belief that a precise vocabulary is easier than any substitute nomenclature and comes just as naturally to the child if he is taught exact terms from the beginning. Therefore jolly little Macie, aged three and round as a butterball, can be heard running to his study with the alarming, "Grandfadder, hurry, hurry! I've cut two of my phalanges." Or picked up in a daze after a daring jump from the porch railing, she wails, "I hit my *occipito frontalis*." Macie learns the bones of the body with no more

trouble than her Mother Goose rhymes. Her father, home
on a visit, says, " With no more trouble *and* with no more
understanding." But her grandfather, who is wise and
simple enough to lend distinction to his title as " educator,"
insists, " You'll be surprised what Macie understands.
Moreover, the words are ready, in place, to be filled with
content as fast as experience comes her way."

If body machines could be depended upon to run
smoothly at all times in spite of misuse, then it might be
less important that children begin very early to understand
how their bodies are made and under what conditions
they appear to function best. But in a land where over-
eating has become the norm — except for the underfed! —
where exercise is largely a matter of whim, and where sleep
is frequently left to the discretion of the Sandman, a little
knowledge of his own physiology does not come amiss for
the child.

This incident happened in the winter of 1928, long
enough ago so that its significance in results can now be
seen. Two seven-year-old boys in the same neighborhood
had rheumatic fever. The father of Howard was a physician, the father of Ben a teacher. Both boys were very
ill and both had heart involvements which required long
weeks of lying in bed.

Howard's father said sternly to his son, " Howard, you
must not sit up. Not for any occasion." And to the boy's
mother: " You'll have to keep strict watch of him because
even one infringement could be serious."

Ben's father, repeating the doctor's orders, said to his son,
" Bennie, you must not sit up. No matter what you want
nor how badly you want it, you must not sit up even
once." And to the boy's mother he said, " No child of seven
can remember this sort of command unless he has some
understanding of it."

Ben's mother, feeling her skill as an inculcator of obedience in question, rose on her wounded dignity and said, "If I tell him not to sit up, he will not sit up."

Ben's father said, "Shucks!"

And then he set to work with his son. The acute illness was passed and the long convalescence lay ahead. He sat by the bed with pencil and paper and drew a picture of a heart, naming its four rooms after their proper nomenclature. Bennie liked repeating "ventricle" and "auricle"; they sounded important; and to think he had two of each! Then his father's pencil added long twisty pipes leading into and out of the heart, and these he called "veins" and "arteries." With the picture before him, father told Ben a story about the heart's really being a pump which works day and night no matter whether its owner is waking or sleeping. The story amused Ben. It was different from the other kinds of stories he knew. He went off to sleep feeling rather comforted that he had such a dependable heart inside his chest.

Day after day, Ben learned new things about the pictures his father drew. The daily "lessons," which Ben did not know were lessons, lasted only a few minutes. Unconsciously he was picking up a new vocabulary and asking intelligent questions. One afternoon when he was decidedly getting better, his father brought home some charts, great, beautiful charts as large as a man himself. They stood on a rack at the foot of Ben's bed. One was marked "The Circulatory System." Ben's twelve-year-old sister Evelyn thought the chart was exceedingly intricate but Ben himself thought it quite plain. By this time he understood in a general way how it was with a heart. The law of resting the heart in acute myocarditis seemed a reasonable law when you considered what a heart had to do.

Unfortunately Ben was known for his huge appetite.

Before his illness, it was the marvel of all the cousins how Ben could eat so much and grow so fast. As soon as he was genuinely getting better this large hunger returned, although he was lying in bed and having no exercise except gentle massage. He wanted to eat " worse than anything else." Sometimes he wanted to eat even more than he wanted to get well. The many little meals which came his way seemed like nothing at all. Then his father drew pictures of the stomach and of " all the appendages there-unto appending." In many ways the chart of " The Di-gestive System " seemed more amazing than the chart of the blood supply. In two weeks Ben was talking glibly of chyle and chyme and confounding Evelyn with remarks about the cardiac orifice and the pyloric orifice. By that time he understood why too full a stomach was hard on a tired heart. He had respect for his amazing organs which so faithfully performed their duties. If the doctor said, " Five small meals each day," then five meals it was and they were small. He chewed the bits of liver, he chewed the sweetbreads, he ate the strained vegetables and didn't ask for cake. Since he was a child whose questions were avid, it would have been easy to give him an unhealthy preoccu-pation with his own internal mechanisms. But the physi-ology lessons were really only a very small part of his day along with color books, sets of pictures, guppie fish, the canary, and many naps.

One day Ben's mother went to call on Howard's mother. They had never been close friends but their mutual problem drew them together. Howard's mother looked ten years older. Howard would not stay flat in bed. He popped up for this and he popped up for that. He had made small progress in ten long weeks. The doctor-father was dis-couraged, Howard was irritable and his mother worn out. Very tactfully, Ben's mother told about the physiology lessons but Howard's mother said, "Howard wouldn't be interested in things like that."

After twenty-one weeks flat in bed, Ben began to get up and move about. When summer came he went to the woods where he swam a little and exercised heedfully. The next fall he started school, under mild restrictions. After thirty weeks, Howard was taken to the seaside with a nurse. At the end of a year he was up and playing some but was not in school. Every time he was really getting better and felt well, he ran too hard and lost the ground he had gained. Today there is exactly the difference between the health of the two boys which one would expect to find.

The moral of a layman's story can be easily overdone. There may have been other factors in the two cases than those which meet the eye, although the father of Howard thinks not. But even though these experiments were not "controlled," the conclusion remains valid enough to be written large across the heavens which shelter parents: To answer as fully as you can a child's questions about his own physiology is to increase his respect for his body and to enable him to cooperate intelligently with nature.

There is also the case of six-year-old Mary who liked peanut butter. From the tips of her animated toes to the end of her freckled nose, she seemed to vibrate with glee every time she saw peanut butter in the offing. Most of the time Mary was an obedient child but whenever peanut butter was concerned her habits of obedience broke down. She had been known to hide the peanut butter under her bed and to eat thereof in the long night watches. She had been known to put peanut butter on her ice cream cone, to dip her radishes in it and to spread it on her gingercake. Whether or not there was a relation between Mary's peanut butter and her many sudden stomach-aches, her mother did not know. But Mary, doubled up in misery, was wont to ask, "How can a good little stomach ache a good little girl so hard?" And then one day it occurred to Mary's mother to explain about stomachs. She made her physiology into a story, but an accurate one, and described the digestion of peanut butter from the stomach's point of view. One physiology lesson led to another until Mary, still only six years old and still liking peanut butter, had learned to manage her appetite intelligently. Mary doesn't know to this day that she "learned a lesson," but Mary's mother knows *she* learned a lesson, one she has applied to other problems many times.

Of course, if too much peanut butter or too little sleep made only a sharp and transient pain in some part of the body, then the child's questions about his physiological make-up would remain comparatively unimportant. But indigestion and weariness have also their close connection with the child's disposition, and the child who feels that his moods are something as entirely apart from his own control as the weather is a handicapped child.

"Why am I so crabby today?" asks Lucille suddenly, with complete ten-year-old candor.

"That's what I'd like to know," says her mother. She thinks a minute. "It may be because you were up so late last night."

"That couldn't have made me crabby because I had such a good time."

"But when you don't get enough sleep, then you're tired inside, no matter how good a time you had," says mother. "Your stomach is a little tired, your liver is a little tired, even your feet are a little tired and hate to run errands. Maybe you don't *feel* tired because you are still excited about the company, but on the inside you *are* tired. And the reason you object with words every time you're asked to move is because your body is objecting inside you."

"Then why do you ask me to move? Aren't you sorry I'm tired?"

"I certainly am. But the day's work has to go on. It wouldn't be fair to throw the whole family off schedule because you don't want to go buy a loaf of bread. The real point is that both you and I will remember after this that it pays to go to bed on time."

Lucille accepts the explanation with apparent indifference but the answer is not entirely wasted for on another day she comes to her mother to say: "Last night I wasn't up too late. But today I feel like disobeying everybody. What makes me that way?"

Mother thinks again. "Did you drink your orange juice for breakfast? Did you sleep well? Did you remember to go to the bathroom before you went to school?"

Lucille has a perfect record.

Mother keeps on trying. "Did you know your lessons? Did you mind your teacher? Did you get along well with the other children? Did anyone make you mad, or did you upset anyone else?"

Again Lucille seems to have a perfect record.

"Then I don't know why you feel so irritable," mother acknowledges. "But there *is* a reason somewhere and we ought to be able to find it."

A little later mother suggests, "Why don't you go up to your own room and read a little while?

"Oh no," says Lucille. "I'm sick of that old room."

"Um," says mother, and goes up to look at the room. There are Lucille's shoes, black and brown, for which her father had given her a shoe-shining outfit, thrown under the bed in need of a shine. There is her laundry bag full of the hose she is supposed to keep washed. In the book-case, the books are upside down and backwards. Her desk is littered with scraps of paper used for arithmetic

problems; her hair-ribbons dangle over the back of a chair.
Nor is it any comfort to open the dresser drawers where
handkerchiefs crowd socks in the place where only pajamas and undies belong. The week has been a very busy
one for mother and she has gone past Lucille's room hastily,
noting only that the bed is made. Now she goes downstairs to Lucille.

" I found the trouble," she sings out.

" Did you? " asks Lucille with interest. " Did we have
pie or something I forgot about? "

" The trouble is in your own room. Your room feels
exactly like a cluttered park after a Fourth of July picnic."

Lucille smiles. And then she frowns. " I just simply
don't even want to go up there. I wish I could sleep somewhere else."

" Let's make a list," says mother as they go upstairs.
Together they list every possible task. " As fast as you
do these things, write down the number of minutes each
task takes. We'll set the alarm for the end of the hour
and see what has happened by then."

When the alarm rings, the room is straight even to the
recesses of the drawers. But Lucille has not finished. She
has decided to sew on three buttons, to take her red dress
to the cleaners, to catch up on her diary called " Weather:
Inside and Out." Seldom has a more cheerful Lucille gone
off to bed at eight simply radiating good-nature and achievement.

In this case, the answer to Lucille's problem did not
lie in understanding the relationship between her bodily
well-being and her emotional well-being but in a realization
that unhappy states of mind may very logically be the result
of her own actions, or of procrastination or laziness or
subterfuge or almost anything which produces a sense of
guilt. School work which piles up day after day be-

comes a burden so heavy that a child unconsciously tries
to "get even" with a world which he feels is treating him
badly.   Never having been taught to do *well* the simple
tasks required of him each day — making beds, washing
dishes, dusting furniture — he may develop continual irritability as well as shoddy work-habits.   Frequently children are aware when something is wrong.   In words or
attitude they ask, " What makes me the way I am? "   And
when they question, or when they should question, they
need to be answered.

It would be nothing short of fatuous to try to suggest
answers which will fit all children's questions about their
moods and inclinations, about their insistent urges to do
this act or to shy away from that.   For one thing, some
children never appear to question their moods.   If they
are joyous, they are joyous and there the matter ends.   If
they feel that they must tramp the woods, they tramp the
woods, or find the next best substitute, and ask no questions as to what they are escaping from or to.   Self-analysis
occupies them very little and their questions pertain largely
to the outside world of matter and event.   But other children begin at a very early age to ask contemplative in-
turned questions.   "Why am I happy when I see something yellow? "   "Why do I jump when I hear a sharp
whistle?   Other children don't jump."   "What makes me
hate to go upstairs in the dark even if I'm not really afraid? "
"Why does that music make me cry when I like it so
much? "   "Why does rainy weather make me want to
sing all the time? "   "Why do I always want to slap
Nellie's uncle as soon as I see him, even if he does give us
pennies and things? "   "What is my mind doing when it
isn't thinking? "   These questions are exceedingly important to the sort of children who ask them.

Some children lean more heavily upon their intuition

than upon their reason, and a parent need not demand scientific definition for intuition and reason to know that there *is* this difference in children. Some children are exceedingly aware of their emotional reactions, and when they ask questions about themselves it is important that their questions be answered. The parent who gives himself to helping them find answers is rendering them a very real service, although naturally he cannot always be correct. The important thing is to answer the questions so that our children are able to utilize their environment, within and without, to their own best ends.

It Doesn't Seem Fair

What shall I say of these save that they stand in the sunlight, but with their backs to the sun?

KAHLIL GIBRAN (*The Prophet*)

Mother is ironing as rapidly as only a woman can when she knows that tomorrow and the next day will be full of other duties. With luck she will be through in time to prepare dinner. Suddenly the front door opens with a bang and Ellen comes running to the kitchen.

"Mother!" She is breathless and wide-eyed. "Mother, what do you think? Nancy Ray fell down in some broken glass at school and tore her stockings and they're the only stockings she owns to her name."

Almost in one breath Ellen tells the rest of her story. After the accident, she and another playmate had gone home with Nancy but no one was at home because her mother "worked out." The basement apartment was cold and dirty; there wasn't any first-aid kit for the scratches. And it is true that Nancy doesn't have any stockings except those she was wearing. Nancy is still crying and refuses to come home with Ellen. "So what shall we do? We can't leave her cold and dirty and all scratched and crying."

Mother, turning off the iron and folding up the ironing board, is thinking to herself much faster than she is speaking to Ellen. How ought she to answer Ellen whose cry for help rises from her first real contact with poverty? She can explain that there are organizations to look after people who need clothes and that she will telephone the

214

proper organization to look after the case. She can say
that nothing she and Ellen could do will be of lasting value.
She can suggest that Nancy's mother may not want inter-
ference, and that there is too much scarlet fever over in
that neighborhood to risk running around in strange apart-
ments, and that she has this ironing to finish. What she
actually says is, "You get the first-aid box while I get my
hat and coat."

"But can't we take some stockings and other clothes
too? "

"Let's see Nancy first."

So they go to see Nancy. She is still crying, dully. She
is a scrawny child and she is not clean. Her hands and
ears and hair are dirty. But she is distinctly pretty and
very shy. Ellen's mother finds a way to heat a little water
to take care of the deep scratches. When the scratches
are bandaged, it is very hard not to say, "Come on over to
our house and play with Ellen until your mother comes
home." But she doesn't say it. The child is *too* unkempt.
If she came once, she would come again. And if she
came again there would soon be the problem of her clothes
and then of her food. There never seems any place to
stop once you let yourself get drawn into these things.

Nancy has dried her eyes now. She and Ellen are talking
about the new art teacher. Mother has an impulse to grab
a broom and do something about the untidy house. She
wishes she dared make a fire in the kitchen stove, but
obviously fuel is scarce. Maybe she can have some wood
sent over — without saying who sent it. That's what she
will do.

"Come on, Ellen," she says briskly, cordially. "I've
thought of something that both of you youngsters can
do."

They look at her. "Something nice? " asks Ellen.

"I hope so. Anyhow, it's something that ought to please your art teacher. On with your hats and coats."

Together they go out into the gathering dusk. Nancy limps a little but nevertheless skips right along with Ellen. Mother takes them to the near-by bookstore and tells them to pick out the boxes of paints they like the best. She knows she is being a little reckless when to the paints she adds a bundle of large sheets of drawing paper for each child.

"Now then," she says as they leave the store, "Nancy will have something to do at home, and so will you. You must each save the best of your pictures to take to school to surprise the teacher."

Nancy is shyly grateful. Her eyes shine. She skips off toward her home still limping but plainly excited and pleased. Ellen and her mother turn toward their own home. Until dinner time the new paints absorb Ellen's attention and she asks no more questions about Nancy. But once they are at the dinner table and father has been told the events of the day, the questions begin again.

"Why does Nancy have to live in that kind of a place? Why does her mother have to go off to work instead of keeping house?"

"I don't know," her father answers. He has had a hard day at the store and he never felt less equal to settling social problems. "I just don't know. I wish I did."

"But it isn't fair," Ellen persists. "Nancy's a good little girl. She does the right things at school."

"There, you see, that's the way people always react," says mother to father. "It's the old superstition that prosperity and goodness go together, that poverty is a kind of punishment for being 'bad.'"

"Some of the children at school used to say that Nancy didn't have any clothes because her father drinks. But that isn't true because her father's been dead ever since she was a baby."

"And there you have the other superstition." Mother sounds a little bitter this time. "'Drink did it.'" She turns to Ellen. "Probably it isn't any fault of theirs at all that they're cold and hungry and dirty and poor. Probably they just never had a chance. All along the line they never had a chance."

"But can't someone give them a chance? Can't somebody get a job for her big brother? He's sixteen and he wants a job. Then her mother could stay home. Can't somebody get them a warmer house or something?"

"I don't know," her father says again. "I wish I did know but I don't. It's unfair all right. People who want work ought to be able to get work. People who live in cold houses ought to have heat. Maybe Nancy's mother would do better if she went on relief. I could phone around and have someone look them up. Maybe your mother could get together some clothes. I don't like to pass by on the other side of the road but I don't know what we can do."

And so Ellen's father summarizes the customary answer to children's questions about economic and social inequality. He would do something (and he really would) if he only knew what he ought to do. Ellen's questions continue through the meal; indeed, they continue throughout the winter as she and Nancy continue their interest in painting. She discovers that there are a good many other children in Nancy's neighborhood, only six blocks away, who live as meagerly as Nancy. There is a little girl across the hall from Nancy who can't start to kindergarten because she hasn't any shoes. There is a family of six who live in one room. She comes home bristling with questions, some of which her parents answer very directly by calling the Associated Charities or the School Nursing Service. But the main answer is always the same: "I don't know what we ought to do. I wish we did know."

There are other parents who feel that they do know what ought to be done, who feel that they have an answer. One hot July day Myron's Scout troop goes on a sight-seeing trip "back of the yards." The troop has been complaining because their camping expedition is cut from four weeks to three and the scoutmaster has decided it would be a good thing for the boys to know how fortunate they are in their quiet, shady part of the city with its access to bathing beaches. They go first down the narrow street popularly called "Tough Alley." Most of Tough Alley is sitting on crowded doorsteps and fire escapes, or playing pantingly in dirty, hot streets. The boys see things they never knew about before: two small children crying over which one shall lick out a banana peeling; a baby sucking a withered orange while his mother fans off the flies; an old man looking hopefully into trash cans. Everywhere the smell of the stockyards. On the part of the troop excitement gives way to depression. When the scoutmaster buys ice cream cones they give them away at their own suggestion to "that bunch of little girls."

On the way home they ask the expected questions. "It doesn't seem fair, does it, that they have to live like that."

"Why should we have so much?" says Charlie. "Not to mention them who've got more than us."

"Why don't we do something about it!" cries Myron in sudden animation. "We're Scouts. We're supposed to do a good turn every day. Why don't we start on something big? Something that matters." In spite of much talk, no one seems to have an answer. Myron goes home. When evening comes, he is waiting for his father with the same questions. "Why should things be like that, dad? Why don't we do something about it?"

"I'll tell you why things are like that," says his father promptly. "It's because the government doesn't take hold. We pay plenty of taxes so that everybody ought to have plenty if the government just did its part."

His father speaks with such authority that the flow of Myron's questions is halted for a moment. But only for a moment. "Just what ought the government to do?"

"I don't know the details. That's what we've got a government for, to figure those things out. They've got plenty of experts. Commissions on this and committees on that. Nobody knows what they do to draw their pay. But one thing they don't do is to get down to business."

"Then why don't we get some new people into the government?" Myron speaks as hopefully as if no one had ever thought of the idea before.

"You try it," says his father. "You just try it. The politicians have everything sewed up. If you could do something about the graft, then maybe the poor people in this country might have a chance."

The conversation goes on for some time, for Myron is still under the shock of his first close touch with economic inequality, but all of his father's answers sum up to the same thing: "It's the government's business. Let them do something."

George's father also feels that *he* has an answer. George, who is a freshman in high school, comes to the dinner table in obvious perturbation. "Listen, dad, today a kid made a report in civics class all about how the sharecroppers got pushed off the land in Oklahoma and places like that. Hundreds of them. Thousands of them. The land is owned by banks and people off in New York or some place, and they just sent out an order for the sharecroppers to get off the land. The owners are plowing the land under with tractors. The tractors just knock over the houses and everything if the people don't get off. Is that fair? Now I ask you, is it *American?* "

" No," says his father shortly. " It isn't fair but maybe it is American."

" Father! that's a pretty dirty dig at your own country."

" Sure it's a dirty dig. But that's us. We just sit down and take it." His father begins to eat a little faster but he does not hurry his words.

" The sharecroppers didn't sit down and take it. They moved out to California. They packed their families into broken old Fords and trucks and they moved all the way to California looking for work."

" And when they got to California — "

" There wasn't any work. At least not enough for all of them."

" That's what I mean," says his father. " We just sit down and take it. They didn't have to go."

" Sure they had to go. What else could they do? "

" They could stay where they were and work the land they'd always worked. They could all stick together. That's the answer. When people aren't getting their share, let them say what they want and then all stick together."

" That might start a fight."

" Then let them fight. It wouldn't be the first time people have fought for their homes and their land. It's the same with them as it is with the factory workers. They've got rights but they don't holler loud enough. Let them stick together and fight if they must."

Which, of course, is another answer.

Hunter is fourteen the year he drives with his father

through the mountain counties of eight southern states. Since he has lived in a northern city all his life, the rural life of the south is entirely new to the boy. Facts, statistics, history which he had learned in school take on human interest. So also does the phrase, " social and economic inequality."

" Why does it have to be like this, father? " asks Hunter, standing beside his father in the cleared patch in front of a mountain cabin where eight tall sons and two daughters live with their parents in two rooms and a lean-to shed. " You'd never think that a fellow who won the declamatory contest for the whole state would come out of that house. Look at how hard they work to go to school. There isn't a boy in our whole school who works that hard. Things don't seem equal."

" I suppose the inequalities are merely the price of ignorance," his father answers. And then, after the car gets under way down the narrow uneven hill road, he picks up the answer again. " Back there I said it was because of our ignorance that some people have so little chance. Maybe it's worse than ignorance. Maybe it's our stupidity. We have enough facts, I think, to make us realize that it would be to the advantage of the state to see that every child got an education regardless of what he could pay."

" You mean state schools instead of schools supported by rich people like these schools we're visiting? "

" State schools or federal schools. Tax-supported institutions."

" But those boys said that no more than two of their family could go to school at the same time because the rest had to work the land."

" That's part of the same problem. The need of a minimum livelihood based, perhaps, on the number of children in the family." His father pauses a moment, as he sometimes does when teaching a class. But the conversation, like the teaching, seems to go right on.

" That's a really swell idea, dad," says Hunter after thinking it over. " Because some poor people have just as smart children as any rich ones, don't they? And your way they'd all have a good chance no matter how poor they are."

" I wouldn't exactly call ' my way ' foolproof, however. Because a great many families have too many children. Sometimes too many for the mother's health. Sometimes too many for the children's own good when the stock is poor physically or mentally. I presume that if the government completely subsidized the education and training of every citizen, then society would have to invent some kind of health certificate for bringing children into the world, and that would have complications, too."

Hunter sighs. It is the slow bewildered sigh of a child who is learning. Twice he starts to speak, stops, and then speaks impetuously. " But we have to do something, father! The world can't go on like it is with so many things unfair."

" You bet we have to do something," his father agrees. " We *are* doing something. Unjust as things are, cruel as they are, there have been a good many improvements since the days when America's first cotton factory was operated entirely by children who worked twelve hours a day. In spite of the hard conditions under which millions struggle for a living, in spite of the other millions who can't even get employment, there probably never was a time when so many people were concerned with the world's injustices. So many people trying, awkwardly or successfully, to do something about the inequalities."

" Well now, father, you're an educator and you *teach*

people what to do. But I really want to *do* something when I grow up."

His father smiles with more wistfulness than amusement. The boy looks so eager, so ready, so capable. He is Youth ready to make a New World; and the least one generation can do for the next is not to discourage it.

"You not only *want* to do something, but you *must* do something. Civilization has always had its ups and downs but just now we're teetering on the brink of a rather steep down."

"What *can* I do?"

"Know what's going on, for one thing. Half our country doesn't know how the other half lives. City people don't know what life means in the country. Country people frequently have a fantastic idea of city problems. Cotton growers don't understand men who raise wheat; wheat growers can't understand fishermen; fishermen haven't the faintest idea what the problems of lumberjacks are.

> Here lies the tragedy of our race:
> Not that men are poor;
> All men know something of poverty.
> Not that men are wicked;
> Who can claim to be good?
> Not that men are ignorant;
> Who can boast that he is wise?
> But that men are strangers.

Hunter thinks for a minute and then says simply, "That's true, I guess."

"Knowing is the first thing, probably. And it's hard work. Just plain hard work. It means reading all the time, reading some of the things you know you won't agree with. It means going out of your way to see things."

"Of course a lot of people *know* quite a bit but that

doesn't make them *do* anything special. I mean people like economists and magazine writers and ministers."

"But telling other people what to do *is* doing something if the ideas are constructively thought out. When people are genuinely informed they can make their routine actions count for something in the cause of social justice."

"What kind of actions?" But before the question is stated Hunter remembers a recent discussion in his civics class. "You mean buying newspapers which pay fair wages to their employees and don't twist the news to mean what they want it to mean."

His father nods agreement. "I also mean the simple matter of voting. After all, it is still possible for the American people to express themselves on the changes they want, and that certainly includes legislation affecting living and working conditions. Social security legislation is a move in that direction."

"What else? I know one thing! Cheaper power — like the TVA. Now how many improvements have been made since I was born? I mean changes that help to even things up."

Thus the conversation turns into a game, but the game is also a lesson and the lesson is something of a social experiment itself. Perhaps the most realistic answer a parent can make to his child's questions about social inequalities and economic injustices is to treat the child as another responsible human being who expects to carry his share of society's burden.

Most children are at some time impressed by the economic inequalities around them and begin to ask questions as to why some people live comfortably, some live extravagantly, and some barely eke out an existence. But their questions may not be long-lived. If their parents can voice the old clichés with enough authority, the children will accept injustice as "just one of those things" which errant human nature is heir to. "There always have been poor people," their parents may say, "and no doubt there always will be." "If things were divided up and everyone started over, it wouldn't be a week until some would be rich and some would be poor." "Prosperity isn't an accident; neither is poverty. Water seeks its own level and money comes to the man who can make it — and spend it." Naturally parents who deal in such answers are not likely to be using their spare time, not to mention their brains and their means, in seeking ways to equalize the inequalities. Therefore their attitudes and actions shout even more loudly than their words the fact that they feel that their children's energy can be better spent than in questioning the inevitable.

Children whose parents are on relief or working for a subsistence wage will ask a different sort of question from children who look at the world from the shelter of comfortable homes. And their parents will answer differently, both in words and in actions. Answers grow out of experience because, as one father puts it to his son, "We don't think with our minds; we think with our experiences." This fact puts an added burden upon the parent who feels that he has a quick-and-sure answer; he needs to test his answer by enough experience to prove that his answer is tenable. For looking about them at the world of people, children are frequently inclined to see human relationships in sharp and vivid outline, the same human relationships which have become blurred and vague to older eyes.

The three Deever children are given permission by their mother to bring home a guest from school for lunch on Lincoln's Birthday. Anna, aged seven, brings a sweet little daughter of New England who is new in the neighborhood. Birch, aged eleven, brings a red-head who can "run like the wind." But Leslie, aged nine, strolls in with his new chum, a Negro boy named John. John happens to be a nimble-witted youngster with a good deal of charm. He keeps the other children laughing and makes the mother of the three young Deevers wish that her children would pick up in their table manners. The children have scarcely gone back to school when the mothers of the other two guests arrive in deep indignation; their children have come to the Deever home for the last time. Echoes of the disturbance reach the children. "Why?" they ask. "He's just as good as anybody. Why can't we eat with John?"

Their questions are fair enough, and no doubt there are fair answers: "sound" answers born of experience and long-time perspective. But who shall be the final authority in setting up those answers? Even when the law speaks, it may speak in the accents of yesterday. Even when the church speaks, it frequently has different answers for different parts of the country. The parent is thrown back again upon his own judgment. But his judgment is useless to the child unless the parent has done his level best to gather as many facts as he can cope with and to keep his mind continually open to new light. Too categorical an answer may prove fatal to the constructive imagination of the next generation.

"Daddy, will you give me a nickel for the slot machine? . . . Why not? Other kids play slot machines. Why can't I?" "Why can't us kids march in the strikers' parade tomorrow? We don't think they got a fair deal. Why shouldn't we say so?" "Why can't we pass handbills for the Citizens' Committee? They're just calling a meeting to force the strikers back to work. If they don't go back to work, the whole town suffers. Aren't we part of the town?" "Lucy's grandfather's too old to work any more and Lucy's house is so small they don't know where to put him if he comes to live with them. Isn't there any place for him? What do you think old people ought to do? Just lie down and die? " " Pat's brother lost his job and now his mother can't finish paying for their kitchen stove. Can't somebody find him another job? He *wants* to work. We can't see our own neighbors lose their stove, can we? " " Rachel's laundress can't take their washing home any more because the water's been cut off at her house on account of she couldn't pay her water bill. Do you think that's right? "

No single answer. No final answer. No sure answer. And yet parents must all the time make answers. For their answers, they need firm honest words. For their words, they need clear courageous thoughts. Back of their thoughts they need sensitive open hearts. How can a parent manage all these things and still have time to earn a living and bring up the children who ask the questions? But how can he do less?

This Hurts Me Worse

> *" I shall never again bid you do violence to your con-*
> *science, my daughter, but to all the commands which*
> *I do lay upon you I shall expect and require the same*
> *ready and cheerful obedience that I have heretofore.*
> *It is my duty to require, and yours to yield it." " Yes,*
> *papa, I know it is," she said with a little sigh, " but it is*
> *very difficult sometimes to keep from wanting to have*
> *my own way."* MARTHA FINLEY (*Elsie Dinsmore*)

" Why do you punish me if you love me? "

In some form or other, every parent has heard that question many times, and many times has wished that he had
an answer which the child would understand. Sometimes
he wishes that he had an answer which he understood himself.

There are many stock answers, of course: " I punish
you because that is the only way you learn that you must
mind." " I punish you because you must learn which things
are wrong." " So that you won't make the same mistake
twice." " Because God says that sin deserves punishment."
" Because you broke a law and man has to learn to respect
law. For you, my commands are the same as the law
of the land." " I punish you because I love you and want
you to grow up to be a good man."

Perhaps the basic confusion about punishment, in the
minds of both children and parents, is caused by the fact
that emotion usually colors our acts of punishment. This
entanglement of justice with anger, of warning with retri-

bution, is no news to parents. The most clear-headed of us has been embarrassed by his emotional reaction to a situation which he knows should be treated objectively. We admire the complete impersonality with which nature metes out her punishments — a stomach-ache for green apples whether they were eaten daringly or innocently, an aching shoulder for too much exercise whether one was playing tennis or saving the furniture from a burning house — but achieving such simple inevitability requires more imagination and restraint than we are accustomed to exercise.

Luella breaks a water pitcher and her mother is angry. The pitcher is part of a set which her mother values. Therefore the quick slap which Luella receives is only half for her carelessness in handling the pitcher; the other half — the part that stings — is because her mother lost something she did not want to part with.

Mary climbs the pantry shelves and eats the wild raspberry jam, after the manner of children since there were shelves, jars and jams. Mother takes one look at Mary and trots upstairs after the hairbrush. By the time she has got Mary and the hairbrush together there is nothing impersonal in her action. Later she explains to Mary's father, "Yes, I was angry but it was righteous anger. I knew she would be sick and I'm simply not going to run the risk of her ever doing that again."

Maybe so. But it was also true that her mother knew that if Mary was sick, gone was the foursome for the afternoon. And Mary would be cranky tomorrow when her grandmother came to visit. Moreover, mother had picked those raspberries with her own hands while off on a camping trip and she was saving that jam as a very, very special treat for luncheon on the day when Mrs. DeWitt Hanover would be coming to speak at the club. Many things were mixed up in that jam. Mary got spanked for them all.

Maybe the spanking did Mary no harm. Many are the Marys who might be different today if they had learned an infantile respect for jam and perhaps for hairbrushes. Maybe Mary grew up and never climbed another pantry shelf. (Maybe, too, she never again ate raspberry jam nor had the least idea why she didn't care for it.) Maybe there actually came the day when she actually thanked her mother for that spanking. But Mary did not learn from the occasion any of the sweet inevitability of nature's laws.

Her mother might have saved herself some trouble, without wasting her adrenalin, by merely seeing Mary as a five-year-old and jam as a confection and life as a game. Then she would have picked Mary off the shelf, led her to the bathroom and washed her face, neck, ears, hands, and maybe her hair. She would have announced cheerfully: "Too much jam makes children sick, as I have sometimes mentioned. There's really nothing I can do about it but get you ready to be sick." Whereupon she would have slid Mary into her pajamas, tucked her in bed, put a washbowl beside her, pulled down the shade, and left her.

Of course Mary may have eaten so much jam that there is something mother can do about it, even to calling a doctor. Or she may have eaten so little jam or have so tough a tummy that her mother knows the chances are against her feeling ill at all. If she cannot count on Mother Nature to look after that punishment (or if she belongs to the uniquely sensible group who throw all of their psychological influence against the very idea of illness), then Mary's mother is put to it to be a bit more resourceful.

She might set Mary on one kitchen chair and herself

on another and talk to the child as one sensible human talks to another. She could tell her exactly how she had made that jam and why it was important, and what Mary had deprived the family of. If she did not use the injured tone of look-at-your-poor-mother-slain-by-your-own-hands, she might accomplish her purpose of making a straight case for the consideration of Mary's straight little mind. Furthermore, she might point out that members of a family have to be able to depend upon one another. Otherwise they are not much different from beasts in a jungle, each going after his own food. She might point out how ridiculous it would be, and how embarrassed they would all feel, if mother had to lock up the jam and cake and candy, but how proud she is to know that she can leave anything exactly where it ought to be, even salted peanuts in the little dish on the reading table beside daddy's favorite chair, knowing perfectly well that Mary would no more take those peanuts at the wrong time than Gyp would jump on the kitchen table after raw meat. Incidentally, when the conversation was over and Mary had gone her sober way, mother might figure a bit to herself whether the child was getting enough sugar in her diet.

Obviously, Mother Nature's punishments are the most satisfactory kind when we do not lay so much dependence upon them that they have to be cruel. The slight cut for the child who handles a knife may be an everlasting reminder of carefulness in handling blades although only a very careless mother would leave the child to get all of his information about sharpness directly from the carving knife itself. Explanation and warning have their place. In an average household in which common sense averts the major accidents, Mother Nature is a great deal more obliging and efficacious than most of us realize. When we learn to team up with her, we save much emotionalizing both for ourselves and for our children.

Helen, aged eleven and old enough to know better, slides down the icy hill on a large sheet of tin. She cuts her hand badly. Mother cleans the cuts and bandages the hand which will be out of commission for a good many days. And then, her surgical duty being accomplished, mother takes down the switch and switches Helen's legs in no uncertain manner. After all, she has told Helen to keep out of the alley and Helen has disobeyed. For months thereafter, Helen carries bitter resentment in her heart, a resentment which upsets her school work and makes her churlish with her family. The resentment is not consciously toward her mother whose punishments she has grown to accept as one accepts the elements. Her resentment is toward God who has betrayed her in allowing a hand to be hurt so badly that it will always bear the scars, when he must have known very well that mother would look after the punishment. She misses the point entirely that icy hills and rusty tin are subject to laws and that one cannot take liberties with those laws without physical danger. It is not pointed out to her that on some other occasion the same laws might have made the icy hill, and even the tin, the helpful servants of man. The child's perspective is thrown askew by her mother's dogged determination to punish where punishment is due. Helen is torn between her desire to assert herself in further disobedience and her sullen withdrawal into a deep inner resentment against the fact that she is powerless to assert herself. No parent cares or needs to risk either reaction.

Father has told David a dozen times he must string up his fishing line back and forth between two large nails prepared for the purpose every time he comes in from fishing. David continually forgets and leaves the wet line on his reel where it frequently tangles and runs danger of rotting. One morning Uncle Spenser appears at dawn to take David's father to a neighboring lake famous for its sporty fishing. David may go along! He grabs up his pole and climbs in the car, excited from head to heels. He has long wanted to get to that lake. But when they arrive, get out in their boat and begin to cast their lines, David's line will not cast. His reel has rusted from standing out in the rain the past two days and his line is tangled in knots. He remembers that he wound his line quickly the last time he used it, expecting to go back and straighten it out later. Now he sits in the boat untangling knots. Through a long hot morning Mother Nature furnishes her own punishment. There is no extra line for David. His father makes no comment. He does not need to. If he had "rubbed it in" then David, whose temper is quick, would have unconsciously turned his resentment against his father instead of taking it smack on his own young chin where it belonged.

In a family which plays the game with Mother Nature, the children do their own impressing of the point. Homer is a college freshman who hates to go to bed at night. He is a very adult looking freshman, having just shot up to six feet two, but unfortunately he needs a great deal of sleep to keep feeling fit. Five nights in succession he stays up very late and on the morning of the sixth day, when he has expected to start on a grand week-end trip, he wakens with a heavy cold. Loud is his grumbling and avid his search for some person or some event outside himself upon whom he can blame his disappointment. But Paul, the younger brother, nips all that in the bud. "Mother Nature's punishment," he chuckles not too gently. "You thought you were so big you could cheat on sleep, but you've got it in the neck."

On another occasion mother tells Paul to do his foot exercises or he won't strengthen the arch on his left foot before he tries out for the team. Paul doesn't listen; his foot doesn't hurt and the arch doesn't show. Homer prophesies cheerfully: "Never mind, kid. Mother Nature will add up your score." And she does. Incidentally — or is it? — a family which is keyed to notice nature's even-handed justice somehow develops a more philosophical set of parents.

But for all the honest playing ball with nature, there are nevertheless times when a parent has to step forth to do his own punishing. If Junior is subject to tonsilitis, he cannot be allowed to get his feet wet. He is too young to remember that wet feet may lead to tonsilitis. He does not even remember, between spells, how dreadfully sick he gets. Apparently he cannot stay out of the water. His father is honest when he says, "Maybe someone could get the idea into his head so that he would have an intelligent response, but we don't seem able to do it. And still he *has* to learn."

Whereupon father says to Junior as he pulls off the child's wet shoes and stockings: "This is the last time, son. You have rubbers which allow you to walk any reasonable place. You have plenty of toys and games and playmates for doing other things than splashing in deep puddles on a cold March day. The next time you get into a puddle, I will take the matter up with your legs in a way they will understand."

For two days Junior stays out of puddles. Then in he goes. And out of the house comes father. He says nothing at all to Junior but takes him into the house to change his shoes and stockings. Fascinated by the silence, Junior says nothing either. When he is ready to go outdoors again, father ties a heavy weight to each ankle, the sort of hitching irons once used by grandfather's horses. Then father speaks to the legs: "I'm sorry for you, legs. These weights are pretty heavy and you won't be able to run worth a cent. But you're so awfully dumb about remembering that you'll just have to have something to help you."

Father goes into the house again. Junior tries the weights experimentally. They are heavy. His two playmates come to look them over. Finding how impractical they are in all the usual games, they try to think up some other games which Junior can play without much moving around. But the stationary games grow stale and, without meaning to, the other boys skip off on their own pursuits. At last Junior slowly climbs the porch steps, goes into the house and calls his father. "Father, they've learned," he announces.

"I'm glad," says father, untying the weights.

And they *have* learned.

Some time afterward in talking to a friend, Junior's mother speaks of the punishment: "I don't think it was very smart, really. But we had tried the other things such as keeping him inside and making him play alone. His aunt thought we ought to whip him and I was afraid myself we'd have to come to it. But whipping seems such an acknowledgment of defeat. We decided we'd try everything else first — and finally this particular idea appears to have worked."

There *is* a good deal of trial and error in meting out punishment. Most parents are in too big a hurry and so do not think through their tactics. Sometimes disobedience is so sudden and so serious that there is no time for prolonged thought. Moreover, all too often parents do not understand what is involved with the disobedience in the child's mind. There are so many urges, so many necessities which pull at the child with more force than any restraining word can have.

Roy is an adopted child, young for his ten years. When he was five and his sister three, they were taken by parents who have much more than ordinary capacity for understanding children. The little sister, Sally, has dark curls and winsome, baby ways. Roy's hair is a nondescript blond and his eyes no special kind of blue. The new parents try to be impartial; they provide toys and tasks, pleasures and responsibilities with generous, firm hands. Still it is Sally who is most often tossed into the air or cuddled to sleep. Now, at eight, Sally still has curls, still talks baby talk, still gets more than her share of cuddling. Roy, lank, lean, ten, cannot get curls no matter how much he tosses his head in his little sister's favorite gesture. But he can talk baby talk. His father and mother most decidedly do not care for baby talk in a boy. They say, " Roy, if you cannot talk like a boy of ten, you can go up to bed like a baby." So Roy tries to "talk his age" but sometimes he lapses and is sent to bed. To a disinterested observer, it is plain that Roy *must* talk baby talk because he must have attention. The child is vaguely conscious of the fact that it is baby talk which helps to get his sister her attention, and so he imitates her. The fear of punishment, of displeasing his parents, is much, much less important than his need of being fussed over.

The wisest parent must fail sometimes. If he sees and understands his failure, then even a failure may be worth while. But he may never know, nor the child ever know, how fraught with disastrous consequences a failure may be. Sometimes we fail when we are most sure we have succeeded — a conclusion which is not so conducive to comfort as to analysis.

If anyone should ask Mrs. Clausen whether or not she

has a discipline problem with her children she would answer with a proud and unhesitating "No." Her theory
is that her children must mind because she tells them to;
after all, she is responsible for their well-being and she
will use her best judgment.   Now Mrs. Clausen understands many modern points of view — all about proper
moving pictures, cod liver oil in winter, large blocks for
small children and tools which actually work. She knows
about the need for rest in growing girls and the need for
fruit juice in growing boys. She has the best parent magazines which she reads from cover to cover and she goes to
meetings of the Parents' Research Association and testifies
to her successes.

Only James, among the seven Clausens, has ever spoken
right out in words and asked, "Why should I mind you
all the time?"   Since he was only eight years old, his question was direct and without guile. His mother, who believes Patience to be a Great Virtue, laid down her pie
crust, looked right at James in the most approved psychological manner and told him a story:

"When I was a little girl, we lived on the edge of a
small town quite near to the railway track. Next door
to us was a family named Smither who had the most obedient children I have ever known, and Jonah Smither was
the most obedient of all. Whatever the father and mother
of those children told them to do, they did — immediately
and without question. In those days when the weather
was bad the roads were likely to be bad too. Sometimes
in the spring the mud was so deep that we could not get
to town by road. Then we were allowed to walk on the
right of way, usually on the railway ties. There was small
danger because the town had only two passenger trains
and two freights each day and all of us knew when they
were due. But one day when Mr. Smither and Jonah, who

was six, were walking to town, Mr. Smither stepped off to the side of the right of way to get something and without warning a special train — a fast express — was almost upon them. It was impossible for Mr. Smither to get back to Jonah or for little Jonah to jump out of the way. So Mr. Smither called to Jonah, 'Lie down where you are.' And Jonah lay down where he was right in the middle of the track between the rails. The train, which could not possibly stop, passed over him *safely*. He was so small that lying flat between the tracks he wasn't touched in any way. It was the marvel of the town how Jonah was saved by absolute obedience. And that, James, is just the reason why God gave little boys and girls their mamas and papas — to give them commands at the right time. And that is why God expects little boys and girls to mind without argument or question."

But James did not hear these latter words about God's gift to little children. His limp yellow hair was still standing on end in sympathetic terror with Jonah. Did the words of James' mother sink into the mind of James? They did! The story has kept him awake nights and terrified his sleep for six long years and he is now entering adolescence with a dread of quick commands which makes him frantically flee the place from which commands are likely to issue. No doubt his case, which is now in the hands of a plump and jolly worker at the Child Guidance Center, has other complicating factors but the lady herself feels that James has been cursed by obedience bought with a price.

When everything else fails, shall the parent whip the child to obtain obedience? Human personality is so sensitive a creation, even when it protects itself with layers of indifference or swathings of rebellion, that the wisest parent hesitates to do with physical force what he cannot accomplish with reason and love. "Besides," the parent asks himself, "I wonder if force can really do anything?" And the child asks, "So you think this will make me want to mind, do you?" or "How dare you do that to me?"

Force can produce fear, of course, and fear may motivate a child's actions. If a parent wants a fear-ridden child, probably he is logical in using physical force to bend the child to his will. Force can produce an outward respect for the commands of the parents, and respect is useful between the generations. Perhaps even an outward respect is preferable to none at all — for certain types of minds. But there is always (always is a long word!) a better way than physical force *if* parents have the physical strength and the spiritual courage to seek until they find it. Hunting the better way is not an easy task; it demands much nervous energy; it requires time. Some parents, in all honesty, have neither the nervous resources nor the time to do the better thing. This sad fact is one of the prices which society pays for throwing too heavy an economic burden upon mothers who must earn the family's support as well as look after the children, or too heavy a psychological burden upon a father who is ill or unemployed, or too heavy a social burden upon the entire household who must live tumbled together in small, cramped quarters. When housing, food, health, recreation, education, all the concerns of the whole of society are borne by the whole of society, then perhaps gradually in time — much time — all parents may learn a wiser way than force.

If there is ever a place for discipline through force, for a "quick smack" or a whipping, that time is surely when the child is very, very small — too small for reasoning and so unavoidably situated that there are certain things he *must not do*. A baby in a crowded household which cannot possibly protect its fires may perhaps need to have his hands, or his legs, smacked right smartly if he insists upon crawling too near the fireplace.

Mother has just come down from putting Alan, aged two and a half, to bed after a hot bath and a stiff rubbing, first aid after his exposure to the cold. She comes into the living room with quick steps. " I wish the weather man would be as quick and relentless as a steam radiator. Two nips cured Alan of touching the radiator. But when he goes out into the snow and takes off his wraps he only catches a cold one time in four because the other three times I ward it off. And somehow I can't think of a good deterrent."

Whereupon grandmother takes up the discussion and the two benevolent tyrants debate possible punishment which will seem to Alan as logical, invariable and instantaneous as a radiator's burn.

" If the punishment's going to make sense to a small child's mind, it has to have some connection with the offense." Mother dusts the living room with impatient little swats, the impatience being directed at her own lack of inventive genius and not at the sleeping child. " I suppose that in his mind going without lunch wouldn't have any relation to taking off his coat."

" It has to be something you can repeat with each offense," says grandmother contemplatively. " A punishment's best when it's inherent in the act, so to speak. As the burn is to the radiator."

" Spanking would be so easy," sighs mother.

" If he were smaller, or not so smart, I'd say yes," grandmother agrees. " Sometimes you have to restrain a child with the sharpest, quickest reminder. But Alan is beginning to reason and he deserves a reasonable punishment."

At this point in walks daddy. Hat on one chair, gloves on another and a kiss for each woman. He hears the tale.

"That's a lot of brain work over one small misdemeanor. What's the difference in one spanking more or less if it works? Or even suppose he slips by now and then without any punishment. You can make it up another time."

His mother looks up quickly. Has all of her twenty-five years of training come to this? But perhaps he has never really been conscious of the methods she used so faithfully on him.

"Son," she says sternly, "how would you feel about your universe if the stars took one course today and another tomorrow? If fire cooked meat today but froze it tomorrow? If today soap took off dirt but tomorrow made no impression on it? If —"

Alan's father can be serious when necessary. "You're right, mother. He's got to have parents he can depend on."

"We've simply got to be dependable unless we want him to feel like an atom lost in chaos," echoes mother almost plaintively. "My aunt used to punish me according to her moods — just the way she played the piano. It made a dizzy world for me."

"Now my idea of a good punishment would be one that works without the child's knowing he is being punished," says the father. "When is a punishment not a punishment?"

"When it's too severe, out of all proportion to the offense," answers grandmother, thinking of the time in her childhood when she was sent to bed hungry for picking the wrong rose.

"When it fails to contribute to the child's growth," says his wife, quoting an encyclopedia on baby culture. "Growth is the primary law of life and the reason nature gave babies parents."

So the three adults finish their discussion on a high note

and feel vaguely that Alan will probably never take off his snow suit in another drift. But the next morning, which is a particularly cold one, the child has not been out of doors fifteen minutes when he has proudly unzipped the garment and stepped out of it. Almost immediately his mother sees him. She goes out after him, leads him firmly into the house, turns him over her knee and spanks him with old-fashioned fervor. He is so surprised that he scarcely cries. When she stands him on his feet, he looks at her incredulously, swallows his sobs, then walks over to his blocks and begins to play with assumed indifference. In all his later years he can never say more plainly to anyone than the expression of his face and body now say, " I'll never let you know what's going on inside my mind because you had no business to do that."

Just at that moment grandmother comes into the room. " I have an idea," she begins, and then takes in the situation and stops. Later, when Alan has gone upstairs, she expresses her idea. " I just wondered if it wasn't the fascination of the zipper that tempts him so; I thought we might get him a sweater which zips and he could play with it to his heart's content in the house. Then we might pin his snow suit with safety pins so that he can't get out of it – if you didn't think that was going too far in taking temptation out of his way."

Mother stands looking at her. " I'll never forgive myself for not thinking of that before I spanked him," says mother. " Now that it's done, I'm not going to be sentimental about having spanked my child but I do feel pretty awful."

Grandmother consoles her sensibly, ending with the whimsical comfort, " Maybe the spanking didn't do a bit of good and we can try the safety pins next time."

But the spanking worked.

Perhaps there is no sure answer to the child's resentful question, "How do you dare to whip a human being? " The parent may answer cheerfully, " I dare because you need it," or honestly, " I dare because I don't know what else to do," or regretfully, " I dare because I have a frightful temper of my own and when you disobey, then I'm angry past all self-control," or blithely, " It's just a family tradition. My parents whipped me and I never minded it much," or confusedly, " I have to show my authority somehow." All the answers are half-evasions and probably the marks of some degree of ignorance or insensitivity. But they are part of the currency of parenthood.

"Why do you punish me if you love me? "

" We punish you *because* we love you and we feel that the penalties we exact now may help you to build habits which will keep you from needing punishment at the hands of a less loving society and a less personally concerned nature later on."

A Law Unto Himself

I would do what I pleased, and doing what I pleased, I should have my will, and having my will, I should be contented; and when one is contented, there is no more to be desired; and when there is no more to be desired, there is an end of it. CERVANTES (*Don Quixote*)

Benny is the country cousin, aged seven, on his first visit to his city cousin Alfred, aged nine. With their mothers, the two boys are walking toward the park, crossing several streets. Suddenly at one street which seems to Benny like all the others, they stop and stand waiting. Benny looks wonderingly up and down the avenue. No cars are in sight.

" What are we waiting for? " he asks impatiently.

" The green light," says Alfred, pointing across the street.

" It isn't green, it's red," corrects Benny.

Then Benny's aunt explains the signals by which city traffic is managed. The boy appears to take in her words rather solemnly and when she has finished he asks, " Who said so? "

" The law said so," Alfred answers quickly. " This city's full of law."

By this time they have crossed the street but Benny is walking backwards in order to watch the changing lights. " What's the law? " asks Benny.

" Yes, what is the law, Alfred? " asks his mother.

" It's what the policemen decide they'll arrest you for if you don't do," explains Alfred.

" The policemen don't decide on the laws," says his

mother. "They only carry out the law. They do what the law tells them to do — arrest people who speed or drive against the lights or break into houses and things like that."

"Then who makes the laws to begin with?"

"Different laws are made by different groups," says his mother, beginning to feel a little vague herself. "Traffic laws are made by the City Council."

"What's the City Council?"

"The City Council is a group of men who govern the city. They get together and decide what regulations will be best for all these thousands of people who live here. If each person had to make up his own mind when to cross the street, there would be many more accidents. On some streets the cars would tear along all day and the people who are waiting to cross might never have a chance. If there weren't any speed limit, careless drivers would speed so fast that careful drivers would be in danger. So the City Council decides the traffic regulations and then lets everybody know about them."

"Do they write everybody a letter?" asks Benny.

"They publish new regulations in the newspapers. Sometimes they also post placards so that people walking along will stop to read the notices."

"They have another way," cries Alfred in sudden excitement. "My father showed me. When you get your automobile license, they send you a little book with all the rules in it."

"But what if you don't get a book and you don't read the newspapers and you didn't see the signs? Then you can drive the way you want to," announces argumentative Benny.

"Oh no, young man," says his own mother. "'Ignorance of the law is no excuse.' When a law is made, it is usually published in newspapers as your aunt said, and copies are sent to the lawyers and honest efforts are made to let people know about it. But it begins to operate no matter whether people have heard of it or not."

" That isn't fair," says Benny. " I wouldn't go to jail for breaking a law I never heard about."

The children having reached the park, law gives way to a war whoop. But evidently the discussion remains in the boy's mind because that night Benny says to his father, " In this city, you have to go to jail for things you never heard about."

" Such as? " asks his father.

" If you never knew you couldn't drive through a red light, why the policeman will put you in jail just the same. Is that fair, I ask you? "

" But practically all drivers know about red lights, Benny, because all of the cities and most towns of any size have them. Only a few people who live as far in the country as we do could possibly be ignorant of them. But there's another thing. Unfortunately there are a good many people in the world who might break a law just because it suited them to break it and then say they never heard of it."

" That would be a lie," says Benny emphatically.

" But maybe the judge couldn't prove it was a lie. If the judge believed one man was telling the truth and let him off, then another man who broke the law would say that he didn't punish the other fellow who didn't obey this same law. The law has to be on the safe side and protect all the citizens by holding them all responsible and treating them all alike."

" I don't want to be treated alike," says Benny to no one in particular. His tone is slightly troubled, slightly defiant, very earnest.

" Why not? " asks his father.

"Because I'm not alike," says Benny.

Of course Benny is not really talking about traffic lights. He is not really talking about any particular curtailment. He is expressing an emotion rather than a thought and his words outreach his years, as children's words not infrequently may do. But he is talking about something which every child has to meet and deal with over and over and over. He is questioning the necessity to conform.

In another mood Benny will express a deep need to conform. He will refuse to wear a sweater with stripes running up and down because "all the guys wear stripes running around." He will want his mother to send his excuses for absence from school "without an envelope because none of the other children have envelopes on their excuses." His clothes, his hair-cut, his vocabulary, his sports — practically his entire world will seem to be held in place by the need for conformity. Nevertheless, and with no sense of contradiction, he will also insist upon being an exception to rules, regulations, customs and compulsions. In reality all his questions are merely different ways of shouting, "Who am I? If I'm too different from the others, I'm nobody. If I'm not different enough, I'm also nobody."

Evelyn is part of a family which always has a prayer at table before the meal begins. In all her eight years, Evelyn has never eaten a meal which did not begin with a blessing. The custom is not only the rule of her family but also the rule of the neighborhood, of the community. Evelyn has never questioned but that prayer before meals is the custom of the entire world; she just takes it for granted. But a new child moves next door, a sharp-eyed little boy of her own age, named Ransom. One rainy day, Ransom is invited to stay for lunch. When the family are all seated at the table the children's chatter suddenly hushes, the grownups break off their remarks mid-air, and Ransom feels an unaccountable silence closing in upon him. He looks anxiously at Evelyn's mother. Her head is bowed, her eyes shut. In embarrassment the child stares from one to the other. Everyone's head is bowed, everyone's eyes are shut. The father is saying something, but before Ransom has made out a word of it the father suddenly raises his head and smiles. The children's chatter begins where it left off. The grownups' remarks are plucked from the air and everything is as it was before. But not for Ransom. If they did that strange thing once, they may do it again. He is half-afraid to eat.

Naturally he is full of questions when he reaches home. His mother explains the custom. But then she must also explain why some families follow the custom and their own family does not. Their family feels that it is nature and man's hard labor which provide the world's food, and that there is no reason to thank " God " for food at stated intervals. Her remarks are logical and reasonable but it is not their intellectual content that sustains Ransom; it is her kindly tone which furnishes the emotional underpinning for his questioning mind. He feels, without putting his feelings into words and scarcely into thoughts, that his family's way is " right " and that the neighbors are a little queer. He never mentions the matter to Evelyn.

But there comes a day when Evelyn stays at Ransom's house for dinner. Ransom's family sit down to table laughing and talking and no one bows his head. Only Evelyn, looking expectantly from one to the other, her hands folded on the table in front of her, waits for the sudden silence which never comes. In amazement she sees the family begin to eat. She picks up her fork but can scarcely take a bite. Not that she has any conscious doubts about eating unblessed food, but that she " doesn't feel right." It's like going to bed without brushing one's teeth or stepping into the bath without taking off one's shoes; the thing isn't natural.

That afternoon Evelyn asks questions of Ransom and Ransom asks questions of Evelyn and both children ask more questions of their parents until finally everybody understands everybody and each family goes on in its own way feeling somewhat superior.

Years pass. Evelyn goes away to prep school. At spring vacation she brings home two roommates. Before dinner she takes her mother aside. "Mother, I'd like to ask you something. Couldn't we skip the prayer at table? The girls aren't used to it. They'll think we are awfully queer. I can't explain it to them before dinner and — anyway I think we can be just as grateful without talking about it aloud three times a day."

In Evelyn's mind one conformity is contending with a stronger conformity. The approval of her own age-group matters more just now than the family custom. She is experiencing the recurrent cycle: Why don't *they* conform with our ways? Why don't *we* conform with their ways? The question is loaded on the side which gives the child the most security at the moment. It is this shifting of the load from side to side which accounts for the apparent paradox in every child's attitude toward conformity.

Sometimes the parent can ease his own resentment against the adolescent's repeated, " Why should I? " by reminding himself how great is the physical inertia of the adolescent. At first it seems preposterous that a boy who can practice football the entire afternoon should find it too much of a strain on his energy to stand up when his sisters come into the room. As a matter of fact, the boy did have the energy to play football, especially under the impetus of team expectancy, but it is also a fact that the boy feels it a physical chore to keep getting up and down out of his chair. The moods of his physical body are as unpredictable as the gymnastics of his voice. If his body had its way, it would not move for quite some time, at least not until some genuine stimulus made it want to move. Therefore he says, either in words or by the reluctant unfolding of his long legs, " Why should I get up every time the women come in and out of the room? "

" It's merely one of the traditions of civilization," his father may return with some asperity. " Some rather busy men through the past several hundred years have found that they are able to bear the burdens of state and still carry on with this quaint tradition."

" Quaint? " asks the son. " It's archaic. What do I stand up *for?* Are you afraid the girls are going to fall in a faint? And don't tell me that it's out of respect to the fair sex because I haven't any more respect for them than I have for my father and brother and uncles and boy cousins and — and the postman."

Every parent of an adolescent son recognizes the conversation. There is the whole argument of what constitutes respect and " wouldn't you rather have a man treat the women as equals than all the time taking off his hat and carrying their parcels? Wouldn't you rather have your children act like honest individuals than like ' ladies ' and ' gentlemen '? Wouldn't you rather feel that a boy was a good person for your daughter to date with than to be certain he was always walking on the outside or opening and closing car doors with the proper deference? "

To all of which the parent parries, " Does one preclude the other? Isn't it possible to be both an honest individual and a gentleman? "

" Yes, sir, but — "

Unfortunately the " but's " are reasonably unreasonable. Maybe the final answer, if there can ever be a final answer, is the Japanese maxim that a certain amount of decorum makes it easier for many human beings to live closely together. Nothing could seem less to need polite custom than taking a drink of tea when one is thirsty, and yet so strongly do these close-packed Orientals feel the need of serving and receiving and drinking the most casual cup of tea with ceremony that the expression " to have no tea " is equivalent to having none of the finer perceptions.

"Do you think, my young son, that you can improve on the experience of the whole human race? Every race has discovered practically the same thing, perhaps in terms of different customs, but with as much finality. It is easier, more comfortable, more inspiring if you will, for humans to treat one another with deference."

" Why can't I spread a whole slice of bread at once? The whole slice has to be buttered, hasn't it? And it takes longer to keep picking up the knife and putting it down again, doesn't it? " " Why not tip back my chair? It rests my legs and my legs are more important than chair-legs, aren't they? " " Why shouldn't people sprawl at the table? The Romans leaned back on cushions and took life easy and they turned out as smart men as the world has ever had, didn't they? " " Why should a person have to lay his knife and fork side by side on the plate? " " What's the sense in always passing things that no one has asked for? " " What's the difference whether you take a big bite or ten little bites just so you chew your food? "

Most parents know answers. Sometimes they know *good* answers so packed with common sense or humor that the child acquiesces. But usually it does not matter whether the answers are excellent or indifferent because the child seldom really hears them. He just goes on nonconforming at table until one unaccountable day it occurs to him to conform and after that he doesn't need the answers anyway. Then perhaps the mother says contentedly, " I knew that if we just kept talking long enough George would begin to understand." And the father says, " I don't think that argument had a thing to do with it. It's example which counts in the long run." George himself doesn't take sides in the debate over his reform because he never has consciously paid any attention to how his parents ate, and he never really felt that either his questions or their answers were important, and besides he doesn't know why he suddenly began to eat like a gentleman. He just began. If his parents feel better about it, that's their luck.

Some of the galaxy of questions on the " why " of conforming with household customs have practical, immediate answers which the child will gradually understand and cooperate with. " Why should I hang up my clothes? I can find them more quickly on a chair." " Why do books have to go back in the exact spot they came from in the bookcase? " " Do I have to walk clear back to the kitchen with this knife? " " Must I go way upstairs to put one spool of thread in the mending basket? " " Can't my toys stay on the floor one night? "

" But after all, darling, there are six people living in this house. Suppose they all left their clothes on chairs. To begin with, it is hard on the clothes and secondly it is hard on the person who tries to clean the house." " If each member of the family used one tool, a hammer or a screw driver or a pair of pliers, and no one returned the tool he used, what would *you* do when you needed one in a hurry? " " How would you like it if the other children took *your* things and didn't return *them?* "

After all, reciprocity is a rather plain and practical argument which even a young child can grasp. Moreover, conformity is freedom. " If *you* must conform, so must the other members of the family, of the community. Then you know what to expect, what to demand. And life is easier for *you* than if every one is a law unto himself."

Sometimes the hardest questions for a parent to deal with are the adolescent's questions as to why he should do certain things which go contrary to the customs of his gang.

"Father, I just have to tell you," says Margot, aged fifteen, "there isn't one girl in the junior class who has to be home as early as I do. Eleven o'clock! *Eleven o'clock!* The party just gets going at eleven o'clock."

"Then the party gets going too late," says her father serenely. "Young people of your age need their sleep. I wish you'd stay home some night and read the study which the Children's Bureau has made on the sleep needs of boys and girls under eighteen."

"Children's Bureau! That's what you think we are, children. You and mother both. I tell you times have changed since you were in school. What difference does it make whether a party runs from seven to ten or from ten to one? Three hours is only three hours whenever you take it."

Usually *this* conversation is limited only by the exigencies of the questioner's time, because the modern parent wants to be "reasonable" and "cooperative" and "open-minded" and he will answer as long as the child asks. He will patiently go over the answers of science and of psychology and of taste. Occasionally such a parent may actually persuade by his arguments. Much more often, he gives in. He says — to the child and to the community: "I don't *like* it but what can we do? We can't expect Margot to be the only child who leaves at eleven." And the fact that Mary's and Martha's and Isabelle's and Ruth's and Helen's and everybody else's parents are saying the same thing never seems to bring them any nearer to concerted action. Occasionally, but only occasionally, there is a parent who says: " Well, it's just too bad that your parents happen to be exceptions in an otherwise broad-minded community. But as long as you live at home and we happen to feel responsible for your health and happiness, you'll come in on time or you won't go out."

Parents who make this latter answer take on a large slice of responsibility because they are then honor-bound to help their son or daughter keep up his end of the game in some other way. If the girl is exceptionally popular, her dates will continue even though she has to come home early. If she is very, very pretty and has what it takes besides, she can capitalize on her parents' stern requirements and make herself seem just a little finer than the ordinary garden varieties. But if she is not so unusual and really is cut off from her group by her parents' requirements, then the parents have to see that the parties she gives are more than ordinarily interesting. They have to see that she has a game room in the basement or a tennis court in the garden or a good cook in the kitchen, *or* a most ingenious mother at the helm to help her to her measure of status and " success." " Limber, loving, and a little bit looney," is the parent's best personal maxim if he wants a degree of conformity to his own nonconformity.

Questions They Cannot Ask

We had fixed habits of activity and industry; we were in ourselves serene and contented; our bodily health and strength increased from day to day; the sentiment of tender attachment was perfect in every heart; we every day acquired some new and still improving channel for the exertion of our physical and moral faculties; we everywhere beheld, and at all times acknowledged marks of the divine wisdom and goodness; our minds were penetrated with love, gratitude, and veneration for the Providence who had so miraculously rescued and preserved us, and conducted us to the true destination of man — that of providing by his labor for the wants of his offspring!
JOHANN D. WYSS (*Swiss Family Robinson*)

Most parents realize that a child's questions are the measure of his growth. No matter how tired or how busy they are, parents can usually gather up a phenomenal amount of patience and ingenuity for answering the questions. They feel that answers are a child's just due. And yet, when a child does *not* ask questions, when he goes about his play content with what he has and proceeds with his daily tasks without a single " Why must I? " the tendency is to feel both relieved and fortunate. But perhaps there is significance in the questions our children have never asked.

Naturally a child's questions are limited by his experience. The boy who has never used a hammer, a saw, a plane, who has never struggled with brace and bits, with wrenches, vises, plumb line — that boy will never ask questions about the law of building things. He will never question the tools themselves. Somehow a boy is poorer who has never questioned tools, who has never resented for the ax — *with* the ax — the fact that someone has dropped it blade down against a stone, who has never rebelled with the saw at not being hung up properly. In tools there is integrity which approaches personality. They not only demand respect but must receive it, just as human individuals must, if they are to be useful to the point of their full stature.

Raymond, who is ten, has gone to visit his grandparents in the country. The first week he learns to use a hammer and nails, the second he experiments with a small plane and the medium brace and bits. Finally he is given for his own a sharp little hatchet with which to whittle tent stakes for his new tent. After the tent is pitched, he goes back to work with hammer, nails and saw as he builds his tent furniture. Suddenly one morning he needs the hatchet. His grandfather has been noting for several days that the hatchet is missing from Raymond's tool rack. He has admonished the boy over and over: "Check up on the tools, Ray. When you leave them for the night, leave them in their places. A good carpenter can't sleep when his tools aren't accounted for, any more than a good shepherd can close the fold with a lamb or two still straying."

"Sure," says Raymond absently.

And then the morning when he needs his hatchet. He hunts, and he finds it in the tall grass back of the tent. The hatchet is rusty. Although he understands that tools must not be allowed to rust, it has never really occurred to him to wonder why tools should not rust. Feeling vaguely guilty, he begins to chop the kindling he wants for his campfires. The wood is hard and the hatchet is dull. He becomes exasperated. Indeed, he is thoroughly disgusted. He hunts his grandfather.

"This hatchet's no good, grandfather. It won't cut. The hardware man gypped us."

His grandfather looks at the hatchet, feels its edge. "The hardware man didn't gyp us. It was a fine little hatchet. But you've broken the law of the hatchet and both you and the hatchet pay the price."

Raymond looks ashamed. But he does need a hatchet. "Could I borrow your hatchet for a few minutes?"

"Sorry," says his grandfather, "but it wouldn't be fair to my hatchet."

By the time Raymond's hatchet is cleaned and the edge reground, his fundamental question about hatchets is answered — by the hatchet.

Perhaps saddest among the questions which many children cannot ask are the questions about green growing things. In the crowded areas of cities, there are many thousands of children who almost never experience full-growing grass into which they may throw their hot bodies for refilling from the earth's deep energy, who have never rested in the deep sweet grass from which they can pull out a blade of timothy to bite off its juicy end. They have never stood knee-deep in the tall grasses when the wind brushes over and the sun leans near. Such children can ask no questions and receive no answers from the grasses.

Certainly, if there is meaning in the heart of the universe, children should have access to the answers of trees, just by virtue of the fact that they are children. A child needs to know how it is to *be* a tree, roots firm in the ground; how it is to feel his straight trunk give to the wind, his branches flung out in ecstasy of sun or rain, his leaves sensitive to the stirring of every mood about him. He should know how it is to be thirsty, and to stand and wait for the rain. No dashing about, no shifting places with some other tree; just pushing his supple root-tips down into the earth where springs of water may be hidden. He should know the tree's response to autumn, the triumphant fulfillment in color. And the tree's acquiescence to winter, its blanketing of snow, its long months of mere " being."

Bunny is five the summer he plays in the grove of white birches. One morning at ten o'clock his mother calls as usual, " Bunny! Bunny, come here and get your milk and cookie."

Bunny does not stir. She calls again a bit impatiently for there stands Bunny very staunchly, looking up into the trees but not moving. " Bunny, run here a minute." Finally Bunny turns his head without changing his stance.

" Sh! Don't call, mummy. I'm a tree. I can't run and I don't want to run. My roots are busy getting their breakfast."

Mary has spent the entire eight years of her life in the country. Her doll house, made of packing box and orange crates, is under an oak which stands next to three silver poplars. One morning her mother comes out to the doll house to visit.

" Today we will have a little program," announces Mary in the accents of the primary teacher. " Mother, you stay right there and stand like an oak. Because I'm going to do the dance of three poplars and you can't understand me unless you are an oak."

Then Mary dances for the three poplars, distinctly taking three parts. Absorbed in watching, her mother starts toward a camp stool to sit down.

" Don't sit down! " cries Mary in alarm. " The poplars couldn't dance if the oak didn't stand up taller than they are."

Fantasy? But of course. And druidry was fantasy before botany was a science. Somewhere in the answers which trees give are the hints of a wonder which " doth not yet appear." No man will wring from a tree its deepest secret who has not first loved a tree with passionate understanding. "Not lightly touching your person, O lord of the land," says one who has asked questions of a live oak and been answered.

Some children never ask questions about money, except to say, "Daddy, gimme a penny," or "Why can't I have a new bicycle?" and frequently those questions have been so poorly answered that the basic idea of income and expenditure never enters their heads. They have never had an opportunity to operate on a budget of their own for which they are held responsible, nor to share in the problems of the family budget. Naturally then they do not ask questions about accounts, about long-time planning, about modifying one expenditure for the sake of another. A girl from an otherwise intelligent family may be turned loose on society as a college graduate, as a bride, as a new wage earner, without ever having looked a dollar squarely in the face and asking, "Whose life blood do you represent? Where can I spend you to make you buy me the most of what I want without feeling that you are buying too much?" A boy may grow to be a man and never have asked his pocketbook, "What do I contribute to the family well-being that you should be so promptly filled each month?" or "How much of a living does the world owe me?"

As long as the current economic system uses money as the basis of exchange, a parent's answers to questions about money are among the most useful equipment with which he can furnish his child. Without sound answers, older children are likely to find themselves in the dizzy position of trying to face in several directions at once. Their desires pull one way, their social convictions another; their prayers speak a language which their pocketbooks cannot even understand. An adequate understanding of the use of money is a correlating factor for many of the other problems in a growing child's life.

Some children have no opportunity to question their study habits; they go through twelve years of school on chance or momentum without ever having been made constructively self-conscious of their poor habits, certainly without being taught the technique of making a new habit. Others are given no opportunity to question their too rigid routine because even their attitudes are regimented. But for every such regimented child there are a dozen who have never questioned the dispersion of energy and the haphazard schedules of the members of their families, including themselves. How can they question an established disorder without having experienced its opposite?

Thus it goes across the entire breadth of experience! Questions denote interest, participation, awareness. Let us list the things our children never question, whether the things belong to the physical world, to the social world or to the world of ideas, and we will have before us a picture of our own limitations. Even the " sure " convictions we pass on to our children need to be questioned if they are to be successfully passed on. If children are to ask the right questions, and enough of them, then they have to have a fullness of life which makes wide questioning possible. Naturally that is what most parents hope for, strive for, wait for: fullness of life for their children. And as the days of our parenthood increase we see more plainly that fullness of life is somehow a shared experience. We cannot share what we do not have, and it is more difficult to be forever making over ourselves than to be remaking our children — more difficult and vastly more effective.

To be a parent is to be perpetually discouraged, especially in moments of success because there are so few of them.   The more clearly a parent discerns what it means to be a parent, the less he feels equal to the task, especially if he *is* equal to it.   But fortunately, no matter how many our failures, even a successful parent may turn over a new leaf, glue it down, and stand on it smiling triumphantly.   There are fresh, unwritten pages ahead.

Bibliography

(*Revised as of January 1, 1946*)

In five years, very few of the books on the list compiled for earlier printings of this volume have become outdated or even excelled in their particular fields. But the discriminating new books just cannot be overlooked. Some present-day writing in the field of children's books comes very near to being lasting literature. All the books here listed are children's books if, as was said before, by children we mean real people from two to whatever. These books are not divided into age-groupings; neither are people. And who could set an age for reading MacDonald and Weisgard's *Little Lost Lamb* or Jones's *Small Rain* or Brown and Charlot's *A Child's Goodnight Book?* When is a child ready for ants and turtles? It depends, of course, upon whose ants and turtles — and perhaps somewhat upon who is reading aloud.

Frequently only one book of a series is listed here, the theory being that when one reads, for instance, *Made in China*, by Cornelia Spencer, one will go right on to *Made in Mexico, Made in Canada, Made in the USSR.* One book of folk tales leads to another, especially the series of "Picture Tales." The present interest in folk tales is one of the hopeful signs of growing insight and appreciation on the part of young American readers. No one tells such tales better than Sophia Fahs, who has a peculiar gift for seeing all life through the eyes of a growing child.

There isn't always a reason why some good book is left

off this list except lack of space, but there is always a reason why a book is *on:* it says something about quality in living. Chances are that it also has a sense of humor in or between its lines. Children are the first to know that information is not enough. *Climbing Our Family Tree,* by Alex Novikoff, is more than an adventure in biology. *A Prayer for Little Things* is more than a poem. Which leads neatly to the observation that some of the quality in children's books is due to the distinguished illustrators who, like Elizabeth Orton Jones and Leonard Weisgard, to name only two, see to the heart of things.

When a book is not available at a local bookstore it can always be ordered direct from the publisher, whose address any librarian will be glad to furnish.

THE WORLD AROUND US

WHAT MAKES IT TICK, by Katherine Britton (Houghton Mifflin).
THE BOOK OF INSECTS, by Edwin W. Teale (Dutton).
WONDER WORLD OF ANTS, by Wilfred S. Bronson (Harcourt, Brace).
TURTLES, by Wilfred S. Bronson (Harcourt, Brace).
THE LOST WOODS, by Edwin W. Teale (Dodd, Mead).
THE LAND WE LIVE ON, by Carol L. Fenton and Mildred A. Fenton (Doubleday, Doran).
A DIPPER FULL OF STARS, by Lou Williams (Wilcox-Follett).
LET'S LOOK AT THE STARS, by Edwin B. Frost (Houghton Mifflin).
WHEN THE STARS COME OUT, by Robert H. Baker (Viking).
STARS FOR CHILDREN, by Gaylord Johnson (Macmillan).
THE EARTH FOR SAM, by William M. Reed (Harcourt, Brace).
BIRDS OF AMERICA, by Louis Agassiz Fuertes (Garden City).
FIELD GUIDE TO BIRDS, by Roger T. Peterson (Houghton Mifflin).
GUIDE TO LAND BIRDS EAST OF THE ROCKIES, by Reed (Doubleday, Doran).
FIRST THE FLOWER THEN THE FRUIT, by Jeanette M. Lucas (Lippincott).
A BOOK OF WILD FLOWERS, by Margaret McKenny and Edith Johnson (Macmillan).
WILD FLOWERS, by Homer D. House (Macmillan).
WEATHER, by Gayle Pickwell (McGraw-Hill).
EVERYBODY'S WEATHER, by Joseph Gaer (Stokes).
FUN WITH SCIENCE, by Ira Freeman (Random House).

FUN WITH CHEMISTRY, by Ira Freeman (Random House).
ELECTRONICS FOR BOYS AND GIRLS, by Jeanne Bendick (Whittlesey House).
HOW THINGS WORK, by George R. Harrison (Morrow).
VAN LOON'S GEOGRAPHY, THE STORY OF THE WORLD (Garden City).
THE CHILD'S STORY OF SCIENCE, by Ramon P. Coffman (Putnam).
ROMPING THROUGH PHYSICS, by Otto W. Gail (Knopf).
PORTRAITS OF THE IRON HORSE, by R. S. Henry (Bobbs-Merrill).
AMERICA'S TREASURES, by Ivan T. Sanderson (Harcourt, Brace).
MAN'S WORLDLY GOODS, by Leo Huberman (Harper).
LET'S GO OUTDOORS, by Harriet Huntington (Doubleday, Doran).
UP ABOVE AND DOWN BELOW (picture book), by Irma E. Weber (Wm. R. Scott).
YOUR FORESTS, by Martha B. Bruere (Lippincott).
FARM ANIMALS, by Dorothy Hogner (Oxford).
THE GULF STREAM, by Ruth Brindze (Vanguard).

ACCOUNTING FOR OURSELVES

MICE, MEN AND ELEPHANTS, by Herbert S. Zim (Harcourt, Brace).
MY BODY AND HOW IT WORKS, by Dorothy W. Baruch and Oscar Reiss, M.D. (Harper).
THE WONDER OF LIFE, by Milton I. Levine, M.D., and Jean H. Seligmann (Simon & Schuster).
CLIMBING OUR FAMILY TREE, by Alex Novikoff (Young World).
THE CHOSEN BABY, by Valentina P. Wasson (Carrick & Evans).
GROWING UP, by Karl de Schweinitz (Macmillan).
BEING BORN, by F. B. Strain (Appleton-Century).
ATTAINING MANHOOD, by George W. Corner (Harper).
STEP BY STEP IN SEX EDUCATION, by Edith Hale Swift (Macmillan).

RELIGIOUS INSIGHT

ONE GOD, by Florence Fitch (Lothrop, Lee).
JESUS, THE CARPENTER'S SON, by Sophia L. Fahs (Beacon Press).
NATHAN, A BOY OF CAPERNAUM, by Amy M. Lillie (Dutton).
SMALL RAIN, by Elizabeth Orton Jones (Viking).
LITTLE LOST LAMB, by Golden MacDonald and Leonard Weisgard (Doubleday, Doran).
PRAYER FOR A SMALL CHILD, by Rachel Field (Macmillan).
A PRAYER FOR LITTLE THINGS, by Eleanor Farjeon (Houghton Mifflin).
PILGRIM'S PROGRESS, by John Bunyan, made into a picture book by Robert Lawson, text shortened and retold by Mary Godolphin (Stokes).
DAVID, by Elizabeth Orton Jones (Macmillan).
JUNIOR BIBLE, by Edgar J. Goodspeed (Macmillan).
THE CHRIST CHILD, by Maud and Miska Petersham (Doubleday, Doran).
BEGINNINGS OF LIFE AND DEATH, by Sophia L. Fahs and Dorothy T. Spoerl (Beacon Press).

MUSIC, ART AND POETRY

MUSIC IN THE HOME, by Satis Coleman (John Day).
CHRISTMAS CAROLS, by Hendrik Van Loon (Simon & Schuster).
ROUND OF CAROLS, by Tertius Noble (Oxford).
SONGS FROM MANY LANDS, by Thomas W. Surette (Houghton Mifflin).
FIFTY FAVORITE SONGS, by Mary P. Graham (Grosset & Dunlap).
CHRISTMAS CAROLS, by Mary P. Graham (Grosset & Dunlap).
BIOGRAPHIES (Bach, Haydn, Mozart, Schubert, MacDowell), by Sybil Deucher and Opal Wheeler (Dutton).
UNFINISHED SYMPHONY, by Madeleine Goss (Holt).
THE STORY OF GEORGE GERSHWIN, by David Ewen (Holt).
CHOPIN, by Antoni Gronowicz (Nelson).
STORIES FROM THE GREAT METROPOLITAN OPERAS, by Helen Dike (Random House).
ART IN THE NEW LAND, by Charlie M. Simon (Dutton).
HOUSES IN AMERICA, by Ethel F. Robinson and Thomas P. Robinson (Viking).
THE CHILDREN'S ART BOOK, by Geoffrey Holmes (The Studio).
THE HOUSE OF A HUNDRED WINDOWS, by Margaret W. Brown (Harper).
GIOTTO TENDED THE SHEEP, by Sybil Deucher and Opal Wheeler (Dutton).
MILLET TILLED THE SOIL, by Sybil Deucher and Opal Wheeler (Dutton).
THIS SINGING WORLD, by Louis Untermeyer (Harcourt, Brace).
SILVER PENNIES, by Blanche J. Thompson (Macmillan).
WHEN WE WERE VERY YOUNG, by A. A. Milne (Dutton).
MY POETRY BOOK, by Grace T. Hefford and Laura M. Carlisle (Winston).
VERY YOUNG VERSES, by Barbara P. Geismer and Antoinette B. Suter (Houghton Mifflin).

LOOKING BACK

THE STORY OF MANKIND, by Hendrik Van Loon (Garden City).
GEORGE WASHINGTON'S WORLD, by Genevieve Foster (Scribner).
ABRAHAM LINCOLN'S WORLD, by Genevieve Foster (Scribner).
THE LITTLE HISTORY OF THE U.S., by Mable Pyne (Houghton Mifflin).
PAGEANT OF CHINESE HISTORY, by Elizabeth Seeger (Longmans).
PAGEANT OF JAPANESE HISTORY, by Marion M. Dilts (Longmans).
STORY OF ENGLISH LIFE, by William Ellis (Putnam).
THE FIRST DAYS OF HISTORY, by Frederic A. Kummer (Doubleday, Doran).
LIFE LONG AGO, by Carroll L. Fenton (John Day).
ANIMALS ON THE MARCH, by William Ellis (Coward-McCann).
BEGINNINGS OF EARTH AND SKY, by Sophia L. Fahs (Beacon Press).

GREAT MEN AND WOMEN

GEORGE WASHINGTON CARVER, by Graham and Lipscomb (Messner).
HAYM SOLOMON, by Howard Fast (Messner).
ABRAHAM LINCOLN, by James Daugherty (Viking).
THOMAS JEFFERSON, by Gene Lisitzky (Viking).
WIDE FIELDS (Henri Fabre), by Irmengarde Eberle (Crowell).
THE MAYOS, by Adolph Regli (Messner).
AMERICAN EMPEROR, by Rose Brown (Viking).
GARIBALDI, by Jean Burton (Viking).
WE HAVE TOMORROW, by Arna Bontemps (Houghton Mifflin).
GREAT AMERICAN NEGROES, by Ben Richardson (Crowell).
TWENTY MODERN AMERICANS, by Alice C. Cooper and Charles A. Palmer
    (Harcourt, Brace).
RUNNER OF THE MOUNTAIN TOPS (Agassiz), by Mabel L. Robinson (Random House).
NANSEN, by Anna G. Hall (Viking).

GETTING ALONG WITH OURSELVES AND OTHERS

STRICTLY PRIVATE, by Elizabeth Woodward (Crowell).
SMARTER AND SMOOTHER, by Maureen Daly (Dodd, Mead).
LET'S TALK ABOUT YOU, by Margueritte H. Bro (Doubleday, Doran).
IT'S MORE FUN WHEN YOU KNOW THE RULES, by B. Pierce (Farrar & Rinehart).
MADE IN CHINA, by Cornelia Spencer (Knopf).
A CHILD'S GOOD NIGHT BOOK, by Margaret Wise Brown (Wm. R. Scott).
LET'S DO BETTER, by Munro Leaf (Lippincott).
THE LITTLE GEOGRAPHY OF THE U.S., by Mable Pyne (Houghton Mifflin).
WE ARE THE GOVERNMENT, by Mary Elting (Doubleday, Doran).
PEOPLES OF THE USSR, by Anna L. Strong (Macmillan).
PICTURE TALES FROM THE JAPANESE, by Chiyono Sugimoto (Stokes).
PICTURE TALES FROM THE RUSSIAN, by Valery Carrick (Blackwell & Mott, Ltd.).
VOYTU'S LITTLE HOUSE (folk legends), by Janina Porazineka (Roy Publishers).
KOOS, THE HOTTENTOT, by Josef Marais (Knopf).
HERE IS INDIA, by Jean Kennedy (Scribner).
STRUGGLE IS OUR BROTHER, by Gregor Felsen (Dutton).
IN MY MOTHER'S HOUSE, by Ann N. Clark (Viking).
SILVER CHIEF, by Jack O'Brian (Winston).
EDRA OF THE ISLANDS, by Marjory Medary (Longmans).
THE GOOD MASTER, by Kate Seredy (Viking).
LITTLE PEAR (China), by Eleanor Frances Lattimore (Harcourt, Brace).
LUCIO AND HIS NUONG (Philippines), by Lucy H. Crockett (Holt).
TALKING DRUMS (Africa), by Waldo Fleming (Doubleday, Doran).

KOBI (Switzerland), by Mary Buff (Viking).

NINO (Italy), by Valenti Angelo (Viking).

OLA (Scandinavia), by Edgar and Ingri D'Aulaire (Harper).

NORWEGIAN FARM, by Marie Hamsun (Lippincott).

LITTLE JUNGLE VILLAGE (South America), by Jo-Bess Waldeck (Viking).

BRIDGE OF CARAVANS (Palestine), by Frances J. Olcott (Wilde).

DANCING CLOUD (Indian), by Mary Buff (Viking).

THE BOOK OF INDIANS, by Holling C. Holling (Platt & Monk).

THEY CAME FROM SCOTLAND, by Clara L. Judson (Houghton Mifflin).

SNOW OVER BETHLEHEM, by Katherine Milhaus (Scribner).

BLUE WILLOW, by Doris Gates (Viking).

STRAWBERRY GIRL, by Lois Lenski (Stokes).

PADDLE TO THE SEA, by Holling C. Holling (Houghton Mifflin).

ROAD TO ALASKA, by Douglas Coe (Messner).

WHISPERING GIRL, by Florence C. Means (Houghton Mifflin).

SHUTTERED WINDOWS, by Florence C. Means (Houghton Mifflin).

LITTLE BOAT BOY, by Jean Bothwell (Harcourt, Brace).

THEE, HANNAH! (Pennsylvania), by Marguerite De Angeli (Doubleday, Doran).

ELIN'S AMERICA (Swedish in Maryland), by Marguerite De Angeli (Doubleday, Doran).

MAMINKA'S CHILDREN (Bohemia in America), by Elizabeth Orton Jones (Macmillan).

HILL DOCTOR (North Carolina), by Hugh Skidmore (Doubleday, Doran).

ALL AMERICAN, by John Tunis (Harcourt, Brace).

A CITY OF LINCOLN, by John Tunis (Harcourt, Brace).

ADVENTURE NORTH, by Kathrene Pinkerton (Harcourt, Brace).

THE STARS CAME DOWN, by Regina J. Woody (Harcourt, Brace).

Acknowledgments

The author gratefully acknowledges her indebtedness to Alfred A. Knopf, Inc., for permission to quote from Kahlil Gibran's *The Prophet;* to Harper and Brothers, for permission to quote from Booth Tarkington's *Seventeen;* and to the Methodist Book Concern, for permission to retell certain incidents originally used in *First Steps in Christian Nurture.*

Especial thanks are due Ruth Tooze of The Book Box, Evanston, Illinois, for sharing her insight and knowledge of children's books and for her generous help in preparing the bibliography.